TQM for Information Systems Management

Other McGraw-Hill Books on Quality

Berry
MANAGING THE TOTAL QUALITY TRANSFORMATION

Cali
TQM FOR PURCHASING MANAGEMENT

Cortada
TQM FOR SALES AND MARKETING MANAGEMENT

Crosby
QUALITY IS FREE

Crosby
QUALITY WITHOUT TEARS

Crosby
LET'S TALK QUALITY

Hart
THE BALDRIGE: WHAT IT IS, HOW IT'S WON, HOW TO USE IT TO
IMPROVE QUALITY IN YOUR COMPANY

Tunks
FAST TRACK TO QUALITY: A 12-MONTH PROGRAM FOR SMALL TO
MID-SIZED BUSINESSES

TQM for Information Systems Management

Quality Practices for Continuous Improvement

James W. Cortada

McGraw-Hill, Inc.

New York   San Francisco   Washington, D.C.   Auckland   Bogotá
Caracas   Lisbon   London   Madrid   Mexico City   Milan
Montreal   New Delhi   San Juan   Singapore
Sydney   Tokyo   Toronto

Library of Congress Cataloging-in-Publication Data

95-79731
CIP

1 2 3 4 5 6 7 8 9 0 DOC/DOC 0 9 8 7 6 5

ISBN: 0-07-023757-3

*The sponsoring editor for this book was James H. Bessent, Jr. It was produced
under the direction of CWL Publishing Enterprises, Madison, Wisconsin. It was
composed at Impressions, a division of Edwards Brothers, Inc.*

Printed and bound by R.R. Donnelley and Company.

This book is printed on recycled, acid-free paper containing
a minimum of 50% recycled de-inked fiber.

To Dora, Beth, Julia, and Georgia

Contents

Preface

This book is written by a member of the information processing profession for managers within the same profession who, like me, are having to deal with profound changes underway in our industry, profession, and enterprises. Reading it also can profit those who either have information technology reporting to them or must deal with this part of the organization. In short, this is a book about management, not about technical issues. The changes are becoming profound, are redefining our roles and our jobs, and are doing so in new terms that should be comforting for the information services world. The good news is that enough is known about these changes to say that they will make it possible for us to thrive in a global economy that offers more customers than we ever had—customers whose rising standards of living leads to more demand for goods and services. The business world in particular and, not too far behind, many government agencies are attempting to organize their actions in a more well-defined way in order to reap the benefits of the Quality Revolution. At the heart of much of this activity is the renewed application of many of the disciplines well known to the information technology (IT) community.

A New World for the Information Systems Community

The IT world is about to enter a new Golden Age of activity characterized by fundamental reengineering of old applications in a Total Quality Management (TQM) mold. IT will become more integrated into the fabric of managers' enterprises through the use of many new technologies. In fact, the process has already started. Lackluster sales of computers and software may be partly attributed to a new emphasis on processes. While large amounts are still being invested in technology, the fact remains that organizations are already shifting their focus away from throwing more machines at their problems and are instead addressing operational inefficiencies and ineffectiveness. The shift is to finding better ways to use what is already installed.

In a recent survey of 407 large companies across eleven industries, CSC Index documented the change. In fact, CSC Index CEO James A. Champy reported that "For chief information systems executives, 1993 began where 1992 left off—with heightened demands from business managers to overhaul woefully inefficient business processes." Everywhere you turn information systems (IS) executives are finding that their organizations are more interested in reengineering business processes than in continuing to automate old ones. In the CSC survey, IS executives listed reengineering as their most important issue, and nearly 300 already had major improvement activities in process. This is not to say that the old focus on applying new hardware, for example, had disappeared, merely that it had changed. Hardware was increasingly being applied within the context of process improvements, such as the application of client-server technology, which facilitates teams working on common business functions. This technology, for instance, is very popular as part of customer service processes because it quickly facilitates multiple organizations focusing on specific customer issues. Imaging technologies are also attractive because of their effect on teamwork. Automated programming tools are also proving attractive as aids to reducing cycle times in processes.

How we move into the new world of process improvement and continuous quality enhancement is the subject of this book. The activities and perspectives involved make up the concept of TQM as applied to the world of information services. I will use a much broader definition of TQM than you might be familiar with simply because of the word "total." I mean it to encompass process work, quality tools (such as statistical process control techniques), and fundamental management philosophy. I include in TQM an organization's culture, concern about strategic planning, technology, and personnel practices. No longer are the concepts of quality and continuous improvement isolated from the mainstream of what people do on a day-to-day basis.

I want you to accept the underlying management principles of quality and to gain the confidence that not only are they applicable to information technology, but they are also essential for your survival and relevance over the next decade. Change in technologies, applications, and marketplace competition are coming so fast that, if there is a loud message in this book, it is to hurry up and apply quality principles now. These will build nicely on the good habits evident over the past forty years in many IS shops and, thus, should not be as shocking a change as experienced in such areas as personnel practices and sales. I promise not to present any harebrained ideas; everything you will read here has been successfully applied. Proposed activities that have yet to be applied will be identified as such. I will also avoid long strings of war stories; they would only make this a fat book that you probably would not have time to read. But I will point to other sources for detailed studies in case you do want to read more.

My second commitment is to keep this book short because it is intended to be a primer on quality management, not a thick user's guide. Although I will discuss corporate cultural transformation, each organization transforms and improves itself in its own way; there is no one right prescription. Common elements of a transformation are discussed, but I do not present an exhaustive methodology. There are basic principles on what is important, what is done first, and obvious errors to avoid. I fully expect that during your transformation to quality practices you will make as many mistakes as others have, but in the end the benefits will outweigh the errors.

But why discuss quality as it relates to information technology in detail? Isn't quality of interest only to engineers and manufacturers worried about how many well-made widgets they can produce more cheaply than the Japanese? What we are learning is that an effective corporation, light on its feet, can move rapidly in and out of markets with different goods and services, provided it applies the same continuous improvement methods originally used only in manufacturing across the entire enterprise. All departments, divisions, and employees have to participate if it is to work.

The ideal is a seamless marketing focus from the mailroom to the boardroom supported by the wise use of IT at appropriate steps on the way that support the critical mission and vision of the enterprise. That sounds very similar to what we have heard for many decades; the difference is that now the entire organization uses a common set of management practices. Those, for example, begin to address an age-old problem in IS: getting the end user to think and talk like the application programmer. In case you have not noticed, quality-focused management practices call for a process view of activities and, thus, we have many end users now flow-charting their actions and defining inputs and outputs! It is a profound transformation of all that we do. My objective is to help you step up to that challenge—maybe the biggest one of your professional life.

IT is an essential part of that movement because IS professionals can automate, streamline, and make more effective those processes that are being reengineered across many enterprises. Indeed, they cannot be reengineered effectively without your participation and leadership. You understand instinctively process reengineering; you can provide "in-process" measurements and data in a timely and effective manner. You also already have the mission to lash together the enterprise with integrated systems in communications, data bases, and critical applications that support such quality values as cycle time reduction and measurements of progress. You can do this by applying the principles advocated by such quality experts as W. Edwards Deming, Joseph M. Juran, and Brian L. Joiner and in a structured mode as suggested, for example, by the Malcolm Baldrige National Quality Award.

So much progress has been made in applying quality management principles in non-IT parts of companies that information services are ripe for renovation. Already firms such as Xerox, IBM, Motorola, and others have seen that improvements in manufacturing are not enough. The total job must be done across all sectors of their companies. Key data processing applications are involved, such as the use of data bases (E-mail-based national bulletin boards, for example).

What This Book Is About

This book describes proven methods of quality management currently being applied in many companies. Having this information, you do not have to reinvent the wheel, but just modify and apply these methods rapidly.

I recognize that IT organizations vary in their commitment to and involvement with quality. Therefore, to serve a wide range of readers, the book offers both basic, even elementary, information as well as detailed tactical advice. If you are familiar with the basic concepts of quality management and the current interest in the subject, you can skip the first chapter. In the second chapter, I begin to discuss implementation—the focus of the rest of the book. If you are a practitioner of quality management today, you will find the subsequent chapters useful as tactical discussions of various topics that you might not have worked with yet.

Thus the chapters that follow reflect a desire to offer balance between the theory of how to run an IT organization in the TQM mold and the need to get tactical about how to bring it alive "on the floor." I end this book with specific suggestions for how to "jump-start" or extend your journey to a quality-oriented, customer-focused environment. I identify some obvious phases companies go through and point out pitfalls and opportunities in case you have already started or need to know where you are on this path of continuous improvement. A short review of publications on related topics, with advice on where to get additional information, is offered at the back of the book. Each chapter also lists publications that deal in more detail with topics just discussed.

Chapter 1 introduces the quality movement in business and briefly describes the Baldrige approach that is sweeping American business. Chapter 2 describes an overall strategy for IT within an enterprise. Chapter 3 shows how to link an enterprise's strategic business plan and a formal IT strategic plan so that IS is in lock step and integrated with the actions of the whole organization. Chapter 4 is devoted to the complex yet critical issues of how to link IT and business planning with emphasis on the quality links involved. Chapter 5 reviews how best to keep up with, identify, and apply emerging technologies to the overall improvement of the efficiencies and effectiveness of a quality-focused enterprise. This is particularly critical today because, after a decade of end users buying tens of millions of microcomputers, they are now looking to IT to make sense of all this technology and help them apply IT more effectively.

With Chapter 6, we move into the IT organization itself in the belief that even the cobbler's children need shoes. This chapter deals with application development as a process reengineering activity. Chapter 7 describes critical IT applications that you should be offering the entire corporation to help its implementation of quality management practices. Chapter 8 looks at IT operations through a TQM lens, discussing such things as cycle time reduction, end-user focus, and customer orientation. Chapter 9 addresses the crucial question of how to manage personnel in this new world—discussions about teaming, roles and education, and finally defining the functions of management in a more empowered, less hierarchical environment. Chapter 10 suggests how to jump-start the quality transformation in an IS organization, while Chapter 11 describes how it can be sustained, primarily through effective measurements.

Appendices offer additional discussion of points not fully explored in the chapters but too important to ignore.

This book succeeds or fails depending on whether or not it is practical, realistic, and wise. Changing any organization is plain hard work. Most people will resist it at first. Leaders of change find this the most exciting period of their professional lives, but there are no clear, researched-based road maps. Yet we know results can be spectacular. Profits grow, end users become more satisfied, and you make a bigger contribution than otherwise might be the case. But nothing is free; there is a cost for change. I will point that out, too.

One additional comment on terms: I use IT (information technology) to mean both hardware and software *and* the people and data processing organizations that use them. I intermix the use of IT with IS (information systems) sometimes to mean the same. However, I also use IS when I want to refer solely to technical personnel, processes, and organizations, usually apart from hardware and software.

A Personal Note to the Reader

I came to the topic of quality in information technology from personal experience. With two decades in this industry and at IBM behind me, I thought I believed in quality—one of IBM's three Basic Beliefs is "Excellence in all that we do"—and have been enjoying a thriving career by practicing those beliefs. My earlier books on the management of information processing also hammered hard on the notion of excellence, focused on end users, and advocated increases in efficiencies and effectiveness. But I found that quality is a discipline unto its own. During the late 1980s I became interested in the body of management principles associated with quality and then, in the early 1990s, I devoted most of my time to the implementation of TQM in "high-tech" environments. Working within IBM and with our clients, I saw many IS executives working with the issue of quality. I learned how crucial it was to apply the principles of quality management in IS, across any enterprise. The TQM role that IT has to play is so strategic that I concluded it needed its own book. Much like my earlier publications on data processing management, which reviewers complimented as being "streetwise," I designed this book to follow in that tradition. I am helped by the fact that many corporations have shown a profound interest in applying quality to all facets of their enterprises, including information services. In short, what you will read here is a report on some of the most wonderful and creative innovations underway in the economy of the western world.

It would have been impossible to write this book without the help of many IT professionals. A wonderful group of individuals at IBM over the past twenty years have taught me a great deal about managing IS organizations. Customers and clients have done the same. However, I would particularly like to thank the IS management team at Appleton Paper Company, led by Vice President John L. Tucker, for demonstrating that the Baldrige criteria really are a valid way to guide IS operations. Tom Jenks, of the IBM Consulting Group, is an unrecognized genius when it comes to measurements. He has quietly worked for nearly twenty years on the problem of how to develop the right measures for guiding performance of organizations; he taught me almost everything I know about the subject and I have stolen his concepts shamelessly for this book. All the illustrations in this book were prepared by John Crema, of IBM, based on my vague notions and scribblings on pieces of paper. He is living proof that good visuals lead to good communications. However, the ideas and views expressed in this book are my own and not necessarily those of the IBM Corporation. Once again, my thanks go to Jim Bessent, my publisher at McGraw-Hill, for showing faith in my work. My copyeditor, Pat Jones, made sure I wrote what I wanted to say, while the staff at Impressions, a Division of Edwards Brothers, and John Woods navigated my manuscript through the production process to finished book. I am constantly amazed at how my family tolerates my isolation from them as I write. They understood my special need to write this book.

James W. Cortada

1

The Quality Revolution and What It Means to Information Services

Good management consists in showing average people how to do the work of superior people.   JOHN D. ROCKEFELLER, 1913

This chapter describes the current emphasis on quality practices around the world, introduces the Baldrige Criteria in looking at an enterprise, and describes the fundamental role information technology must play.

We are told that the Quality Revolution is upon us! Our junk mail is filled with flyers about seminars on empowerment, Total Quality Management (TQM), books on process improvement, new methods for programming, and on Baldrige assessments, and we are becoming aware of such organizations as the American Society for Quality Control (ASQC). In the growing roar about the new management style, we are seeing a rebirth of customer focus while our customers question us about our commitments to quality. Automobile dealers pay attention to their rest rooms, companies you buy from survey your staff. Government agencies have caught the quality "bug," and even local schools are talking about the "Deming approach." Service is the byword, used as if it had never existed before. We have finally realized that competition is global and that our competitors come very quickly, from unexpected corners of the world, and often with outstanding products and services.

From an information technology (IT) perspective, we have seen other changes that influence corporate cultures and the way IT is operating. For example, downsizing of corporations has been made possible by the availability of computing in many sizes and shapes across the enterprise, from PCs to mainframes. Frequently these are networked from satellites to local area networks (LANs). Programming rapidly has been shifting away from being an art form to being a disciplined practice, from being done locally toward wherever it makes good economic sense, such as India's low-cost programming centers. IT is available to everyone. In fact, a recent survey in the United States indicated that 30 percent of the population used computers directly in their jobs and that over 70 percent of all American workers were dependent on computers to get his or her work done. So your world is also changing profoundly. In a large enterprise, your activities have become more integral to the strategic performance of the firm. In small organizations, everyone seems to have his or her own data processing applications on a PC.

The point is that the roles and structures of organizations are changing quickly, and IT is increasingly one of the most important levers of effective change. The driving management principles for controlling or reacting to these changes are TQM principles.

The purpose of this chapter is to define the quality emphasis and explain briefly some of its terms and concepts. Chapter 2 provides the formal description of quality management as it appears in an IS world.

Shift to a Quality Emphasis

Since World War II, technology has made it possible for just about anyone to produce a high-quality product that is competitively priced. Second, the enormous improvements in telecommunications and transportation have made it possible to move data and products to any location very quickly. Third, barriers to trade around the world have come down, making it possible to do business anywhere and at any time. To a large extent, that capability has been facilitated by the use of computer technology. The focus has increasingly shifted, therefore, to speed in execution of activities and, as a strategic imperative, to leading with quality. The growing emphasis on quality of products and services has led companies to embrace a body of management principles that increase the reliability and excellence of goods and services. Companies are learning several important lessons about quality.

The First Lesson

The most effective way to gain and sustain competitive advantage is to shorten the amount of time it takes to design, build, and deliver a product. In the new parlance, this is called cycle time reduction. Studies have shown that reducing the amount of time it takes to get to market or to performance (to get something done) is the single biggest advantage of quality practices. It is the most important pillar of the quality movement. You know, for example, that getting a large application designed and programmed in one year, instead of in three, is of greater advantage to your end users. If a new application is needed to support a new service that your firm anticipates offering for only two years, you can see the necessity to deliver the software support in months, not years; otherwise the original offering cannot even be contemplated. It used to take several years to design and then build a new line of computers; now you see IBM, Compaq, and Apple, for example, refurbish their product lines at least once and often twice a year. Companies have learned that the largest number of opportunities to improve cycle time lies outside manufacturing (where cycle time reduction has already occurred in from 60 to 90 percent of the cases).

The Second Lesson

Sustainable competitive advantage cannot be achieved just by having better-quality products. Everyone is using robots and computers, for example, to ensure consistently high quality. Rather, they needed to add value to the products to differentiate their goods from those of others. Warranty and service agreements with home appliances, computers, and credit cards and additional services rapidly became the norm by the end of the 1980s. Evidence is now appearing that many of these services were more profitable than the actual products.

The Third Lesson

The only difference-maker is people. Everyone has computers and robots. However, how companies capitalize on their human resources differentiates them from competitors. Every nation has access to cheap labor, technology, and fabrication plants. But work forces vary widely from country to country. Robert Reich, U.S. Secretary of Labor, argued in a book he wrote while at Harvard University (*The Work of Nations*) that as economic activity has become globalized, a country's "most important competitive asset becomes the skills and cumulative learning of its work force."

That realization led corporations to focus more on the quality of their work forces: their skills, efficiency, and attitudes. All through the 1980s and into the 1990s, investments in training rose while you were asked to make more computing tools available to ever-larger pools of employees. The idea was to increase the effectiveness of employees not by working them harder, just differently. How the process of encouraging, delegating, teaching, and managing people changed is the subject of most discussions about the quality movement. We will have occasion to discuss those issues in subsequent chapters.

The Role of Managers Is Changing Dramatically

A new model of the role of managers began to emerge in the 1980s and early 1990s as changes made it more difficult for them to keep up. In a nutshell what happened was that managers found it more effective to get things done by delegating increasing amounts of authority to well-informed employees. As Figure 1.1 shows, their role shifted from telling employees what to do to facilitating employees' getting things done. That shift called for managers to train their employees well, to provide tools with which they could get work done, and to foster the use of teams to approach problems and projects. Managers found they could have larger spans of control while improving the overall speed and quality with which their missions were carried out.

It has been difficult to achieve the process by which change has come to the role of managers. Managers were asked to push aside a body of skills they had developed over successful careers and to adopt another that called for giving away their authority (although in a disciplined manner) and to acquire new roles. They were asked to foster participatory decision-making, to allow mistakes to be made (providing lessons were learned and improvements applied), and to reward the application of quality principles and skills development—and not just for getting things built, sold, and delivered. Layers of management were eliminated, downsizing became the management byword of the 1990s, and organizations moved toward creation of more horizontal structures with more cells of organizations operating increasingly on their own in a matrix formation. These structures are kept together by common visions and practices, and with your technology. Such organizations focus on creating a shared cul-

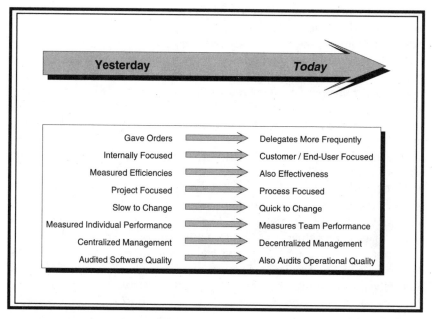

Figure 1.1 Changing role of managers.

ture in which ownership for results is granted to the lowest parts of the enterprise.

By the early 1990s we began to see changes in management philosophy on how to work and make judgments. They began to move in the direction of management by methodology rather than just management by objectives. Essentially, this means that managers focus more on improving how things are done rather than just on what is accomplished. Scores are kept on how well things were accomplished, not just on what was done. For example, instead of just worrying about how many lines of code were programmed, software managers began to worry more about how quickly programs were developed and how error-free they were.

The Value of Processes Is Becoming Very Evident

In this new environment, it becomes essential to have a system of processes that allow functions to support each other efficiently. All parts of the enterprise must help each other at peer levels without having to go up and down an organization to hand off work from, say, design to manufacture, manufacture to distribution, and so forth. The approach must be to see all activities as processes interdependent on each other. In the world of quality practices, it is crucial that a system of matrix-based processes exist from one end of the organization to another and, to a large extent, IT provides the consistency and communications required.

But why do it? Tinkering with a corporate culture is very risky. We do know that the benefits outweigh risks and costs. Today, we know that traditional management overhead drove operating costs up because at least one-third of a manager's time was spent inspecting employees' work—hence the rising tide of complaints that companies were becoming too bureaucratic and too inwardly focused. By reducing the number of managers, one could get rid of inspective work, simplify activities, take out steps in a process, and thus drive down costs and time to get things done. Companies discovered that this approach forced them to have better-skilled employees and that these employees worked more efficiently and enjoyed greater morale. Technology was applied to support processes rather than to perpetuate existing structures and practices.

Companies also found they had to become more market-driven. As economic activity accelerated, inwardly focused organizations found themselves in trouble. They had to pay more attention to customer requirements and respond more quickly to stay in business. Surveys in the 1980s and 1990s showed that customers were increasingly less brand-loyal than in the past, and were simply demanding better quality at better prices. Quality and functionality became more important to customers than ever before. Markets came and went faster, as products became "hot" and "cold" quickly and globally.

Definitions of Quality

There are many definitions of quality; however, they all accept the notion that quality is defined by the customer. Quality management is a body of practices defined by both quality theorists and practitioners. The gurus created the overall philosophical content of the subject and now practitioners are filling in the "how-to" details. The term "quality" increasingly requires a comprehensive, organization-wide embrace of a definition or set of processes for implementation. That is why you will hear phrases such as Total Quality Management, Total Quality Control, and so forth.

W. Edwards Deming, a leading quality guru, called it "continuous improvement," while many executives say they know quality when they see it. Another expert, Joseph M. Juran, speaks of "fit for use," while Philip Crosby uses the phrase "conformance to requirements." Americans speak of value received for dollars spent, while Europeans emphasize quality engineered into their goods. Kaoru Ishikawa, another guru, thought in terms of products "most economical, most useful, and always satisfactory to the consumer."

Companies also have their definitions, in order to give the enterprise common standards. Definitions extend beyond quality products to quality in processes. For example, recall "the moment of truth" when an employee deals with a customer. How that interaction takes place will define quality in the mind of the customer. The same applies with a fellow employee. For instance, if the service an end user gets from your help desk is a positive experience, a quality service has been rendered. In other words, quality is created at the moment of performance, not in a factory designing in functional quality or just in the programming department.

What is received is often the focus of quality, but so too is *how* someone receives quality—a crucial distinction for service organizations such as those in IS. IBM defines quality as a "delighted customer," Xerox in delivering "innovative products and services that fully satisfy their requirements." Definitions are crafted around what customers perceive to be quality rather than just performance to a set of standards. However, many useful engineering paradigms still exist: zero defects, six sigma, defect-free, conformance to requirements, and so forth. These are terms commonly used today—for example, in the management of software development—that borrow from quality principles long used in manufacturing. But they apply across your entire organization.

Such definitions require you to understand who your customers are. In the case of IT, they are more than just end users or management. They include suppliers linked to your company via electronic data interchange (EDI), customers who buy goods to whom you bill, and government agencies to which you send electronic data on taxes and workers' compensation. A great deal of concentration is focused on service delivery definitions. We know that service work involves performance more than products and has a very large labor component (see Figure 1.2). In addition, since consumption of a service occurs as it is performed, consumption and production are inseparable and perishable—they occur once, as an airplane flight or a restaurant meal. Customer-oriented definitions therefore call for focus on the reliability of services provided, willingness or responsiveness to service someone quickly, ability of employees to offer trust and confidence, empathy, and a good business environment.

How to Develop Your Definition of Quality

Developing a definition is an early step in the implementation of quality. If your company or agency does not have one, the first step is to get an enterprise-wide definition. If that is not possible, develop one for your

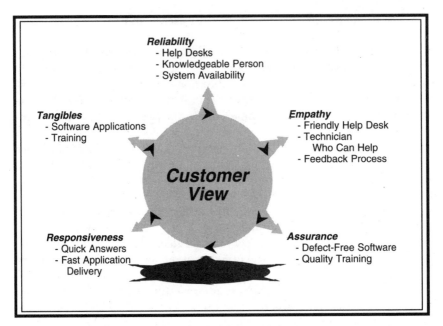

Figure 1.2 Components of a service quality delivery definition.

own department with an eye toward its potential adoption by the entire enterprise. Three basic steps are effective in developing a useful definition:

- Ask your customers or end users what they think quality should be.

- Solicit ideas from your employees, particularly those closest to customers and end users.

- Determine what your competitors worldwide use as a definition.

There are several good rules of thumb to follow in defining quality.

First, think of two types of customer-focused quality or satisfaction: for "big C" customers, the individuals who select and pay for your goods and services, and for "little c" customers, all employees whose work you depend upon or who depend on the output of your efforts.

Second, make your definition general enough so that it fits your entire enterprise and is consistent with your vision of the firm's future. It is imperative that your employees "buy into" the definition because they have to develop strategies for implementing it and measurement systems for determining success. You will know how effective the definition is over time by how your customers react to your services.

While more will be said about vision, suffice it to say that a good vision speaks to an ideal state that an enterprise wishes to achieve. For example, an IT organization can visualize an environment in which its end users turn to it whenever there is any kind of process problem to solve. The information processing department at Lands' End speaks of providing world-class service to the rest of the corporation. At IBM, end users come first. Visions, like definitions, must be plausible, generate confidence that they are attainable, and be important enough to be worth all the hard work necessary to attain them. They are statements about the future and provide a focus for all activities.

Third, make sure each employee understands the definition. Do that by communicating, by having executives constantly discuss it, and by having employees participate in the original definition and support of the vision.

Fourth, apply the definition to strategic planning and measurements. Effective strategic planning today embodies visioning anyway, so current methodologies already take this step into account. When armed with a vision, you can ask: How are we going to apply quality principles to our daily activities? Building strategies and tactics that address how you are going to implement your quality definition and corporate vision is integral to making quality management part of the fabric of your business.

Management Insights from Quality Gurus

The most influential quality expert, W. Edwards Deming, spoke of "constancy of purpose" as a critical management imperative. His phrase implies that the definition of quality is not one that changes frequently, but it is one that you have to get right. Being in the computer business is a bad definition if what you are really in is the information processing business. He argued that you must be careful and pick the right definition.

Continuous improvement is another concept that he proposed. This means that everything constantly changes; therefore you must develop processes that lead you to improve everything. Nothing ever reaches perfection; customers and suppliers change needs and services and so must you. If you can reduce software bugs by 50 percent this year, next year you should reduce them by 75 percent, the third year by 95 percent, and so forth.

Deming argues that profound knowledge is important. This idea involves understanding systems, a theory of variation, psychology, and knowledge. In his mind, systems are collections "of functions or activities" that are clearly understood within an organization. People working within a system work as a team on common goals. Variation is simply the application of statistical analysis to understand what is going on and why, so that corrective actions can be taken when appropriate to improve performance.

Deming's theory of knowledge is that no insight or fact is absolute or definitive. If you change the way you count something, the results change, too. There are no right answers, just answers generated by the methods used to generate them. Knowledge is good for predicting outcomes based on measuring data.

Philip Crosby, author of *Quality Is Free* (1979), contributed the obvious but important idea that doing things right the first time is cheaper than correcting errors. He emphasizes the value of prevention, of avoiding problems before they occur, by building prevention-based steps into our processes.

Joseph M. Juran emphasizes understanding who your customers are and what they want. He believes the charge has to be led by senior management, that all employees need to be trained in how to improve quality, and that quality must be improved rapidly to be effective. More than the others, Juran urges speed in improvement as a way to remain competitive, even if it means revolutionary changes. He argues for "fitness for use"— a Juran pearl—as his way of saying that what the customer wants is the starting point for any quality program.

What Quality Experts Have Learned

What we have learned over the past two decades can be summarized quickly:

- You must approach quality specifically and systematically.
- Quality takes time to implement; quick fixes do not work.
- Involve all employees and make sure they are all empowered to make decisions regarding quality.
- Quality requires focus and concentration.
- Quality is a management process and a business strategy that leads to competitive advantage and to less-expensive products of superior quality.
- Customers are the central focus of all improvement processes.
- Managers often get in the way of an organization's transformation and are at fault if the workers do not produce quality in all that they do.

Baldrige Approach to Quality

Many models are being developed on how to implement quality. These models invariably have an assessment or report-card function associated with them. The design that is becoming the standard of choice in the United States, and that will serve as the model for subsequent discussions in this book, is the Baldrige approach. Many organizations are finding that this approach serves as an effective tool to measure the performance of IS organizations. Since IS has to be measured in the context of how an entire enterprise is performing, our ability to view IT through the Baldrige lens allows management to integrate the activities of IS and the measures of its performance into other parts of the company or agency. Furthermore, customers and stakeholders are increasingly insisting that their suppliers use the Baldrige approach in defining their quality efforts. In short, the Baldrige criteria offer a measurement of commitment to quality and a framework for discussion and improvement.

The recognition associated with the Baldrige approach is the most prestigious award in American industry, worth a fortune in free advertising. Japan and Europe also have quality awards, and in the United States over thirty states have their own awards, most of them modeled on the Baldrige. The point is, every industrialized country in the world also now has a national quality award.

The Malcolm Baldrige National Award was established in honor of the secretary of commerce in the Reagan administration who espoused the need for quality improvement in business to enhance U.S. competitiveness. It is administered by the National Institute of Standards and Technology and the American Society for Quality Control (ASQC), and is awarded annually to as many as six firms: two in manufacturing, two in services, and two small firms. Selection is based on a rigorous measurement of quality achievements in seven categories worth varying points not exceeding a total of 1,000. Its underlying assumption is that quality is defined by the customer; thus category 7 (customer satisfaction) is worth several times more in points than, for example, category 3 (planning). Figure 1.3 is a flowchart of the Baldrige framework.

Key Elements of the Baldrige Criteria to Apply

Senior executives are charged with creating the values and goals of the organization and the environment that makes possible sustained pursuit of quality improvement. They move the organization toward use of quality tools and practices. To fulfill the vision of quality improvement, the enterprise gathers and analyzes information to judge performance, plans implementation of improvements and quality, deploys and improves employees, and manages the quality process, which constitutes the system or activities of the organization. Operational results and customer satisfaction are critical measures of outcomes and effectiveness. The Baldrige

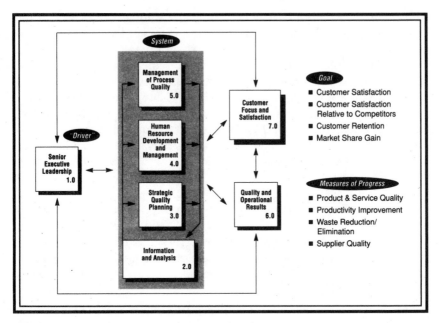

Figure 1.3 Baldrige Award Criteria Framework.

examiners look for a system of well-defined and well-designed processes that actualize the quality vision. In categories 6 and 7, they look for success in quantifiable terms.

The model values continuous improvements in results over time with "ever-improving value to customers." It does not suggest how to improve, but rather how well you are doing on your journey toward ever-improving quality performance. Those familiar with the process argue that its greatest benefit is in providing a structured view of your strengths and weaknesses in your terms. Thus it can lead directly and confidently to an agenda for improvements. For IS organizations, for example, it can serve as an approach to deal with your issues (both technical and operational). The model prizes fact-based decision making, measurement of process improvements and results, a customer focus, cycle time reduction, better products and services, more skilled employees, and a long-term view of the business—all attributes long considered good management principles in the world of IS management.

Because the Baldrige criteria are so widely accepted and serve as a useful way of measuring progress, a more detailed description of the categories can be found in Appendix A.

What Baldrige and the Quality Emphasis Have Taught Organizations

Consumers Want Quality

Surveys done by the ASQC, Gallup, and others have conclusively shown that consumers in Europe, Asia, and North America have been increasingly demanding higher levels of quality in both products and services. This insistence on quality has also appeared within enterprises where end users are demanding greater levels of performance by other departments.

Companies Find Quality Profitable

A variety of empirical studies shows that implementation of quality practices does in fact improve profitability. Without taking up pages of this book to review those studies, suffice it to point out several conclusions. There is a direct cause-and-effect relationship between the kind of quality practices supported by the Baldrige criteria and actual performance of corporations. Quality-successful organizations focus on:

- customer satisfaction
- leadership from senior management
- empowerment and training of employees
- fact-based decision-making processes for continuous improvement
- the Baldrige management model

These observations are just as true within departments as across entire enterprises.

Best Practices Are Valued by Corporations

The number of surveys and studies done to identify what are best practices in the world of quality has grown almost exponentially during the early 1990s. Some studies, like those currently underway by the American Quality Foundation—Ernst & Young, IBM Consulting Group, various U.S. government agencies, and university professors and consultants—are leading to a corpus of reliable management techniques, many of which will be presented in subsequent chapters. However, several important insights applicable to IS organizations are worth listing now:

- Quality is a critical factor in strategic performance.
- Quality is in the eye of the customer.

- Awareness of competitive activities is critical.
- Process improvements are a strategic imperative.
- Employee involvement is crucial and on the rise.

Quality Improves an Organization's Competitiveness

Given the demand of both little c and big C customers for quality, those who provide it are in a better position to succeed. Increasingly, the vehicle for delivering quality goods and services is through process improvement. As mentioned earlier, an important factor in quality process work is the role of IT, particularly in supporting cycle time reduction. Thus, more than ever before, the effectiveness of an organization's performance is dependent on the role of IT. The application of IT can be either by the IS organization or directly by end users. Increasingly, the evidence suggests that both IS and end users need to apply IT to their process work to get the benefits desired.

Be Patient for Quality Results but Push Hard for Action

Surveys of company-wide quality programs all have led to a similar conclusion: It takes at least two years of emphasis on quality improvements before you get tangible results, and it takes an additional three to four years before you can be "best of breed." The first three years are the most difficult for quality programs, and this period yields less at first, while people learn and apply these principles. This is when the skeptics and cynics within an enterprise feel rewarded because all the available data suggests that there are no benefits "so far." In addition, costs will actually go up if for no other reason than retraining—all expenses incurred before benefits become apparent. After about three years, a snowballing effect becomes apparent as basic process improvements and reeningeering give back benefits.

Since in the early stages the going is slow, and even confusing, anybody three years down the path is now gaining momentum that allows them to run ahead of your organization. By definition, therefore, because quality is a competitive advantage, they have a quality edge over you. The message is to start the process now, and if you are already engaged in quality practices, to speed up the effort as much as your culture allows. You should not assume that all other departments and companies have started at the same level of quality or that they evolve through various phases at the same rate. Until you get in the habit of comparing your performance to that of, say, other IS organizations, you will not really appreciate how far behind or ahead you are. However, we do know that avoidance of quality improvement can be lethal. The Baldrige framework can help define the rate of progress you are making and how that compares to efforts in other parts of your company and against your competitors.

Why Information Technology Is Critical

For years, information technology was justified solely on its ability either to reduce operating expenses (through automation of work) or to help people make decisions. The first approach was obvious and clearly understood; the second was done more on faith than on facts. As a result, many IS operations have been under the sharp analytical eyes of frustrated CEOs wondering what they were getting in exchange for their investment of anything from 1 to 5 percent of the organization's total operating budget. The ability to cost-justify information technology changes substantially when it is viewed as a tool to support quality activities. If an organization uses process improvement or reengineering as the primary strategy for quality improvement, and accepts the kinds of ideas put forth by Deming and Juran (such as using statistical data to make decisions), then information processing has a very important role to play. This role is played out in three fundamental ways.

First, one can do "in-process" monitoring. As a process is being used, computers can track its effectiveness, generating data that allows a process owner to improve the process itself. For example, telephone systems can tell how many rings it takes before a phone is answered or how many suggestions management responded to and by when.

Second, computers can store in data bases information useful in executing tasks or processes important to a customer. For instance, having on-line access to information on your products and their availability makes it possible to explain immediately to a customer the features of your products and when they can get them. IS shops can tell their end users what data is available or use the information to analyze how to improve an application's performance.

Third, they can shorten lines of communication and speed up how things are done, buying you cycle time reduction. Electronic mail systems (all computer-managed) allow people to communicate instantaneously across the enterprise regardless of its organization, bringing together (if you want) product designers, manufacturers, and sales people. These systems can also be linked to customers and vendors. In each instance, communications—which are a very time-consuming part of most processes—are shortened dramatically.

Then there is the IS organization itself, long recognized as the cobbler without many shoes. As you catalog the tasks an IS organization performs, and then improve all of those tasks by process improvement, you quickly find that you, too, can use computers to reduce cycle time (for example, speed with which programs are written), communicate more effectively and quickly with end users (such as through bulletin boards and E-mail messages), and monitor your work (through such tools as in-process monitors).

Seven Benefits Your Company or Agency Derives from Using Computers

This is not the place to talk about modern applications; you can turn to many books and articles for those. However, in the world of quality, companies are exploiting seven generic benefits to the application of computers. One generally achieves these benefits by ensuring that all significant process improvement efforts include an assessment of how to exploit them and then by designing in IT uses that create these benefits.

1. Computers shorten lines of communication. The two obvious examples are electronic mail and report generation. More important to the culture and operations of an organization, computers can eliminate geographic distance within your enterprise. Where people are is no longer relevant as long as you have telephone links to them through computers, and a nearby airport! This is most evident with such large work forces as salespeople (often now called members of the mobile work force) and customer support representatives (CSRs).

2. Computer-based applications can be designed to make sure the right information is at the right place at the right time. An obvious example is making airline reservation information available to someone trying to sell you a flight ticket. Another is having diagnostic information available real-time during a medical operation or while repairing a car. The military needs such data to determine status of combat action (for example, artillery and bombing systems). Benefits include cycle time reduction (your view) and faster service (customer's view).

3. Computers can gather data on transactions and also on how processes are doing (effectiveness), then do basic statistical analysis for you. Much of the useful operational data that historically you gathered in a glass house (for example, CICS utilization, CPU availability, and so on) are examples. Computers can also merge processes to provide new insight into your operations or those of your end users. In sales, for example, opportunity identification processes and data bases are being

merged with skills availability processes and data bases to help organizations determine their capability to go after specific market segments. In IS, I am beginning to see processes merge together as well. The most obvious example is the total view becoming evident of on-line applications availability by merging the end user's view, that of telecommunications, and computer operations as one seamless mega-process.

4. Computers help increase your awareness of your environment. An early and still expanding application of computers is to perform competitive analysis (benchmarking), and to tap into data bases maintained by other firms (such as DIALOGUE, Standard & Poors) to learn more about rivals and customers. In IS, we have seen network analyzers at work for decades, but now also with real-time status of how various on-line processes are performing. The most popular of these are computer-based telephone systems that monitor how long people are kept waiting on calls, the number who hang up because they could not get into an organization, and types of line usage (such as fax versus voice).

5. Computers make it possible to provide new or additional services. New services enable many organizations to achieve competitive advantage over rivals. Technology is a major tool for facilitating delivery of those services. Providing data bases that inventory the repair history of products, dispatch service personnel, or integrate multiple data bases on customers are well-understood applications. In the public sector, IT is used to track repeat offenders of state workers' compensation or civil rights laws and to provide user-friendly kiosks in shopping centers for information on state programs and services. Linking your computer to a bank's so that customers can pay for goods and services or so that you can deposit employee paychecks are others. Increasingly, alliances among companies have been formed largely by merging applications and data bases. You see it in airline, hotel, and car reservations all merging, but obviously involving at least three companies (four if you are the travel agent). Thus, this is more than EDI: It is the merging of processes, services, and strategies across organizations, agencies, and companies, using IT as the facilitator (the extended enterprise concept). Implementing that kind of strategy effectively requires rigorous project and process management.

6. Computers can give you a fuller view of customers and clients. As you build the number and complexity of computer systems with growing data bases and multiple levels of processing (for example, on the micro and then in mainframe platforms), it becomes more and more possible to merge these to provide links leading to more complete views of customers and processes. For example, look at customer master records. The first on-line data base records were typically customer

name, number, address, and accounts receivable files. Then came records on order-entry and purchase history. In the 1980s, people added access to commercially available data bases to determine who to sell to, what prospects' buying habits were, and their demographics. Simultaneously, there came the technical capability of splitting screens on a terminal into four or more windows or a dozen or more open files. You can now get that kind of information to a salesperson online over the weekend for a more effective customer call on Monday morning. In fact, you can safely assume that some of your competitors are doing that right now. In IS, large systems-development projects are benefiting routinely from such applications of technology.

7. Computers improve efficiency of services and operations. Repair services today are increasingly being tracked and managed via computer. Packages are delivered with bar codes serving as tracking mechanisms. IS shops post in real time on consoles current CPU utilizations, number of CICS transactions, and network volumes. Giving employees communications vehicles allows them to work together better and management to include more people in the organization's activities.

Conclusions

The theme of this chapter—that IS must be and already is central to the quality transformation underway—is not an idle thought. A recent survey by Dun & Bradstreet (D&B) Software found that 59 percent of the IS respondents were implementing process improvement strategies. Most IS executives also reported that they expected significant benefits from such an approach in their own organizations. So, on the one hand, you are pulled into the process work being done by your end users because they need your technology, but on the other hand, you cannot avoid applying the same techniques to your own operations for the same reasons. There are many models of how best to perform. Some of the IS organizations in the United States most widely recognized for their application of quality methods include American Express (customer service), Boeing (IS metrics pioneer), Caterpillar (quality tech support), FMC (continuous improvement strategy), General Electric (function point analysis), Hughes Aircraft (programmer productivity), IBM (quality strategies), J.I. Case (use of metrics), Motorola (metrics and system availability), Prudential Insurance (low-cost IS services), Travelers (end-user orientation), and Xerox (metrics linked to best practices).

At the same time, there has been as much, if not more, resistance to applying Total Quality Management principles in IS. As with many end-user departments, lack of knowledge about these principles is one issue. A second is a reluctance to pick up new habits and new ways. But there is growing evidence of other issues. For example, IS is often fractured and exists in many departments, making it difficult politically and organizationally to pull things together.

Another problem has been the lack of really good statistical quality-control software that could serve as tools for IS to apply to quality implementation, particularly for networked personal computers. Also some tools are applied by end users first, without IS being in the loop. That circumstance alone has frequently served as a barrier to coordinated activities as, for example, plant quality-control experts implementing TQM software without any regard for the benefits of having organization-wide networks that use common TQM software and metrics.

The bottom line is simple: Today quality practices are being adopted at warp speed by organizations of all kinds in the industrialized world. IS is central to the success of any organization's quality implementation. Therefore, IS is looked to for support and, also, is expected to implement these same strategies in its own house for the same reasons. The evidence is clear today that the disciplined process management techniques we see all around us constitute nothing less than a fundamental shift in management practices. These are at least as significant as the introduction of mass production techniques in the early 1900s, such management techniques as Management by Objectives (MBO) after World War II, and the use of computers in business by the 1960s. Our challenge is to apply proven techniques to the operations of IS. We begin to examine that process in Chapter 2.

References

Cortada, James W. "Jargon and Business Transformation," *AIXcellence* (July 1994): pp. 10–12.

Cortada, James W. "Quality Movement Is Here To Stay," *The Total Quality Review* (March/April 1994): pp. 7–9.

Crosby, Philip B. *Quality Is Free: The Art of Making Quality Certain.* New York: McGraw-Hill, 1979.

Deming, W. Edwards. *Out of the Crisis,* 2d Ed. Cambridge, MA: MIT Center for Advanced Engineering Study, 1986.

Dobyns, Lloyd, and Clare Crawford-Mason. *Quality or Else: Revolution in World Business.* Boston: Houghton Mifflin, 1991.

Ishikawa, Kaoru. *What Is Total Quality Control? The Japanese Way,* translated by David J. Lu. Englewood Cliffs, NJ: Prentice-Hall, 1985.

Joiner, Brian L. *Fourth Generation Management: The New Business Consciousness.* New York: McGraw-Hill, 1994.

Juran, J.M. *Juran on Leadership for Quality: An Executive Handbook.* New York: Free Press, 1989.

Maglitta, Joseph. "Re-engineering the Workplace," *Computerworld* (October 3, 1994): pp. 94–97.

Nanus, Burt. *Visionary Leadership.* San Francisco: Jossey-Bass, 1992.

U.S. Department of Commerce, Technology Administration, National Institute of Standards and Technology. *1993 Award Criteria: Malcolm Baldrige National Quality Award.* Gaithersburg, Md.: U.S. Department of Commerce, 1992.

U.S. General Accounting Office. *Management Practices—U.S. Companies Improve Performance through Quality Efforts* (GAO NSIAD 91–190). Washington, D.C.: Government Printing Office, 1991.

Walton, Mary. *The Deming Management Method.* New York: Perigee, 1986.

2

An Information Systems Strategy for Quality

Never tell people how to do things. Tell them what to do and they will surprise you with their ingenuity.   GEORGE S. PATTON, 1994

In this chapter I explore the early steps toward a quality-driven information systems (IS) strategy. I look at the theory of quality as applied to IS, define the role of processes and process reengineering, and describe the role of measurements as a change agent.

Briefly stated, Total Quality Management (TQM), or quality management practices, dictates that an organization should have a comprehensive master plan for continuously improving quality. The emphasis should be on the word "comprehensive" because to work these practices must cut across all functions and levels of an organization. While TQM may start in one department, no real or substantive successes are possible without everyone participating because there are so many interconnections between departments. For example, for management information systems (MIS) to implement its principles effectively, it must ensure that end users apply the same tools and management systems. Otherwise one cancels out the other. For many IS executives, the single biggest obstacle to implementing quality practices in their own operations is getting the rest of the enterprise on board. The problem must be addressed early. Thus it is critical that the IS executive leads the charge, if necessary, in senior management ranks to disseminate TQM principles across the board before going too far within his or her own organization.

Quality Is a Strategic Tool

TQM is a strategic, long-term set of practices that make it possible for management to introduce continuous improvement initiatives across all functions. While it may start with one's own department, over time it must seep through to the four corners of the enterprise because most activities are interrelated across departments and divisions. Quality practices integrate various techniques and management principles. These usually include quality function deployment, statistical process control, just-in-time practices, root-cause analysis, and vision-based strategic planning. The ultimate aim is nothing less than the implementation of quality practices in all activities throughout the organization.

If this sounds to you like the kind of sea change that will forever alter the culture of your organization, you are correct. This is serious business; therefore, it is imperative that management appreciate the consequences of applying quality principles and understand their effect on the culture of the enterprise. Once started, it is hard, if not impossible, to reverse the process.

To be effective, you must systematically apply order and common sense to all activities. Successes are predictable, while failures become opportunities for learning and improving, not for punishing. Focusing the heart and soul of an enterprise on customers leads to better overall organization-wide results.

Black & Decker's corporate information services, for example, used TQM principles to help the firm increase cost-effective product yields. One by-product the IS department experienced was improved stature within the firm because both IS and end users began using common language, tearing down traditional barriers between them.

Monsanto's Fiber Division applied TQM across all departments, including IS. Combined with computer integrated manufacturing (CIM), the division achieved a 50-percent increase in productivity. When applying TQM principles to projects involving automation, management learned that a detailed vision-based strategic plan was crucial; that one could and should analyze and define key "cost drivers" at every step of the way; that measuring results at each step was essential to continuous improvement; and that effectiveness increased when management focused on the overall process and quality improvement, not just on how to save money.

Appleton Papers, Inc., used IS in a TQM-driven strategy to improve the efficiency and effectiveness of all parts of the business as it moved profitably from some maturing product lines to specialty papers. IS replaced all its major systems in six years to support effectively the company's various operations while weaving TQM principles into daily work.

Each of these strategic initiatives in successful companies and agencies are multiyear, multidimensional approaches that lead to new measurements, different personnel practices, a changed culture, and new levels of results—many of which are different from earlier ones.

All good IS TQM strategies incorporate four basic ideas:

- continuous improvements
- zero defects
- doing it right the first time
- reliance on employees closest to the situation to improve it

At the center of all such strategies is the customer; everyone inside and outside the organization is a customer (see Figure 2.1). An enterprise can achieve the greatest set of competitive advantages by reducing the cycle

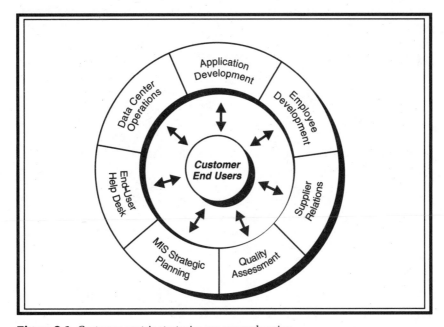

Figure 2.1 Customer-centric strategies are comprehensive.

time required to design, develop, sell, and service products. From an IS point of view, cycle time reduction means helping all other functions of the organization (such as manufacturing) reduce their cycle time. In IS it also means getting backlogs of programming reduced sooner, maintenance done faster, and availability made continuous.

Measurements of performance track quality indicators, not just financial numbers. Measurements indicate how quality is improving and also suggest areas for enhancement.

Whatever your quality targets were this year, to continuously improve, you accept the notion that next year's will be higher. You prize measures of defects (errors and mistakes) and root them out so that you get fewer per unit of measure, such as fewer per million transactions (the sigma measurement approach). The objective is to get to zero mistakes or defects. As children we were raised with the idea of "do it right the first time." It turns out that was good advice. Fixing a problem by avoiding it in the first place is far less expensive than allowing it to grow. For example, anticipating a defect in the design of an automobile component might cost only an additional $35 but, if let go, could lead to the recall of hundreds of thousands of automobiles. In IS a software bug could result in customers being under-billed for goods. Trying to collect the difference by re-billing would cost a fortune, not to mention be awkward and possibly reduce customer satisfaction.

The notion that employees closest to a situation are probably best equipped to improve it has been borne out by empirical research. As organizations learn more about how to train and empower employees—and this is a process of its own—the more delegation makes sense.

Heroes are people who practice the new thinking and achieve improvements. More frequently than not they function as teams. The currently fashionable description for groups of employees who are most knowledgeable about a process is natural work teams. When effective they are almost self-governing groups of employees who set their own goals, measure their own performance, and decide what activities to perform: They may work in IS and in end-user departments or even with customers and suppliers. In their world managers are facilitators who knock down barriers. Natural work teams allow supervisors to spend less time inspecting and more time coaching. This is a powerful new paradigm for IS management and an enormously effective one because of the extensive requirement to rely on technically skilled employees to decide what gets done and how.

In this world, gathering information about what is going on is crucial. Also, as already mentioned, is the need to reduce cycle time in all that gets done. The notion of processes is likewise important because it is central to any quality strategic approach.

Tasks and Processes Provide the Best Way to Look at Your Activities

View your tasks as processes, as families of activities. For example, to document all the steps required to design a new system to meet your end users' needs means that both the IS professional and the end user must speak the same language. Using common IS flowcharting techniques allows both groups to find new ways to reduce time to perform tasks, to simplify procedures, and to improve service to customers. What is new is that the end user is using some of your techniques and language, such as flowcharting!

When you look at tasks as processes you find that they can be improved. This notion is called entitlement; that is, all existing processes have built into them room for improvement that you are "entitled" to, since the process exists today in an imperfect form. You measure the time it takes to do it today. Next you make improvements, measure the effect of your changes on cycle time reduction, make more improvements, measure those, and so forth. You also define defects and make changes to reduce their number as well. The easiest way to improve a process is to eliminate unnecessary steps, such as multiple signoffs and redundant inspections by supervisors. Also useful is simply deleting duplicate copies of files and data that various participants in a process use.

Eventually you cannot improve the process any further. It is as "tuned" and stable as it can be with little variation in performance. To improve beyond this point requires that you replace the process with a radically new one. This is known as process reengineering.

In practice a new process can only succeed if you set goals for defect elimination and cycle time reduction that you absolutely cannot achieve by improving the existing approach. In short, with such goals you force those working with the process to find a better way. That may be as simple as looking at what other firms have done (a benchmarking activity). But it also involves your employees applying their knowledge of what customers or end users want. Their knowledge of costs and tasks, plus their creativity and benchmarking, also can get you to a new process. Checking with competitor data can spur the imagination. For example, if your rival or peer organization can maintain availability of CICS transactions at 99 percent with response times of under 2 seconds, while yours is 95 percent at an average of 8 seconds, you know there is a way to get better performance, because someone else has already figured out how to do it!

When you treat tasks as processes you can gain profound knowledge of a function (Deming's idea), design out defects (Crosby's suggestion), and create an atmosphere of constant improvement and customer focus (Joiner's notion). Sharing ideas with end users and customers to validate that a particular process is worth changing, and doing your share in an organized manner, is in itself a process.

Figure 2.2 (a Deming concept) illustrates continues process improvement as a natural work team would execute it. You spend a great deal of time planning an improvement, make it, study the consequences, and then plan additional improvements. What is a new idea for most people is that the process never ends; the wheel keeps turning.

Figure 2.3 can serve as a strategic overview of how your organization can do all its process work with one fundamental focus: to serve your stakeholders (customers)—the people who either depend upon you for your work or who judge your performance.

What's New, What's Business as Usual

For forty years management has demanded that data processing serve the strategic requirements of an organization and the best IS executives have attempted to implement this ideal. In a quality-driven world, businesses apply a variation of this strategy. They first tackle the problem of reconfiguring the non-IS aspects of the enterprise to conform to market realities

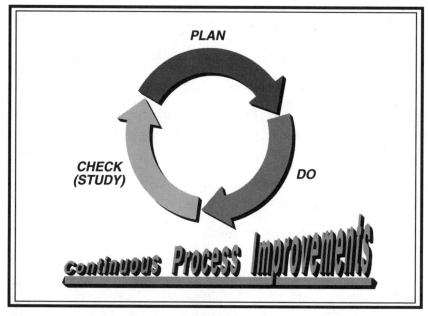

Figure 2.2 Continuous process improvement.

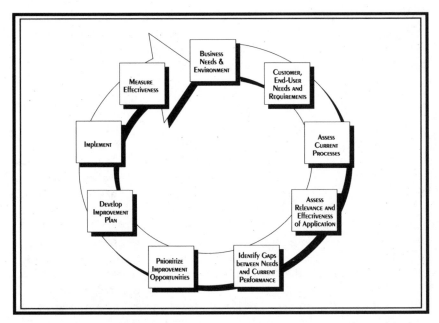

Figure 2.3 Strategic overview of process work.

and to a strategic plan. Next they reapply IT to support the functions of the business as effectively as possible. Finally, to support the use of IT correctly, they restructure the IS function to match.

IS Structure is More than Hardware Implementation

From the point of view of IT, managers typically find that to bend technology effectively to their businesses' goals they must formulate strategies in five areas:

- applications
- hardware
- information (data)
- business
- work

Not so clear is work flow. This basically calls for examining how non-IS employees implement their processes and how IT can improve them. Do you automate a process? Add CRTs? Do you outsource?

Business flows lead essentially to a precise set of actions once non-IS management has figured out how it wants to organize the enterprise. IS then determines how to support the new structure. If, for example, a company breaks itself up into a federation of stand-alone legal entities, should each have its own IS organization and independent applications? If the structure moves toward a more decentralized form, must you give up glass-house strategies in favor of collections of local area networks (LANs) of PCs?

Viewing the enterprise through the prism of information or data is yet another way to examine how IS supports the organization. This means identifying what the organization needs to function, especially in terms of sets of processes. For example, a university knows it has to have a body of information about students (registration, grades, dorm address, parents' address, hours taken, library fines not paid, and so on). Understanding this requirement and knowing where these pieces of information need to be within processes helps IS determine what strategies can make such information available. The library will need to know in real time if a student habitually returns books late; the administration will want a batch billing capability; campus police need on-line access to dorm address information, as does the student health center. Professors need a way to submit grades and possibly homework assignments via computer.

Interestingly, most management books on IS focus on technology. They look at how it is changing, call for IS management to focus on platforms, discuss fourth-generation tools, and so forth. However, in a quality culture, technology is only one of several issues IS must take into consideration to arrive at a holistic view of how it supports an organization.

Finally, looking at applications through use of quality management practices calls for us to think of them as processes. In fact, I would like to see the word "application" driven out of the vocabulary of the IS community and be replaced with the word "process." Process implies a broader perspective, because it includes activities that may not be automated, whereas an application view traditionally focuses only on automated tasks. By using the notion of process, IS then has to concern itself with where to apply technology within a larger flow of events, recognizing that not all things are automated, while others are completely taken over by machines. It forces IS to be like the carpenter who looks at a construction assignment thinking about what tools to use, not limited to just a hammer and saw. Previously, this carpenter might only have worked on a project if he or she could rely on just hammer and nail. In short, limiting one's view or, as we see in IS so often, just working within specific IT constraints, is a problem. I will have more occasions later to talk about the role of IS in process improvements and reengineering.

IS Organization Conforms to Enterprise-Wide Models

While this is not the place to have an extended discussion on how IS organizations will look in the 1990s, it is important to note that if you conduct process reengineering with heavy doses of IT, you will find that the IS organization may have to change to become more effective.

Several issues drive all businesses to examine organization. One early concern is a business's strategic plan and its long-term goals or vision. The plan should answer the question, how do we align resources to achieve objectives?

Another issue is how personnel are recruited, trained, managed, and rewarded. I have devoted Chapter 9 to this issue because it is an important lever that affects how you organize an IS shop. Since people tend to work hardest at those tasks on which they are being evaluated, measures of IS and enterprise success as a whole influence profoundly how IS organizations evolve. While this concept is not a new one, the fact that you have in-process measurements and not just measures of output does influence your structure. For example, do you align some of your resources by function (such as people assigned to work with manufacturing and accounting)? Or do you align your structure and people around processes that may be cross-functional (such as order fulfillment)? As you move toward a more process-oriented view of your role, IS organization shifts away from just a functional alignment, although a core group remains aligned the old way (such as operations staff to run a glass house).

There is a growing body of knowledge about when IS organizations need realignment, and how they should conduct it. Some of this research is listed in the references at the end of this chapter. Suffice it to say that the bigger the enterprise, the more IS management must look at organization, changes in applications and technology, management of people, and strategic planning as formal ongoing processes in their enterprises. Increasingly these activities become less annual or occasional events and more often continuous. They are linked with actions that occur every week or month through a fact-based "plan-do-check-redo" approach. This is how you end up applying statistical process control and process improvement tools and techniques to renew your organization and its activities on a continuous basis. The notion of continuous revitalization of organizations and processes is a fundamental imperative in quality-based practices.

It is the process view that leads you to discussion of centralized versus decentralized, outsourcing versus in-house, glass house platforms or PCs, from one set of software tools to another, and so forth. As Figure 2.4 illustrates, you move from your vision of the business as a whole, and its role in the economy, to a structure of the enterprise. From there you can

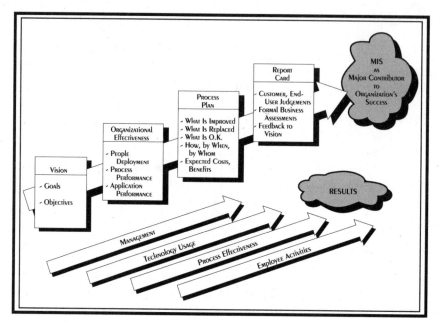

Figure 2.4 From vision to results.

determine what IS must do to support processes, and what processes, and finally to its own organization, platforms, and processes.

IS Executives Become Process Leaders

Finally there is the role of IS management. While Appendix A reviews some concepts on the role of managerial leadership as defined in Chapter 1 of Baldrige, there is an old responsibility that becomes even more important today. CIOs and IS managers are moving away from serving as technocrats and more toward thinking and acting as business managers. Increasingly they need to facilitate process views of their operations. The rest of this book is devoted to the activities they must take on to implement improved operations. It clearly is appropriate for the IS executive, particularly the senior manager, to view his or her role as that of a business leader integrating IS activities into those of the rest of the enterprise and, more specifically, into processes where they make sense.

Second, such executives still have the traditional role of managing deployment of their resources (people, equipment, software, and information) to support the enterprise. While both a management and a technical function, the process view linked to a strategic business plan is critical.

Third, and usually underemphasized, is the responsibility of the senior IS manager to make everyone within the enterprise aware of how IT can support customer service and process improvements. Some of the best IS executives take the initiative to go to functional departments and suggest new approaches. Today the requirement in a quality world is for that same executive to take the initiative in showing his or her staff how to use IT to improve processes.

Five Components of an IS Quality Strategy

Whether you are just embarking on the path toward quality practices or are well on your way, a number of areas require constant attention to ensure continued progress in implementation. They generally fall into five categories of activities:

- processes
- measurements
- organization
- rewards and incentives
- education

For quality management to work in any organization, management must address these five themes because they provide the environment in which employees can implement quality practices and techniques. The challenge, simply put, is to get employees to behave in ways that quality-driven enterprises value. To a large extent you must begin with a clear list of attributes that you want in all that gets done. These are woven into the five critical areas just listed.

Key Attributes of Quality-Based IS Activities

The list of quality-based IS activities is short but important:

- service to customers (internal and external)
- leadership involvement (directs, rewards, and inspects)
- continuous improvement (process focus)
- employee involvement (empowerment and commitments)
- quality assurance (assessments)
- measurements (including self-assessments)

- supplier partnerships (shared management disciplines)
- strategic quality planning (involves everyone)

By making sure all of your process work involves each of these eight attributes, you can change your culture, improve your effectiveness, and ensure your link to the mainstream of the enterprise's mission.

From a tactical point of view, it is wise to catalog processes and give them owners. Process owners play a special role. They are the key change-masters in the organization. They "own" responsibility for improving a process and, when they are properly empowered, can cross all functional lines (even inside and outside IS if necessary) to get the job done. In practical terms, these responsibilities often mean that process owners have to be high enough in the organization to understand how the corporate coordination of activities across various departments and divisions will affect their work. Process owners have to understand the context in which their responsibilities lie. Ownership seen this way is crucial to the successful implementation of a process because it uses many of the same motivational tools—such as compensation, rewards, and accountability—that are important in delegation of responsibility.

Figure 2.5 summarizes the kind of behavior desired in a quality-driven organization. These attributes are just as relevant in IS as in manufacturing

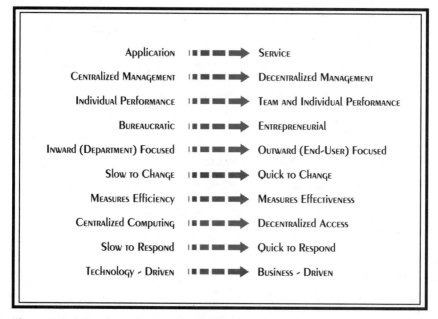

Figure 2.5 Cultural transformation in IS organizations.

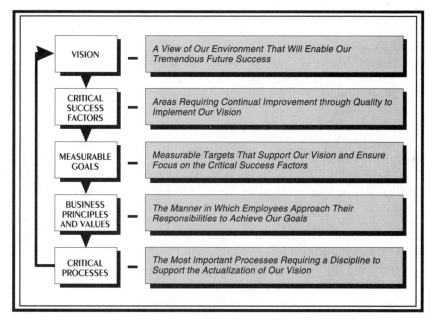

Figure 2.6 Continual improvement.

or sales; indeed, you want them consistent across the entire enterprise so teams of employees can work with shared values and culture. The left side of the chart describes behavior as we generally see it in many organizations today. You might want to draw one up for your company or agency as it is now; it will probably have many of the same features. The right-hand side reflects the ideal of a quality-driven organization. To achieve this ideal focus on the eight key attributes of quality listed above, add a messianic focus on customer satisfaction, and emphasize cycle time reduction in all that gets done. You can then accomplish the required improvements in tasks and processes using process management reengineering techniques.

There is a growing body of preferred practices to accomplish these tasks. However, to list all of them here would confuse the issue because each organization must emphasize one over the others and change that emphasis over time as circumstances evolve. No two enterprises are ever quite the same. So to provide a cookbook for the cultural change I am talking about is not realistic. We must instead think in terms of strategic initiatives and areas of emphasis to get to where we need to be.

Figure 2.6 illustrates how the various elements work. One specific tactical step that is universally effective is documenting your actions as you develop a plan for quality improvements. A visual representation makes it easier for staff to understand how their specific actions and roles fit into the larger frame of what the organization is attempting to accomplish. This is very important. Many organizations that fail to place employees' activities into context create confusion among their people about what they have to do. As a result, their effectiveness is degraded. So it is very important to build a model, even a very simple one, of what is going on in your organization to help delineate everyone's roles. Figure 2.6 is a simplified blueprint for excellence and can be drafted that simply. You can make yours more detailed and certainly different, but have one.

Figure 2.7 looks at IS as one large process and uses the Baldrige framework to illustrate some of its various components. Yours, to be realistic, could look much more complex. As in Figure 2.6, common elements become obvious:

- senior IS executive drives a vision that is heavily value-based (customer-focused, quality-dependent)

- information collected is used in fact-based decision making, planning and deployment, and improving processes of the enterprise

- measurement of results and customer satisfaction become routine

Results then influence the organization's vision and the process begins all over again.

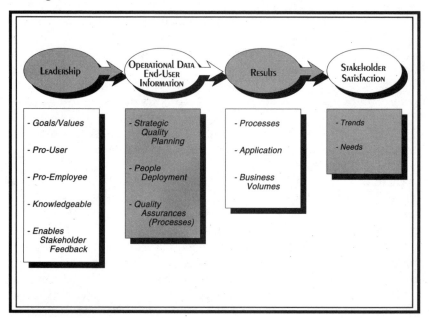

Figure 2.7 Baldrige view of IS.

Role of Processes

Because processes are at the heart of what people do in a quality-driven organization, they require management much like any assets of the enterprise. They are the vehicles for channelling the daily activities of all employees from CEO down. The sooner you can identify existing and desired processes, the faster you can get on with improving them. The sooner you can establish measures of their effectiveness, the more quickly you can set goals and measure progress toward them. Thus the tasks are to catalog processes, assign process owners, and begin improving processes. Here I will focus on management's role in using process work.

How to Apply Planning Elements

Because it is much easier to run an organization if you have a plan, taking some of the best practices of planning and applying them to the quality transformation you want is an effective strategy. Begin by creating a vision of where your organization is going. The organization must have a clear sense of where it wants to go by what date, followed by a statement about what the IS organization should do.

Craft the IS statement to be customer-driven. For example, "Information Services supports the company's strategic intent to be a world leader in specialty chemicals, high value-added customer services, and customer-focused quality." Many organizations also add a statement about how they carry out their mission and may include something about employees. One firm uses a simple statement to describe its mission: "Information Services leverages the effectiveness of the company by providing information resources that create competitive advantage, better decision making, and improved internal and external communications." Another company decided to add: "We are also committed to continually improving the skills, performance, and job satisfaction of all employees." You might consider adding some statement that indicates the measure of overall success. Customer satisfaction surveys are the most popular and effective. Customers of IS are defined typically as employees of the company or agency. They may also include big C customers and suppliers. Regardless of who they are, their satisfaction is measured by surveys and by their definition of quality.

Since organizations that do strategic planning invariably also identify critical success factors, in a quality-driven world management concludes very quickly that continuous improvement of customer satisfaction is most important but is followed very closely by employee success (morale, skills, and so forth). Others include effective application development, deployment of teams to get things done, and use of process reengineering.

The most widely used set of measures of results consists of four categories:

- customer (usually end user) satisfaction or success
- employee success or morale
- company revenue or profit
- budget attainment or taxpayer satisfaction (if government)

Well-run IS shops develop measures of continuous improvement within each of the above four areas. Success depends on meeting these goals to fulfill the mission. Examples of measures include numbers of telephone calls answered (such as by a help desk), line drops on the system, and speed with which application changes are made from initial end user request to full operation.

Goals for IS help point to processes that need improvement either to be more efficient or effective. Goals also allow an organization to link their activities back to a vision and to the categories of success listed earlier. Common goals can be statements of values and expectations. Examples in IS include:

- improving customer satisfaction with IS services
- improving employee skills
- implementing new systems faster
- implementing "world-class" processes
- applying state-of-the-art technologies

There Is a Big Difference Between Process Improvement and Process Reengineering and When You Use Them

Writers, consultants, and professional quality experts use the terms "process improvement" and "process reengineering" interchangeably. However, there is a distinction that you need to understand because sometimes you will simply want to improve a process and other times you will want to replace or reengineer it. Improving an existing process is sensible when you have one that is performing relatively well and you just need to add enhancements to capitalize on your entitlement. However, if the case for action is compelling—that is to say, you need something radically different—process reengineering is the ticket. Improved processes tend to focus on many but small incremental changes that have a cumulative effect over time; however, with business reengineering, dramatically different, even

Process Improvement vs. Process Reengineering		
Process Improvement	Attribute	Process Reengineering
Continuous	Velocity	Rapid one time
Important at the start	Management	Active throughout
Inspection	Management	Leadership
Incidental	Technology	Intensive/Cornerstone
Incremental/Cumulative	Change	Periodic/Dramatic
Improvement of steps, tasks, all processes	Work effort	Redesign of significant process

Figure 2.8

outrageous results are the goal (see Figure 2.8). Risk of failure grows as you move from continuous improvement to reengineering, so the need for major change must be more acute as you move toward the reengineering option. An example might be an application development process that goes from an average cycle of three years to three months. You have to find a better way!

If you are just improving established processes, pay attention to tasks and little steps everywhere along the path; otherwise reengineer by picking a major activity and redoing it all at once, moving instead from the incremental to the order-of-magnitude change. You will find that with existing tuned processes end users just want to add automation and data processing almost as an incidental application, to bolt on technology to existing methods of work. In a reengineering situation, technology can be the cornerstone of the new process. For instance, if people interact generally by mail with state government or by walking into an office, how you deal with them might simply be a gradual improvement over existing approaches. Putting kiosks in shopping centers where citizens can renew their drivers' licenses with a VISA card is process reengineering.

Most IS managers do not realize that there is a distinction between gradual and radical change. Each approach has its own disciplines for process work, and each requires a different implementation. If process improvement is the only objective, senior management might be casually involved. In a reengineering situation, senior management is intensively involved throughout because the changes are profound. Understand the difference and realize that each one is treated differently, but both are part of the world of quality.

IS Management Should Set Priorities for What Gets Done

You cannot boil the ocean. Attempting to improve all your processes will feel like you are taking on too much. Well-run IS organizations at Motorola, Xerox, IBM, DEC, and AT&T, for example, have learned to pick their targets carefully. Attempting to do too much simply takes focus away from the day-to-day business to an extent that is unacceptable. By prioritizing processes you want to improve, you apply your resources more effectively. It is not uncommon to find that just working on a half dozen or fewer is effective. Going beyond ten is risky although I have seen IS organizations do more. If you are just starting down the quality path pick fewer, easier-to-do projects and then, with experience, broaden your attack on more complex problem areas. Once a set of processes is improved, stabilized, and put on a course of continuous improvement (with early results to encourage others), then you can pick up a few more to work on with little risk of failure.

You will have to make an initial list of the critical processes of your organization, prioritize their relative importance to the enterprise, probably also grade their current health, and then pick the ones to improve. It is normal to see a list of fifteen to twenty critical processes in any organization. You can easily also develop a list closer to fifty. However, initially you should emphasize a list of the most critical. Figure 2.9 lists some of the more obvious ones in most if not all IS organizations. Your organization will probably have others as well. The traditional planning methodologies that companies and government agencies use include techniques for prioritizing lists linked back to customer satisfaction and continuous improvements in the efficiency and effectiveness of operations. The output you want is a list that blends that which is important to customers, your employees, and the firm as a whole.

However, experience would indicate that there are several very obvious areas to focus on first. These are both processes and areas for management emphasis; you must address all of them simultaneously to jump-start the quality process or to sustain it. They are:

- measurements
- organization
- rewards and incentives
- education on quality

All are inward-focused, pay too little attention to customers and end users, and allow maximum politicking in the existing culture. But they are the basis of incentives that historically have encouraged employees to

Strategic Planning	Compensation
End-User Support	Personnel Management
End-User Feedback	Employee Feedback
Supplier Relations	Recognition
Communications	Facilities Management
Skills Development	Application Design
Service and Repair	Application Development
Budgeting	System Support
Telephones	Software Maintenance
Measurements	Hardware Conversions
Resource Deployment	Software Acquisition
Organization	Technology Acquisition
Quality Assessments	Data Base Management
Systems Assurance	PC Administration
Complaints	Case Tools Use and Application
Telecommunications Support	

Figure 2.9 Critical IS processes.

perform. As a manager attempting to change cultures and practices, you need tools with which to shift employees' activities. These are the most effective collections of tools available to you. Apply them first to get employees to do the sorts of things discussed throughout this book. By managing these tools as processes, you can also learn how to improve other processes, implement quality improvement techniques, and ultimately change behavior to conform to the objectives of the enterprise. Organizations already recognized as leaders in quality have found these initial focus areas to be crucial to any transformation, although the literature on quality is only now beginning to reflect their importance.

Role of Measurements

People focus on those tasks for which they are being measured. Since people perform the tasks in processes, measures of processes and their results are, in fact, measures of human performance. The subject of measurements is not yet sufficiently understood in the world of quality but, because of the profound effect it has on people and processes, is constantly studied and debated. What the quality experts agree on, however, is that to improve constantly, processes must be measured statistically.

It is increasingly evident that a firm's or department's measurements profoundly support or inhibit its cultural transformation. Thus the measurement system in an enterprise ought to support the vision, goals, and objectives in terms that are quality-driven.

In addition to providing focus, at the process level measurements allow us to understand what is going on. Statistical analysis of many activities within a process also permit us to see patterns of performance not otherwise obvious. For example, if you measured the causes of downtime on terminals over the course of a year, you would learn enough to identify the primary and secondary causes. If you run a help desk and track how many people you help within two hours after they contact you, then it would be relatively easy to gauge your performance. Well-structured in-process indicators also can serve as early warning systems that something further down the pike is going to break. In software, defect rates and types have long been a source of many effective measurements.

How Measurements Are Established

For any process or result, process owners should ask, what do we want to accomplish? Having settled on that, then ask the question, how will we know that it is accomplished? The answer should be some numbers. For example, I want to produce thirty lines of tested code per programmer each day. I would like to do this consistently each day. In this very simple example, I would measure the number of finished lines of code, track that performance over time to see if it goes up or down, and then, to get to continuous improvement, ask how I can get the output up to thirty-five lines. To achieve that, I would create measurements of the various programming activities to determine what critical activities a programmer does that gets him or her to thirty lines per day. Statistical tracking will point out what in a programming process varies too much and is too influential overall. Once identified, those elements of the process can be improved or controlled either to increase a programmer's capability of writing more lines of code or to ensure no drop below thirty lines.

Many organizations have learned a few "tricks of the trade" that help in the overall strategy of implementing measurements.

1. Measure anything worthwhile numerically. Though it is sometimes very difficult, everything can be measured statistically. For example, if you have an activity that is repeated frequently, each action can be treated as a statistic.

2. Measurements should indicate progress toward goals, not hurt the individuals who gather the data. Thus, for example, measuring im-

proved end-user satisfaction with the network is far more effective than simply assessing the downtime.

3. Define the process, then formulate measures. This ensures that your priorities are in order: the process, not the measurements of it, is most important. Measurements should always be subservient to the goals of the organization and to the process. They thus can be measures of progress toward goals already identified as beneficial.

4. Expect measurements to change as circumstances and your experience evolve. If you improve continuously, then, by definition, processes must change. That circumstance will cause you to need different measures from time to time. In fact, as your rate of change increases, so too will the variety of measures, creating a problem of constancy of measures. Ideally you want the same set of measurements over a long period of time so that you can judge increases and decreases in performance. But you may find that impossible for very specific measures, in which case you must find ways to aggregate measures to produce quality indicator indices. For example, if you have an employee opinion survey in which a number of questions keep changing each year, you may want to express responses as percent satisfied, then aggregate all of these into one satisfaction percentage.

If It Exists It Can Be Measured

While I will have more to say about measurements in discussing software, it is important to reiterate that every process in information systems can be measured. At first organizations find this fact hard to accept, let alone implement. Very quickly, however, they find ways to prove the point. Examples of measurements actually in use in IS organizations include:

- average annual hours of training
- training evaluation scores
- ranking of development methodologies
- DASD error recording
- CICS availability
- help desk response time
- data base optimum space utilization
- data security requests completed
- total defects by operations

- downtime by system, by application
- system response times
- peak times
- network availability by location
- abandoned telephone calls
- end-user satisfaction with IS timeliness
- end-user satisfaction with IS service attitudes
- percent DASD growth
- CPU utilization
- paging rates
- cost center rate in dollars per unit of CPU
- MIPS per programmer
- MIPS per data center headcount
- trends in customer dissatisfaction

Moving Your Organization to Shared Measurements Is Possible and Essential

All IS organizations have measurements today. Typically these derive from mainframe systems software in operations and from the network functions. In large part these measures of performance are built into software and hardware provided by vendors (such as CPU utilization, line hits). However, these are not enough because they do not link specific actions to processes or to the overall mission of IS to support the entire enterprise. So for all practical purposes in most IS organizations, measurements as a strategy for improvement start at ground zero and must be jump-started.

The first step is to understand the measurable goals of the company or agency that everyone has to support, both inside and outside IS. This information can lead to very specific discussions about what measures IS needs to ensure its overall activities are synchronized with those of the corporation. Figure 2.10 shows a hierarchy of measurements linking corporate goals down to transaction levels. The conceptual architecture of measurements you construct is both unique to your organization and begins from the top down. So you begin by understanding corporate goals, then move down to department objectives, then to process measures (discrete or aggregated). Finally you get to transaction-based measures, which are most often already present.

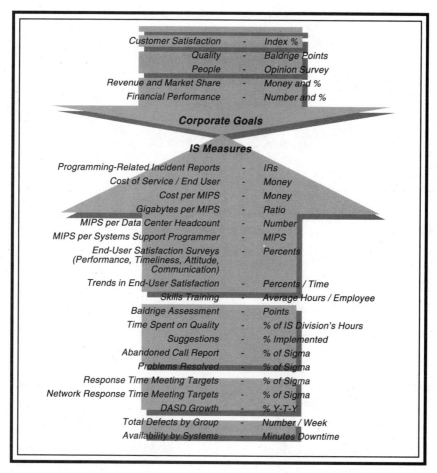

Figure 2.10 Sample hierarchy of measurements.

Having a chart as simple as Figure 2.10 will help you satisfy one other major requirement of good measures: clearly understood relevance. Figure 2.11 is yet another example of how to track programs. Blindly putting measurements in place without having employees understand their significance is useless. The problem is that without giving your staff a frame of reference, it is virtually impossible to have them continuously improve operations through their own insight into what the measures say. Empowered employees without a common vision of where the entire enterprise is going are simply anarchists. Measures help link small actions to grand purposes.

A set of measurable goals shared among departments should not just

Function	Major Indicies	Goals
Tech Support	Planned Outages Unplanned Outages CICS Error Network Availability	Least Business Impact Zero Six Sigma 100%
Help Desk	Calls Abandoned Calls Answered Quickly	Zero 90% in 12 Seconds
Data Base	IDMS Errors Optimum Space Utilization	Six Sigma <60%
Planning	Adequate Processor Adequate DASD	<85% Utilized <70% Utilized (Minus Work Pools)
Data Security	Requests Completed	≤ 1 Day
Administration	Meeting Mail Delivery Schedule	Within 5 Minutes of Schedule

Figure 2.11 Summary of support-function quality indicies and goals, IS department, Appleton Papers, Inc.

include technical performance criteria but also managerial information. These can include data on expenses, resource allocation, and overall customer satisfaction. Enabling employees to help each other succeed in order to thrive personally allows management to link performance back to measurable departmental and corporate goals. Experience suggests that shared measurements of this type should not be held at just management levels but ought to flow down and across the entire organization. Many IS shops also plaster their walls with various measurements and present them as trends so people can see progress and defects over time.

Measurements in quality-driven organizations tend to move from just the discrete (transaction-specific) to broader indicators of progress. Thus instead of just measuring uptime on the computer, one might add skills improvements, team participation, and company measures of profitability. As you move to broader measures, you will find it absolutely necessary to change your reward and recognition systems. By doing this an IS employee can actually thrive because of superior contributions he or she made to the overall success of the enterprise. For many, this approach is radical, and particularly disturbing to those employees who just want to work in a narrow area and be left alone.

A Case of the New Measurements

The IS organization of Appleton Papers, Inc., illustrates a well-defined strategy for linking measures of corporate success to those of its own operations. John L. Tucker, Vice President of IS, focuses the mission of his organization on several activities:

- development and enhancement of information systems
- continuous availability of hardware and software
- customer-focused application development

These three areas of emphasis tie neatly into corporate objectives to use IS as a strategic tool to improve efficiencies and effectiveness. Over a period of a half dozen years, Appleton Papers developed specific goals with metrics for each. "Quality Scoreboards" helped track their progress. They began by focusing on high availability of hardware, then added software-defect elimination, number of employee suggestions (Bright Ideas for Improvement—BIFI), and participation rates. They followed these with six sigma for computer operations and targets and measures of employee involvement and teamwork. Now the organization imposes on top of all these measures an assessment based on the Baldrige Award criteria.

Along the way, this IS shop visited other IS organizations at Milliken, Motorola, IBM, and elsewhere to learn about specific measures and strategies. For example, BIFI grew out of suggestion process work at Milliken, while Motorola taught the IS organization about Six Sigma, and IBM Rochester infused IS with its customer focus. Tucker sees no end to the process of looking at how to link IS operations to corporate objectives measured in quantitative terms. He also communicates results on bulletin boards, through a newsletter to all Appleton Papers organizations, in staff meetings within IS and to top management, to vendors supporting IS, and, if asked, to customers of the company. It took nearly a half dozen years to get to where he is with measures and he expects that these will continue to change as his operations evolve.

The Basic Lesson: Focus on Measurements

Early in your transformation to a quality-driven enterprise, focus on what gets measured. Then change or add measures to reflect what the IS organization wants to accomplish as a whole. Build process measurements underneath those as you implement or shore up your process work. Changing measurements of organization-wide objectives may be the easiest element of a transformation because a senior executive can almost single-handedly implement these. (On the other hand, staff would have to figure out what data to trap and how to present it, making sure it was linked to goals.) The senior manager can catalog what each department is doing to support the measurable organization goals and then to map the processes that either are unique to a department (programming or running the mainframe), that cut across the entire IS organization (for example, personnel practices), or that encompass the whole company or agency (such as end-user computing support). Putting in place appropriate measures of performance with goals for acceptable rates of improvement links activities effectively as long as measures are outgrowths of key processes.

Enlisting first- and second-line management to help develop goals that include measures of organization and process-level performance is crucial to managing the "buy-in" process for both IS and end-user employees. Let the managers lead the detailed efforts first, then later engage employees and end users in the detailed definition of specific process measures and goals. When goals are not met, let IS and end users work with the process owners to root out the causes of defects and malperformance. Let *them* suggest and implement changes that will enable performance to improve.

Initiating these kinds of approaches, with root cause work done at a process level in response to measurements, usually takes less than a year. However, it does take approximately two to three years to have all functions of an IS shop so linked. The smaller the organization the more quickly the process can be fully functioning since there are fewer people to engage in the effort.

References

Ceridwen, Janice. "Using Quality's Tools: What's Working Well," *Journal for Quality and Participation* 15, no. 2 (March 1992):92–99.

Covey, Stephen R. *The 7 Habits of Highly Effective People*. New York: Simon & Schuster, 1989.

Darst, Donald. "Balancing Productivity and Quality," *Datamation* 36, no. 18 (September 15, 1990):117–119.

Henderson, John C., and N. Venkatraman. "Understanding Strategic Alignment," *Business Quarterly* (Winter 1991):72–78.

Hronec, Steven M. *Vital Signs: Using Quality, Time, and Cost Performance Measurement to Chart Your Company's Future*. New York: Amacon, 1993.

"Information Systems: The Risk and the Return," *I/S Analyzer* 29, no. 12 (December 1991):1–12.

Keyes, Jessica. "New Metrics Needed for New Generation," *Software Magazine* 12, no. 6 (May 1992):42–56.

Kouzes, James M., and Barry Z. Posner. *The Leadership Challenge: How to Get Extraordinary Things Done in Organizations.* San Francisco: Jossey-Bass, 1990.

Manning, Mitch. "Managing TQM Information Overload," *Journal for Quality and Participation* (December 1990):76–77.

3

Applying an Information Systems Quality Strategy

Take time to deliberate, but when the time for action has arrived, stop thinking and go in.
NAPOLEON BONAPARTE, 1815

In this chapter, I focus on major areas of activity that must be organized early in an IS process of transformation: organization, rewards and incentives, education on quality, and a way to begin to know if things are moving in the right direction.

In Chapter 1 we looked at where IS fit in the quality management activities of the 1990s, and in Chapter 2 we examined several basic components of an IS quality strategy at a high level. Now we need to focus on those clusters of activities that allow senior management and its employees to transform an IS organization into a quality-obsessed one. This is done by using traditional management tools: organization, rewards and incentives, quality education, and inspection of results. The actual "how to" in many cases is business as usual; the new elements answer the question "what to do." With the "what to do" list worked out, it becomes much easier to link IS operations to corporate or agency business plans. That linkage addresses the question of how IS supports the overall aims of the end-user community.

This sequence of events has a very simple assumption built into it: Before your IS organization can go back to its company to announce it is prepared to be a quality player, it must get its own house in order. Before touching Big C or little c customers, it must suit up for play. While the process of getting ready to participate occurs simultaneously with the overall evolution of the company or government agency, nonetheless, IS management must focus early on making its employees capable of performing along the lines suggested in Chapters 1 and 2. That calls for internal housekeeping activities.

Organization

This is not the place to discuss organizational theories nor how to organize IS to support the business function. It is sufficient to note that today many organizations are using the Henderson and Venkatraman model in which IT is aligned to reflect the realities of an organization's processes. Figure 3.1 shows the interrelationship among business strategies, IT strategies, organizational infrastructure, and finally how IT's organization fits.

However, there are similar questions IS executives ask themselves when aligning IS to business objectives and when creating a structure that fosters continuous improvement and quality. They include:

- How must the organization be structured in order to satisfy the requirements of the overall business-based IS strategy?

- How well is this strategy being executed within the current IS organization?

- To what extent are IS skills being developed that support the IS business plan?

The questions could go on; however, notice that the main emphasis is on linking the organization to what the institution is attempting to do.

The operative strategy is to organize IS to carry out its mission. If that mission changes, so too must the organization, and that involves more than restructuring an organization chart. It involves allocating resources, investing in skills, and finally in defining roles of individuals. The other lesson learned from quality-driven IS organizations is that they change more frequently today than in the past.

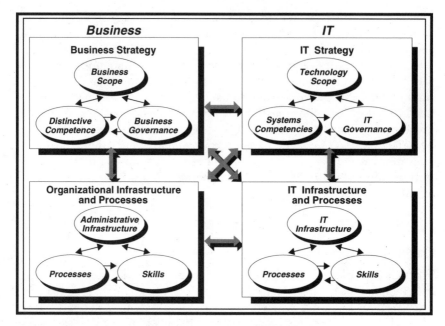

Figure 3.1 Henderson and Venkatraman alignment model.

What Today's Organizations Are Beginning to Look Like

Increasingly, organizations are being structured to meet several basic requirements:

- to place the majority of employees in direct end-user or customer support, with fewer in staff functions
- to reduce the layers of management, driving down overhead costs while shortening the decision-making process
- to enhance flexibility to change quickly to support new functions and opportunities
- to continuously improve the effectiveness of the enterprise

These kinds of intentions lead to organizations that make decisions quicker and in which employees have far greater responsibility and authority to define what they do and how than they did a decade ago. Consequently, management's role is less to police and to allocate and more to help define the IS business strategy for supporting the company or agency, and to facilitate development of skills and investments in technology that employees must work with.

Some functions remain constant on an organization chart: operations, systems development, and so forth. But depending on the size of the IS organization, more people are spending time as members of cross-functional teams populated primarily by end users. Spans of control within departments have been creeping up from five to ten people to over twenty people per manager. Using some assessment tool, such as the Baldrige criteria, gives an IS organization a framework with which to constantly test its effectiveness.

How to Change an Organization

Enough with great theory—the real question is how do you change organizations? The fastest way is to reduce their size. Take out layers of management and change spans of control. Any IS executive can perform these actions. You will have to do it in a series of waves, to avoid chaos, but stripping out a whole layer of middle management, for example, is an excellent first step. Second, extending the span of control for managers so they have more people reporting directly to them forces altered behavior and different ways of looking at structure. For example, combining programming and systems development into one function in a midsized IS shop can be very effective. In a large IS operation, setting a goal of not having more than three layers of management is productive. So the first step is to reduce the number of managers.

The span of control issue is a tricky one. If managers go from having ten employees working for them, as an example, to thirty, they must learn how to lead a larger group or they will attempt to manage it the same way they managed the smaller group. As you extend spans of control, you must also revisit your personnel practices and look at your managers' roles to see what has to change. The answer invariably is that you must teach your managers to delegate, to enhance the skills of their own people in managing process improvement, and then link them directly to the end users and fellow workers who they support.

The Need to Focus on Five Critical Success Factors

If your work force is intelligent, motivated, and has good morale, these two steps work well. However, several critical success factors should receive special attention.

First, all employees must understand and support the overall vision and business plan for IS because they need to make decisions within that frame of reference. Furthermore, with fewer managers there are fewer people from whom to ask permission, thus employees end up taking ownership for their own actions.

Second, make sure these employees are trained in process improvement techniques. These tools will help them improve the day-to-day functions of their departments and give them the confidence to make new changes.

Third, performance plans, rewards and recognition, and compensation must be aligned to support this new world. These can include rewards for team-based activities, for developing new quality-oriented skills, and for process work.

Fourth, employees must want to accept responsibility, authority, and management support for their new roles. Not all are willing to do so; recognize that they may never change and, thus, may have to leave your organization. Those who perform with effective initiative need to be protected and rewarded. They should be assured of job security if their own positions disappear because of some process reengineering results. Participatory environments where they get help to set goals and directions also facilitate development of this kind of culture.

Fifth, management has to facilitate the exchange of ideas and dialogue between their staffs and those of other end-user departments, customers of the firm or agency, and with peers outside the enterprise. Too often workloads are created that do not permit these kinds of activities. Without spending time outside the traditional IS organization, it becomes very difficult for employees to maintain either a customer focus or to learn about new ways of performing IS functions.

Management should take advantage of another continuous process involving the "unofficial" changes that occur within organizations. Traditionally, management announces a restructuring and publishes an organization chart with people's names in boxes. Yet we have all seen how people cluster together differently than on the "org chart" to perform tasks. Today, the informal organizational structure is more the norm, and it changes much faster. Experts on organization argue that the best organizations are those structured to support tasks, and that is exactly what happens with "virtual" or unofficial organizations. Our job is to legitimize these unwritten structures wherever possible because they are usually more effective than official ones.

What drives these underground structures is exactly what we provide to the rest of the enterprise: telecommunications, fax, E-mail, data bases, PCs, air travel, and continued delegation of authority and responsibility down an organization. Over the years, democratized structures have been created, in effect, taking away from senior management some of its authority to design an organization. Management's challenge now is to make those changes public in order to improve their efficiency and effectiveness while blending them with the official organization. In an ideal situation, the new organization should reflect the business objectives of the entire company or agency, not just of IS. Today, an enormous amount of research is being done to define how best to do this (a summary of some of that research is listed in the references at the end of this chapter).

Thus, as you begin your journey to a world of continuous improvement and quality practices, organization must be an early high-priority candidate for transformation. If you are attempting to transform the IS function in context with the rest of the company, then you will find that organizational changes are a most effective way to propel the conversion across the entire firm. If other parts of the company are also changing structures, your early transformation of organization is critical in order to avoid conflicts of interest and/or discontinuities of support and teaming. Many IS shops use TQM tools to help constantly change their organizations. The most important of these tools are measurements of success, root-cause analysis to determine why structures are not as effective as they might be, and process definition and redesign techniques to establish what tasks to do and how best to deploy people.

Rewards and Incentives

TQM literature focuses little on motivating people in the world of quality. Overwhelmingly, the discussion at seminars focuses on process work, measures, and outcomes of activities. All the documentation I have seen on software and TQM looks at the application of process work in programming. All of these approaches are important. But effective IS managers know that before any are operative, they must bring along the people who are to do the work, to make the transformation, to improve continuously. To win the hearts and minds of staffs, IS executives make it in the best personal self-interest of their employees to come along on the quality journey. You must put those incentives in place at the same time you work on organizational changes. The process of creating positive incentives and rewards also is continuous. We have learned that before you can expect significant process improvement, your culture must change. Put more tactically, how you motivate and reward your people will determine to a large extent how much progress can be expected from IS staffs.

While I devote a whole chapter to employee issues later (consistent with Baldrige criteria in that it also devotes a whole chapter to people), we must deal with institutional motivation early in this book.

The essential question is how you get your employees to perform in a quality manner; specifically, how you get them to do the following:

- focus on customer and end-user requirements
- build relevant skills

- participate on teams
- do process improvement work
- take personal ownership for specific and enterprise-wide success
- welcome change and even craft it
- work well with others
- continuously challenge themselves to do better
- exhibit a work ethic that makes their activities exciting

Many techniques have traditionally worked to create the positive environment we all seek for our staffs. However, recognition plays a very special role in the process.

Role of Performance Measurements and Plans

An effective first step is to make sure that all employees have a documented performance plan that includes the requirement that they contribute to the quality activities of the organization. Then you can tie evaluations of that performance to merit pay systems, rewards, and recognition. Such plans can call out the need for individual and team results.

With performance plans in place, the organization can implement a series of rewards to reinforce quality-based recognition. Management is responsible for developing a recognition process or at least starting it; employees should participate in the development effort. A variety of monetary and nonmonetary methods can be used, often in combination. Figure 3.2 lists a wide variety of recognition in existence in IS organizations.

With performance plans and a reward process in place, you can then standardize values and practices that are measured and recognized. Essentially, the amount of emphasis on appraisal and recognition allocated to quality-based activities goes up. You emphasize quality results of processes, individuals, and teams more than before to determine appraisals and recognition. Employees can help create measures of success both in processes and through jointly developed (with management) performance plans so that there is clear communication of expectations and results. Management and employees can publicize quality successes of individuals and teams, and ultimately those who exhibit quality work habits can be promoted. Make sure that you measure performance and recognize achievements at both the individual and team levels so that you encourage both being effective.

How do you know that the effort is working? Employee opinion sur-

Examples of IS Recognition Programs

Department, Division, HQ Awards	Money, trips, mementos, bulletin board notices
Team Award	Money, trips, mementos, department/ team parties
Individual Awards	Money, expensive mementos, mention in company newsletter
Suggestion Awards	Cash, bulletin board announcements
Training Awards	Memento, certificate, certification
Performance Awards	Bonus for quality work, salary increases, gifts
Customer Satisfaction Award	Framed customer letter, HQ awards, mementos, merchandise, "night out"

Figure 3.2

veys will tell you if the performance and recognition processes are having desired effects. You also can count the number of teams and the results of each major process to see what is happening. Constantly comparing results to your performance and reward processes will tell you if one is helping or hurting the other. Some IS departments also measure effectiveness of recognition by the enthusiasm displayed by award recipients. Are they emotional when they receive an award? Do they display recognition mementos in their work space? Do they alter their attitude and exhibit different work habits as a consequence? To what extent do peers congratulate award recipients? How many thank-you notes sent by employees and managers to each other for an award is another indicator of acceptance and effectiveness.

Many organizations have a permanent recognition process team representing all levels and functions that continuously improves, monitors, and implements recognition programs linked to the kinds of behavior and results the enterprise or department desire. Frequently these teams also participate in company-wide recognition process teams. The same is true for performance planning and evaluation, usually driven by the firm or agency human resources community with representation from IS. Increasingly, IS organizations are establishing their own human resource management teams to ensure integration of rewards, compensation, performance, skills development, and education.

What Your People Want You to Do

An enormous amount of research has been done in the past two decades to understand what motivates employees. The IS community has not been immune to these kinds of studies either. Knowing what your people want is very important in creating a quality-based culture in IS. There are four sources of information upon which to make fact-based decisions concerning your transformation:

1. You can go to the literature on managing people.
2. Your own company's human resource or personnel department will have information.
3. You have the experiences of your own enterprise.
4. You can ask your people.

The first three you probably do today. But do you ask your own people? Confidential opinion surveys of how people want to be compensated, rewarded, recognized, and measured are very valuable sources of information. Having employee roundtables to explore these issues is also effective. I recommend doing a combination of both periodically (for example, roundtables quarterly, surveys annually) because issues change. For example, young staff with families want practices and programs that support their roles as parents and confirm their technical capabilities. Older employees may want you to focus on monetary issues and personal recognition of achievement.

Managers can ask their own employees, on a one-on-one basis, what motivates them and what they want. You would be amazed at what you hear. For example, some employees consider education on their area of responsibilities as a reward; you and I see that as a necessity. Others are motivated by public recognition of accomplishments, while some just want to make more money. Some want more vacation time. We have all met IS people who are most effective when working on state-of-the-art systems. An understanding between an employee and a manager about incentives and motivation can help both work together in harmony and for the implementation of continuous improvement. There is little substitute for the one-on-one communication. The opinion surveys will then provide measurable data on effectiveness of management, results of goals and objectives, and effects of recognition and compensation programs.

Having said all that, a number of values most IS personnel would subscribe to should be reflected in incentives and rewards. The various industry surveys over the years have repeatedly confirmed the list:

- People basically want to do a good job.
- Employees want to feel good about the work they do.

- Employees want positive recognition for their results.
- Public acknowledgment of achievement is more valued than private acknowledgment.
- Peer approval is very important.
- Employees usually prefer help (teamwork) to reduce risk of failure.
- There are always lone wolves in every organization, but they too want recognition (but won't admit it).
- Employees want management encouragement.
- Money is not the only incentive.
- Skill development opportunities are very important.
- People like to believe they are working on important things.

Develop a Compensation Plan that Supports Your Vision

Performance plans and recognition processes are also intertwined with compensation systems. Typically, IS personnel are salaried and their income is tied to how management perceives their performance, skills, and sometimes the value of seniority. However, as previously suggested, when transforming an organization, management has to employ a variety of tools to move along the desired changes. Using compensation is important in the early stages of the transformation and, later, in sustaining it. Using compensation along with a combination of other tools (for example, recognition, organization, and education) can increase the rate of transformation. Two strategies are useful.

First, use teams of employees with management to develop a compensation methodology consistent with what the enterprise expects in rewardable behavior. They will do the job better than any personnel or compensation consultant could because they are closest to the realities of their organization. The most obvious rewardable behavior is a profound procustomer emphasis with an eye cast on expenses and process results. Profit-sharing bonuses have become popular and effective approaches employed in the private sector.

Second, treat compensation as a critical process that needs to be studied and continuously modified as circumstances warrant. If employees realize that it is their process, too, they can be expected to take ownership of tying its rewards to your (and their) business objectives. Case after case indicates that this is a reasonable approach. This strategy will also inevitably factor in the value of working with state-of-the-art technologies and collective needs of classes of employees (for example, men versus women, young versus old).

You also will have to appreciate that people's needs change over time. Your personnel department focuses on this reality continuously as it changes benefits, for example. Simply put, employees between roughly the ages of 21 and 30 are developing, learning, and exploring possibilities. Therefore, they are very interested in things such as improving skills, job satisfaction, and positive feedback. Those between the ages of 30 and 45 value career enhancement and view their managers less as guides and more as role models. Compensation and rewards cannot be money alone; promotions are crucial. In the period from the late forties to the early fifties, competition for success and promotion generally declines, employees see themselves as guides, and immediate rewards have to be monetary more frequently than not. They worry about putting children through college, getting their houses paid for, relationships with coworkers, and how their jobs identify with specific organizations. As they approach retirement, people begin to identify with other interests outside of work. They are more interested in what psychologists and sociologists call "lower-order rewards," like money (see Figure 3.3).

So why worry about all these reward and compensation issues? As you change your organization into one valuing continuous improvement and renewed customer focus in a service-based world, each age group has to be treated differently. This is particularly difficult with older employees, a problem since 22-year-old programmers are becoming harder to find due to changing demographics throughout North America and Western Europe! And what happens if you decide to have your programming done in India, where it is far less expensive than in the United States or Germany? What effect does that strategy have on continuous improvement and personnel practices? We do not know the answer to that question

How People's Needs Change Over Time	
Ages	Needs and Wants
21–30	Improve skills, job satisfaction, positive job feedback
30–45	Career enhancement, promotions, personal victories
40s–50s	Serve as guides, monetary rewards, identify with organizations, prepare for retirement or alternate careers

Figure 3.3

today. I suspect that a combination of time-proven personnel practices and process disciplines will do the trick.

Quality-focused IS organizations find that they can develop compensation strategies that support business objectives. Hewlett-Packard and IBM pay better than the average company and pay for merit, which is measured by results against objectives. Later in this book, we will explore these issues in more detail. For the moment, suffice it to say that in order to make the transformation, compensation and recognition actions cannot be ignored.

Quality Education

Another process that you must address early and with enthusiasm is education on quality. Although most organizations recognize they need to work on education, they usually mismanage it, forget that it too is a process, and operate it as a program with no definable measures of success let alone goals. Most transforming organizations forget to develop good business plans, to define organizational structures well, and instead run to education and technology out of context. But at least they understand that education is a useful tool.

In short, education is useful in making employees aware of the principles of process improvement and reengineering, the realities of changing markets and circumstances for their enterprises, and the definition of their role. Skills transfer also can be achieved in this early stage of movement to a more quality-driven company culture. It can reinforce the goals set out through compensation and recognition processes by explaining how to achieve success in a TQM form.

Just as measurements, organizational changes, and compensation systems remain a permanent part of any organization, so too does education on quality. That is the same requirement that we have always taught IS personnel about new IS technology and new techniques. Each of the Baldrige winners in the United States and the Deming Prize recipients in Japan have found their education budgets rise. It is not uncommon today to see organizations spend between 4 and 6 percent of their budgets on quality education in the early years. Why make this enormous investment? If done properly, results can lead to a 10 to 40 percent reduction in waste and associated costs while gaining market share or productivity within the first three to four years of investment. Money in the bank or invested in stocks can hardly match those yield rates. However, the risk of failure is high because most organizations have implemented quality education poorly.

Every case of quality transformation I have studied has placed education at the forefront of implementation. This education is over and above the normal training one sees on programming languages and techniques, computer operating systems, and telecommunications. The best education strategies I have seen involve training that is similar across the entire enterprise, not unique to IS. The reasons you have enterprise-wide training are to develop a company-wide vision of the business, interchangeable team functioning techniques, and common quality implementation methods. The initial step is to change everyone's attitude toward a shared perspective of the business or enterprise, followed by skill-based training that focuses on quality tools appropriate for each individual's job. Figure 3.4 illustrates the kinds of topics provided by effective education processes in the beginning of a quality transformation (usually within the first eighteen months).

Two Strategies for Quality Education Are Effective

There are two widely applied approaches to quality education that work. The first angle of attack, which is increasingly being seen as the best, involves a one- to two-day awareness class on why the organization needs to apply quality principles, identification of TQM's basic elements, and some exposure to statistical methods for measuring activities. This class

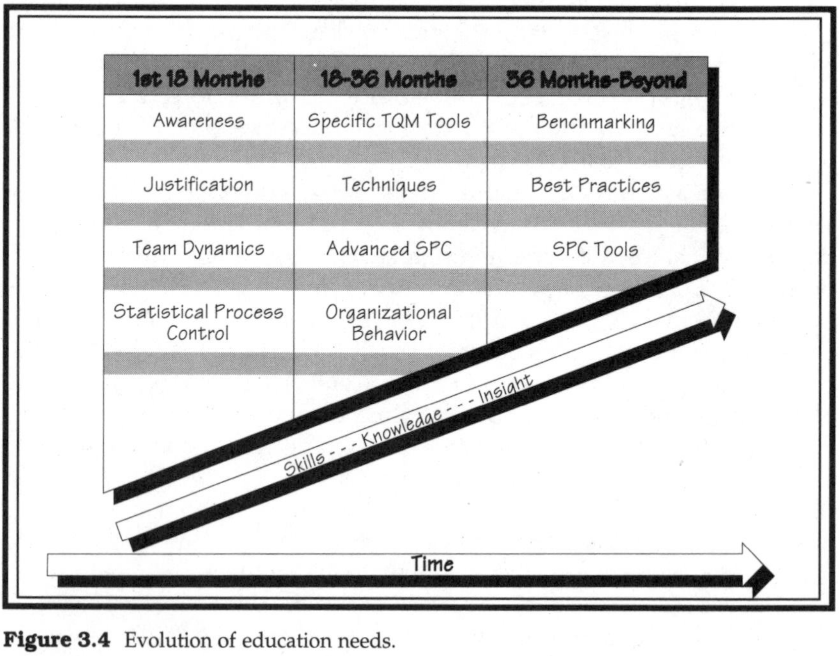

1st 18 Months	18-36 Months	36 Months-Beyond
Awareness	Specific TQM Tools	Benchmarking
Justification	Techniques	Best Practices
Team Dynamics	Advanced SPC	SPC Tools
Statistical Process Control	Organizational Behavior	

Skills - - - Knowledge - - - Insight

Time

Figure 3.4 Evolution of education needs.

is typically followed up in a few weeks or a month with two- to ten-day seminars on process improvement or process reengineering. Specific problems are worked on using seminar and case study teaching techniques. At this juncture, employees are exposed to statistical process control (SPC) techniques (usually called tools) such as Pareto charts and fishbone diagrams. After such training, management can expect employees to begin applying TQM principles in their work on the process. Often application is literally the next day!

Whether they do or not is a function of how the education is handled: as a program, in which case application usually does not occur, or as a process, in which case expectations for application were set and someone is following up to make sure the lessons are applied. In this scenario a process team first is formed, meets at least a couple of times, gets its process education, and then goes to work.

Education is provided either by consultants or by staff within the enterprise charged with the responsibility of educating all segments of the organization. If you are a small firm or agency, you would probably find it more cost effective to hire a consultant to teach the material on process improvement. You would still need to build the one- to two-day awareness education yourself because you know your business. Consultants can help, however. As the organization gets larger, it makes more sense financially to do your own education, although you might rely on consultants to develop the materials for you.

A second path is the fire-hose approach. A company sends everyone off for five to fifteen days of education on "quality-related" topics and then drops them back into their work environment. If the measurement system has been altered to give incentives for process improvements and so forth, then results can reasonably be expected. If not, you can count on having wasted your employees' time while frustrating their hopes that things will change. In short, you will have set expectations too high and not delivered a mechanism by which to fulfill them. Almost every organization I have studied has tried the fire-hose approach; it is expensive and bad pedagogy.

What American, Asian, and European companies have found most effective is incremental education delivered in various doses over time. Their messages are more permanently etched in the minds of employees, and skills learned are more effectively applied. Providing audits with training when needed—a "just-in-time" approach—works better and creates expense only when needed. Each successful education offering recognizes that employees need hard skills to transform their business and that those skills involve process improvement/reengineering, problem identification, analysis, and resolution. Education must allow employees to link their quality activities to their real jobs and to the main purposes

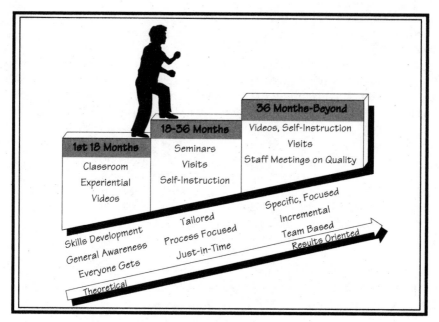

Figure 3.5 Stages of education delivery.

of their organizations. Finally, good education programs must, by necessity, evolve over time as the skills and needs of each employee change (see Figure 3.5).

With either approach, it is imperative that specific outcomes be defined and tracked. To send everyone off to quality education is absurd. In the spirit of common sense and good quality practice, specific goals should be set for results. These should be measurable. For example, sending people off to awareness education should result in increased appreciation for why the enterprise is transforming itself. That can be measured through specific questions asked in an employee opinion survey. Looking at how many employees educated on quality are on process teams, and then later at the results of those teams, can be tied back to skills education as measures of education's results. However you do it, expect and measure results. Simply measuring what percent of the employee population went off to class is not good enough; in fact, it is a mistake since you have no benefit to show for the effort.

Better programs, like those at Xerox or Federal Express, are aimed at altering cultural values as well as teaching skills or arguing the case for a particular organization's need for change. For example, at IBM, a two-day class, known as "The Journey Continues," is given a year after initial quality exposure to show employees the power of vision, the benefits of working more closely as a team, and how to encourage and support each other in quality improvements. It is based on the work of James M. Kouzes and Barry Z. Posner. Theirs is a simple but powerful message: To get extraordinary things done in an organization, five practices must be alive and well:

1. changing processes
2. inspiring a shared vision of a successful future
3. enabling others to act
4. modeling the way for others
5. encouraging the heart

The leaders' role is to make these five practices come alive. By challenging processes, you search for opportunities to change the status quo, with risk-taking allowed and encouraged. Inspiring a shared vision calls for envisioning a better, specific future and attracting others to the common purpose of implementing the vision. This vision can be departmental or corporate; I recommend both. Enabling others to act is simply fostering collaboration and teamwork and sharing power and information to get the best out of everyone. Modeling the way is setting the example—leading by doing. Encouraging the heart is recognizing contributions, linking rewards to performance, and "valuing the victories." All employees, from the CEO to the newest employee on the team, are encouraged to work on all five.

The class is unique in its focus on the values of employees as applied to quality rather than on the mechanics of applying process reengineering principles. Many of the same sentiments are found in Stephen R. Covey's *The 7 Habits of Highly Effective People*. Approximately 25 percent of the course content is directed to altering attitudes, another 25 percent to teaching skills, and the remainder to transmitting knowledge about transformation, vision, and so forth.

In the best managed organizations (either departments or companies), nobody is exempt from quality education. In many enterprises, the standard approach is for the initial awareness education to be taught by the highest ranking official of the firm to his or her direct reports; they in turn teach their direct reports, and so forth down the organization until everyone has been through the material. This approach ingrains in management the principles and values involved and is proof of their commitment to employees up and down the organization from one end to the other. Later, when skills such as statistical analysis and problem solving are of greater importance, instructors on staff, fellow-employees with skills, or consultants can do the training more effectively. Management, however, has to be seen taking these skill-focused courses and applying their techniques.

Increasingly, customers and stakeholders outside your firm or agency

---

Proofs of Quality Commitments

Written Baldrige Assessments (more than one)
ISO 9000 Certification
Process documentation and measurements
Public display of quality performance measures
"No questions asked" product and service guarantees
"No questions asked" money back policy
Quality awards your organization has received
Amount of training on quality issues per employee
Mandatory customer surveys
Continuous expansion of end-user training and support services
Establishment of service standards

Figure 3.6

are asking for proof of your organization's commitment to quality. This is done not only to ensure quality goods and services, but also because some customers are finding it more cost effective to have fewer suppliers, who they now depend on more. A supplier not dedicated to providing high quality goods and services can be disastrous. Thus, just to compete, many organizations have to prove what they are doing to implement quality principles. This is a well-documented phenomenon. And the test is how many departments are participating—including yours. Baldrige assessments, educational programs, and process work all help persuade stakeholders and customers that your enterprise is serious about continuously improving all of its activities using fact-based, scientific approaches, and sound management principles (see Figure 3.6).

Knowing If It All Is Working

A large number of processes have to be improved continuously if an organization is to enhance its effectiveness significantly. Because the process of reformation is rigorous and extensive, it is best to assume you do not know how well things are going just based on your observation and casual feedback. You should conduct a number of tests to gauge progress, especially to measure to what extent your organization is becoming more end-user or customer focused. I prefer testing the temperature of the enterprise at about six month intervals, forever.

You can begin by looking at the four areas that I targeted for early attention—measurements, organization, compensation and rewards, and quality education. All four are inward looking and are contained within your organization. They must be working well before you start touching end users and customers or suppliers. These are preparation, much like practicing football during the week before the big game on Saturday. Initial measurements are simply a tool to measure and alter behavior and will be replaced with others more specifically tied to tactical processes that concern your stakeholders. Organizational and compensation actions are taken to align resources with your organization's vision. Education provides the skills to execute the transformation.

While your intentions might be noble, and the suggestions made throughout this book interesting, the fact remains you will run into resistance from some of your employees. A few will take the position that things are fine just as they are, so why change? A second group will conclude that the kinds of changes being asked of them are a far cry from what made them successful in the past. A third opinion will hold that these new approaches are at best a fad, and at worst will not work. These cynics will tell you they have seen it before: quality circles in the early 1980s, excellence programs of a large variety, posters, and so forth. The cynics are your enemies; they usually cannot be persuaded. The skeptics are your best allies because once converted they can form the nucleus of a new way of running the department, while ensuring that reality does not give way to euphoria over quality practices.

But change is difficult for people, and we must recognize that reality. Formal assessments of their attitudes and progress help us measure the nature and rate of their transformation.

How to Assess the Status of Quality among Employees

The easiest tool to use is the opinion survey, either within your organization or across the entire company or agency. If you or your enterprise do not currently use such a tool, go to work on getting one right away. Proper use of such surveys requires a special skill, but one piece of advice: Whatever tool is used, ensure absolute anonymity of the answers no matter what the cost. The knowledge gained can set the quality agenda for years. Employees must feel that they can express the truth as they see it without fear of their managers knowing what they said. As you preach the gospel of quality and the necessity for customer focus, you can ask two to three questions on the employee survey to measure buy-in and degree of application. If the questions are asked exactly the same way over several years, the first round of questioning serves as a baseline against which to measure progress. The whole exercise can be done through computer systems using E-mail. The kinds of questions you might ask include:

- To what extent do you believe senior management is committed to quality improvement?
- To what extent are you personally willing to apply principles of quality improvement to your job?
- To what extent is your manager (or department) committed to quality improvement?

Get the data back on these responses in two groups: managers and nonmanagers. If management is not on board with quality, it will not come on its own. They are the leaders who must implement quality practices with their employees. Such surveys should not include questions about quality until after you have started making changes in the four areas previously suggested.

Responses should be translated into statistical measures. Questions about the roles of management that are measured this way tell you how far along one level or type of management is versus another and suggest which groups need more or less help on their transformation. Statistical answers to the following questions are also very useful:

- To what extent do you understand the company's quality improvement strategy?
- Which of the following best expresses your views on being end-user driven? (Pick three to five variables relevant to your department or business.)

Figure 3.7 illustrates the kind of data you can get.

The first time such a survey is done the typical buy-in ranges from a low of 20 percent to as high as 50 percent. The lower number is more realistic and grows out of little or no experience with quality values and practices. Incremental improvements in buy-in and experience of five to ten points per year are not uncommon, although higher rates are frequently possible. These rates of transformation mean that, on average, it takes a minimum of three to five years to change people's attitudes and activities. As successes mount along with peer pressure from the converted, some employees will leave your company or agency, others sadly will have to be dismissed for taking too long to convert (they either slow a team down too much or are a negative influence), and the rest will embrace the new approach at their own pace. It takes time to get buy-in

---

Examples of Employee Survey Data Types

Degree felt empowered
Buy-in on IS quality strategy
Understanding of IS quality strategy
Trust and confidence in management
Satisfaction level in department's performance
Satisfaction in one's own quality skills
Degree to which change is accepted
Problem areas by unit, by type
How opinions have changed over time by topic, by unit
Rate of progress on issues over time, by type of employee
Percents on degree of commitment, severity of issues
Numbers by issues and organizations (quantity, rating)

Figure 3.7

and to change habits, but once done, you have altered your culture in a way that will stick for a long time.

Quality Indicators Help Measure Progress

A second way to measure progress is to develop a short list of quality indicators that provide a quick snapshot of how your organization is doing against its objectives. Over time you can add to or change these indicators. Practical criteria for these include:

- one page of measurements
- quarterly or monthly publication
- numeric (percent, index, ratio, etc.)
- easy-to-understand trend indicators
- this year's achievement goals (a number)
- measures from IS executive on down

These measures are indicators, not necessarily explicit reflections of how individual processes are doing. You want a set of measures that tells everyone what your trend is toward effective implementation of your goals. For example, you could set growth in employee morale as a goal and show that number, or goals on end-user satisfaction, financial performance, or community involvement. These measures could also be performance indicators of applications and systems. You could reasonably have two to five measures for each goal, but do not exceed one page per goal. By listing goals on the same page, you present a complete, integrated package to your employees. Figure 3.8 lists sample measurement elements.

Begin with existing measurable data, such as system performance, and add on measures as you determine how to implement your goals. Surveys of end users, customers, suppliers, and employees are useful. Data on number of hours or days of employee training or skills certification also are effective. The number of employees submitting suggestions, or the number of suggestions implemented, is an important indicator of buy-in and commitment.

For quality, departmental and company-wide, Baldrige assessment scores are most effective as a quick "sniff test" of progress. Financial contributions are obvious, and you have that data today.

Many organizations find that it is effective to have a team of employees representing various departments and functions to advise, preach, and report on progress. In short, they own the effort to prepare and publish

Indicator	This Month	YTD Average	Target	Trend
Customer				
- Satisfaction	82%	82%	88%	Flat
- Complaints	15	20	NONE	Down
Employees				
- Morale	80%	82%	84%	Lagging
- Skills	94%	90%	98%	Up
Programming				
- Error Rate	5%	7%	5%	Improved
- Cycle Time	90%	90%	92%	Flat
- Overtime	5%	5%	1%	Poor
Operations				
- Abandoned Calls	19	21	15	Poor
- Average Response	3 Sec	5 Sec	3 Sec	Improving
- CPU Utilization	35%	45%	45%	Down

Figure 3.8 Sample quality indicators.

the one-page "Top Sheet" set of measurements. They can enhance their effectiveness by trading ideas with other IS organizations.

Ask peers in other enterprises about how much progress they have made and over what period of time. Hear their war stories of frustrations and successes. Their advice is nothing less than priceless; they too will want to know about your experiences. Many IS organizations already have another source of input: customer or end-user councils that can be asked to look at performance using rigorous quality management disciplines. More about quality councils later—suffice it to point out that asking others about their initial processes and programs is just good benchmarking and effective management. Outside feedback encourages and gives confidence to employees in the early stages, while at later stages, the feedback is compliments.

Conclusions

Rosabeth Moss Kanter, a Harvard Business School professor who specializes in the transformation of companies, put it very well: "Cowboy management is a disaster for the company that seeks quality." Deming argued that, if there is a problem, it is usually in the processes or environments in which we place people, not in the employee. A growing number of CEOs and quality experts argue that management is the greatest impediment to quality transformations. So the message is clear: All managers must lead the charge, do it by personal example, and apply the tools of the quality world.

References

Berry, Thomas H. *Managing the Total Quality Transformation.* New York: McGraw-Hill, 1991.

Champy, James. *Reengineering Management.* New York: Harper Business, 1995.

Covey, Stephen R. *The 7 Habits of Highly Effective People.* New York: Simon & Schuster, 1989.

Daniels, Aubrey C. *Performance Management: Improving Quality Productivity through Positive Reinforcement.* 3rd. ed. Tucker, Ga.: Performance Management Publications, 1990.

Davis, Stanley M. *Managing Corporate Culture.* New York: Harper and Row, 1984.

Feher, Bela, and Mark F. Levine. *Organization Redesign for Productivity Improvement: Method Case Study.* San Diego: Navy Personnel and Research Development Center, 1985.

Juran, J.M. *Juran's New Quality Road Map*. New York: Free Press, 1991.

Kanter, Rosabeth Moss. "Managing the Human Side of Change," *Management Review* (April 1985): pp. 52–56.

Lawton, Robin L. "Creating a Customer-Centered Culture for Service Quality," *Quality Progress* 22, no. 5 (May 1989): pp. 34–36.

Tapscott, Don, and Art Caston. *Paradigm Shift: The New Promise of Information Technology*. New York: McGraw-Hill, 1993.

Tishman, Michael L., Charles O'Reilly, and David A. Nadler (eds), *The Management of Organizations*. New York: Harper and Row, 1989.

4

Business Planning
and IT Planning—
The Quality Links

*Achieving quality in products and services is
critical. The problem is that many companies
are chasing this goal without a clear sense of
where they are trying to go or how difficult a
journey they should expect. Quality
improvement is a slow and difficult journey.
It would be a tragedy if we let our impatience
and our appetite for the next quick fix
smother the most promising idea to come
along in a decade.*
COMPUTERWORLD, November 26, 1992

This chapter is devoted to a review of key elements of modern strategic planning. I describe how this kind of planning is a crucial component of any quality-based improvement effort. Issues that management should focus on as part of the planning process are also
presented.

For decades professors and consultants have been telling people to link
how they use information technology to their business goals. At the same
time, executives have been variously successful at it, some using IT as a

necessary evil to automate paperwork, others using IT creatively as a strategic marketing tool. But rarely has anyone displayed a high degree of confidence that computers were linked tightly to business plans and results. That situation came about in large part because there was no way to link business and data processing activities in terms as specific as was possible with activities such as manufacturing and logistics. But that is all changing rapidly because today more effective methods exist to draw together quality, IT, and strategic plans.

Trends in Quality-Focused Strategic Planning

The biggest change underway is the evolving role of information technology in process improvements and process reengineering, both of which are specific enough to make it clearer to all exactly where IT should play to advantage. IT becomes an integral part of critical business processes—some almost go too far and argue it is the cornerstone. These processes, in turn, are some of the bricks and mortar of modern strategic business plans. As Figure 4.1 illustrates, seeing IT as part of a group of activities such as process redesigns or linkages between organizations and processes, while feeding information to decision support applications, allows IT to participate specifically in the strategies of an organization.

Looking at IT as a strategic weapon makes sense. Nearly a decade ago, Michael Porter began to harp on the point that technology could affect competition by:

- altering industry structures
- supporting cost and differentiation strategies
- spawning entirely new businesses

In recent years, others have discovered the value of time-based strategies as levers of competitive advantage. With the realization that reducing the time it takes to do things provided profound benefits, IT could be looked at differently and with a greater sense of urgency. As we saw in earlier chapters, linking IT to actionable items is done most clearly through process work.

From an IT perspective, linking to business plans becomes easier if your organization begins with a shared sense of style of how the enterprise is run. That style involves all of the topics discussed in the first three chapters:

- a commitment to quality-based values and activities
- an emphasis on process management
- a body of personnel practices that rewards quality performance

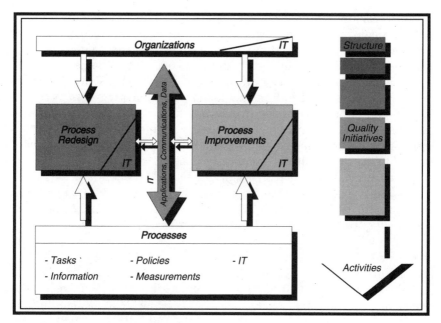

Figure 4.1 IT and strategic planning.

Management Still Faces Problems with IT

Despite the new perspective that IT can tie in nicely with processes, management still faces a long-standing set of problems with computers.

First, most organizations have an aging portfolio of applications and other ineffective systems. Given the growing speed of change today (due to new technologies and changing business structures), they are getting older faster. As a result, IT is actually a barrier to future business initiatives because systems are too cumbersome and difficult to change to support new structures, applications, and processes. If this problem was ignored in your organization a decade ago, it is worse today.

Second, with technologies changing so quickly and businesses attempting to move in and out of markets equally fast, many organizations are discovering that their IS organizations and other infrastructures do not lend themselves to rapid change. This is less of a problem for small new businesses, but a major one with large corporations, higher education, and government.

IS organizations are finding more technology deployed outside their traditional boundaries than ever before, causing the data processing community to restructure to conform to new organizational boundaries within their companies and agencies. Natural resistance to such organizational changes poses a continuing problem for senior management.

Third, IS management frequently continues to operate without a long-term strategic plan despite the fact that they normally aspire to implement long-term technology-based architectures. The problem continues to be that their plans are not sufficiently linked to business strategies.

The answer has long been obvious: link concurrent IT and business planning. This is made more possible today by new practices in organization-wide strategic planning that better link business plans to business processes across an entire enterprise. Enterprise models incorporate data, applications, and technology all within a framework of processes deemed critical to the success of the organization (see Figure 4.2).

The traditional thick IT plan is almost a thing of the past. Instead, business-wide strategic planning is incorporating IT as part of the whole, which means that independent IT plans are retreating. More companies are moving from a situation in which IS performs independent planning to one in which business functions incorporate IT issues into their own. Planning is moving from being an annual event to being a continuous process involving many parts of an enterprise. Plans that once reflected just the organizational structure of the enterprise are now increasingly reflecting processes and functions. Instead of being static, with multiyear strategies, they are becoming more dynamic and fluid, many even have a tactical flavor.

	Product Design	Product Manufacturing	Product and Service Marketing/Sales	Delivery	Support
Processes	Engineering Design	Parts Logistics	Opportunity ID	Logistics	Maintenance
	Customer Feedback	Shop Floor	Order Entry	Tracking	Repair
	Performance Reviews	Work-in-Progress	Customer Feedback	A/P	Customer Feedback
Data	Part #s	Part #s	Opportunities	Order Tracking	Product Performance
	Designs	Schedules	Customer Records	Prices	Defects
			Complaints	Costs	Repair Time
Applications	CAD/CAM	CAM	Order Entry	Truck Scheduling	Dispatch
	DB	Data Collection	Configurators	Billing	Parts Inventory Management
		MRP	Billing	A/P	Product Performance
Technology	CASE	TP	PCs	DB	DB
	PCs	Analog Instruments	TP	PC	CRT
	TP	Robotics	FAX	TP	TP

Figure 4.2 Sample high-level enterprise model.

As planning seeks more integration across functions and through processes, drivers of such planning, not IT executives, increasingly are becoming process owners. As teams reflect on the style by which processes are managed, their approach to technology becomes iterative, changing their views on how best to use technology as they apply TQM-like principles to the implementation and management of processes. The common vision of the team or enterprise regarding the ideal end state of a process provides the beacon of light used to clarify which IT decisions are made.

As implementation of process views expands, enterprises find their borders changing. Where does the corporation end and a supplier or a customer begin? The use of EDI, for example, has made it possible to shift responsibilities outside the traditional walls of a company. Customers can enter their own orders, check on the status of deliveries, and even pay bills electronically. Suppliers are increasingly part of the forecast system, ship on their own decision, and collect bills electronically. EDI is a wonderful example of a growing application of technology to compete against time, link customers and suppliers to our organizations, and simplify processes.

Cost justification of IT in this new world changes. For one thing, a process owner considers expenditures in IT as only one of several that are a part of his or her overall implementation of a strategy. For another, measures of success, while still overwhelmingly financial, also change. Some companies, for instance, are beginning to measure how much time it takes to get something done, even setting time reduction quotas, translating improvements into monetary terms. That approach leads to a quantifiable measure of justification for IT. Vision and value-based planning are now critically important.

Over the past decade, a number of changes have occurred in strategic planning. Figure 4.3 is a schematic of modern strategic planning. To function in a decentralized environment with teams running around, management has increasingly found it necessary to ensure that all functions in an organization are in alignment with everyone working toward a common set of goals. This effort begins by defining the organization's style of operation (values), followed by a specific bought-in vision of where the enterprise is going, and by when. Goals are established that, when achieved, will mean the vision has been actualized. Then comes development of strategies to implement goals, and finally tasks within strategies.

From a practical point of view, this approach is then implemented through the key enterprise processes. At each step, process measures ensure that work done is profitable and effective, and always linked directly to the fulfillment of customer expectations.

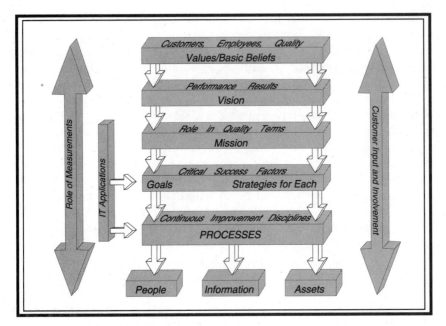

Figure 4.3 Modern strategic framework.

How IT Links into Modern Strategic Planning

Aligning with a formal enterprise-wide strategic planning effort is crucial to ensure quality improvements in all that is done. Normal practice is to have a Fall Plan and a Spring Plan process. IS participates in both to create a two- to three-year plan, with some planning as far ahead as five years.

It is increasingly becoming attractive to involve customers and suppliers in this process. Often IS must follow the enterprise-wide planning efforts with some of its own to fill in technical and support details. These usually involve suppliers and customers in quality-focused IT shops. Issues that are discussed by IS and influence its planning include such quality-oriented concerns as:

- feedback from end users and customers
- employee opinion surveys
- performance measures for applications and hardware
- benchmarking

Quality objectives are set and plans are developed for meeting them. These are compared against the business plan of the enterprise to ensure conformance both in terms of timing and performance.

As part of the planning effort, today, the trend is to identify an ideal state, assess where the organization is against that ideal, and then identify the gaps that need to be filled. Those gaps represent opportunities for IT's improvement or contribution to the organization. Common gaps occur, for example, in:

- process performance
- end-user and customer support
- speed and quality of service delivery
- feedback and appreciation of customer needs
- efficiency of organizational structure
- capability of IT's culture to change sufficiently
- knowledge and skills of IT personnel

The role of customers has been rising in IT strategic planning. For example, they are increasingly being asked to identify requirements, determine priorities of activities, assess acceptance testing of new applications, and assess results. Their participation validates the relevance of plans, brings in new ideas and issues, and reduces development time for applications. Overall customer satisfaction tends to increase because of improved productivity, reduced cycle time, and a visible effort to respond to customer requirements. Customer satisfaction feedback processes confirm to what extent IT is performing against these criteria. The same is done with suppliers.

Three Key Quality Tasks Are Aligned with Planning

In quality-driven IT organizations, management must identify customer requirements, develop plans to commit resources to implement plans, and then improve planning itself. To do those things, management finds it useful to carry out three activities:

1. Benchmark applications and performance. Benchmark customer satisfaction, service reliability and availability, performance, cost of all systems and applications, and application development time and cost.

2. Benchmark IT organization and overall effectiveness. This is done by looking at the overall performance of other IT organizations. You want to know such things as what applications they have, their role in the organization, how they are organized, what they spend, and how they manage IS applications. Criteria for selecting who to visit include:

- quality leadership in applications and functions relevant to your operations
- outstanding business results of the enterprise and of IT specifically
- leadership in the application of technology
- measurable outstanding performance in provided services

The most aggressive IT operations go beyond comparing themselves to shops within their own company or even in their own community. They try to study systematically best practices for IT organizations first in their company's industry and then across many industries. We have learned that the greatest number of new ideas for improvement often come from outside of your own industry.

3. Define clearly anticipated results. All strategic initiatives should have three types of outcome-based measurable results:

- customer success or satisfaction
- employee success and high morale
- company revenue or profit success

Typically, indicators of success and continuous improvement are developed for all three categories, as it is impossible to do well without performing effectively in all arenas. Those are quality indicators for processing that lead to the business results usually required by stakeholders. Examples of quality indicators set for each year in the planning cycle might include percent of telephone calls answered and the number not answered, measures of how fast processes perform over time, surveys of how customers feel about a particular service over time, efficiency to process changes, and extent that a process performs within statistically acceptable levels.

Goals help point to the specific processes that must become more effective. They are also a good link back to your vision. In IT organizations, effective common goals are statements that blend values and expectations. Examples include:

- delighting end users
- improving employee technical skills
- implementing "world class" quality
- linking supplier to enterprise, enterprise to customers
- reducing cycle time to get things done at lower unit costs

Setting Priorities for What Gets Done

Like their parent enterprises, IT executives who have positive experiences in implementing quality practices argue that (1) you cannot fix all processes at the same time because boiling the ocean takes too much focus off day-to-day business, and (2) thus you must set tactical and strategic priorities on processes targeted for improvement or replacement. Experience shows that working on a few at a time (a dozen or less), in a disciplined manner, is effective. Once a set of processes is improved, stabilized, and put on a course of continuous improvement (with some early results achieved to encourage others), then the next tier of processes can be addressed. What gets improved first is a function of what is most critical in satisfying customers, what makes business sense to the enterprise as a whole, and what you are capable of doing based on your resources and skills. Too often we hear "run out and satisfy customers" from management who forgets to take into account the enterprise's needs and limitations of capability.

Contemporary IT Strategic Alignment

The heart and soul of quality-based strategic planning in IT is its alignment with the enterprise as a whole. We just saw that if the enterprise applies vision-based planning, IS must be in the same time frames. Such actions lead to common approaches that bond IT to the enterprise. For example, if the corporation is downsizing, IS will be asked to support the effort. We are all aware of many cases of IT's role in downsizing, involving large-scale software applications moving stiffly to networked desktop workstations. While these have offered such benefits as significant cost savings, flexibility, improved employee productivity, and congeniality between the "style" or culture of the company and how IT is implemented, there have also been problems. Cost savings frequently are not realized unless well planned, and then often exceed implementation costs by a third to over 200 percent.

Culture is as much at the heart of an IT organization's ability to respond effectively as its ability to implement effective processes. If an organization is very hierarchical and bureaucratic, Deming-based ideas and process improvement strategies will have tough going in the beginning. Too much analysis can slow IT's ability to apply technology. For example, if it takes over six months to make an implementation decision involving desktop products, you could have a problem. Life cycles of such products are now less than six months, so by the time you are ready to implement, you could be installing outdated machines or back-level software!

Changes of enormous magnitude require infrastructures and cultures to be in alignment. The architect of one of the largest downsizing and restructuring efforts in recent years, Ralph Szygenda, vice president and manager of Texas Instruments' Information Systems and Service Division, confirmed that he and his staff underestimated the effort it would take, learned to align their infrastructure correctly, and that it was worth it. He expects TI's costs for applications to be between one-half and two-thirds less than in the past. He also anticipates overall improvements in effectiveness of end users.

These kinds of strategic implementations of IT call for careful alignment of how technology functions within an enterprise. Fortunately, considerable amount of work has been done to identify critical success patterns. Effective ways to align IT to what the enterprise does is crucial if any organization wants to (a) use IT to improve the quality of the enterprise's own operations or (b) wants IT to improve its own internal affairs (for example, operations, processes).

Some of the most recent interesting research on how IT can deliver value in exchange for corporate investments has come from John C. Henderson and N. Venkatraman. Simply put, they have demonstrated "that the inability to realize value from IT investments is, in part, due to the lack of alignment between the business and IT strategies of organizations." In order for IT to contribute to the transformation of organizations, they have concluded that IT planning must be an integral part of the enterprise-wide planning for performance that we talked about earlier in this chapter.

Given that satisfying customer requirements calls for a cross-functional process view of an enterprise's activities, it becomes obvious why IT cannot plan in isolation, apart from the core activities of an organization. Therefore, management must answer quickly a number of basic questions:

- What investment criteria should be used with IT?
- What context should be used in prioritizing proposed investments in IT?
- How are others doing it?
- What leverage points exist in using IT to accelerate implementation of business strategies?
- How should one measure quality and productivity of IT?
- What emerging technologies are crucial to achieving a specific business strategy?

Henderson and Venkatraman have answered these questions by developing a useful Strategic Alignment Model (Figure 4.4) that recognizes the realities of the processes of an organization on the one hand, yet on the other attempts to gain alignment within this context. Their useful perspective has four components: business, IT, organizational infrastructure and processes, and IT infrastructure and processes.

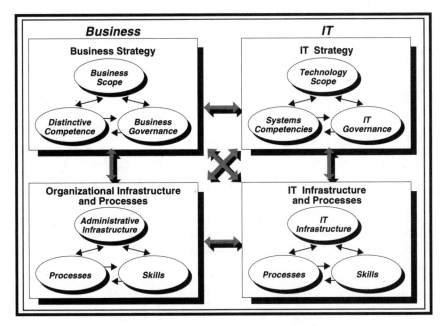

Figure 4.4 Alignment model. (Reproduced with permission. © 1993 IBM).

The business strategy defines how the enterprise will compete and acknowledges the well-understood and obvious questions about what business you are in, how you are positioned relative to competition, what you should be doing, why customers buy from you, and so forth. The second perspective is the definition of structure, people, processes, and assets of the corporation. You need to ask such basic questions as what is needed to do your work; what skills are required; what kind of people, values, and culture are essential; and what your core capabilities are. While looking at these questions, you would reasonably ask how to apply quality practices to your business and to what extent existing processes are optimized—are they dangerously weak, or simply lacking?

The authors argue that you need a strategic fit between your business strategy and your organizational infrastructure and processes. I and many others have found that as part of the process of ensuring strategic fit, you have to answer such questions as how do you change your organization to achieve your strategy, how well do your employees understand the overall game plan, to what extent do they understand their role, and how do you best communicate plans to everyone. The two authors go the extra step of arguing that strategic fit calls for understanding the reality and opportunity for an organization to successfully implement its business strategy.

More clearly than others, they have shown that IT strategies are the definers of key technologies and competencies critical to an organization achieving its strategic objectives. This realization begs some obvious questions:

- What new technologies must you invest in?
- What technical skills must you have to be competitive?
- What skills can you buy?
- To what extent does IT understand the needs of your business strategy?
- What does IS have to do to support the business?

The capabilities of an IS organization are always defined by the characteristics of its only assets: people, hardware, software, and processes. Good IT strategic planning requires that you answer several basic questions:

- How can you deliver systems and applications faster?
- How can you improve the flexibility of new and existing systems and applications?
- How do you prioritize all the possible applications and projects involving IT?
- How do you squeeze the most out of your IT investments and expenditures?
- Are your investments in technology cost-justified in normal business terms? By using ABC accounting?
- What is the most effective architecture for your IS operations?
- Can your IS community successfully support your business strategies?

As with business strategic fit, a strategic fit must exist between IT strategy and IT infrastructure and processes, so that what happens with the application of technology fits into what IS wants to do, and in turn into what the business needs to have happen. Here very specific questions must be answered:

- How must your IS organization change to support the IT strategy? (Assumes it is a business-based one.)
- How well is your IT plan being implemented by and within the IS community?
- How well are technical skills crucial to the successful implementation of your IT strategy being developed or acquired?

- And, as with business alignment, there are questions about how well IS understands and communicates the business strategy.

Answers to these questions and the resultant actions leverage current and anticipated IT investments to support the overall business plan.

What Henderson and Venkatraman point out is that when you look at IT through any of the four perspectives, you get different views of IT's strategic alignment. Put another way, different strategic perspectives taken during any planning process can generate a different focus on IT's role. For example, on the topic of strategy execution, once it is set the enterprise wants to implement it. From an IT perspective, you ask what IT can do to implement the plan or improve existing processes across the enterprise. On the question of competition, what can IT do to enable new business strategies to be implemented effectively? Service levels are always of major concern (particularly to customers) and thus beg the question, how can IT deliver better goods and services? That again is a process-oriented question. Also related is the question, to what extent does IT need to be world class in order to deliver the kinds of support and strategic advantage necessary for the business to carry out its plans? Finally, what are the organizational and cultural implications for your IS organization caused by the introduction of new IT?

Building on the strategic alignment concept that these two professors developed, one can quickly see that what the IS community does for a living can be linked to what the business at large does. Looking into the IS organization itself then allows you to judge the extent to which what you are doing is tied to what the business needs. You can do this in a number of areas:

- applications
- data
- communications

You can look at these areas both in terms of what you have and what you want (sometimes called blueprints). The business strategy represents a top-down effort to define where the organization is going and how, while the analysis of IS's infrastructure and operations is both a top-down and bottom-up activity. The reason for the bottom-up involvement of employees is that they best understand the nature, function, and current use of IS's assets in a broad range of activities: hardware, software, data files, communications, existing processes and procedures, personnel, and user practices.

As Figure 4.5 illustrates, good IT strategic plans incorporate all aspects that constitute and define the requirements for information systems, and always within the context of a business strategy.

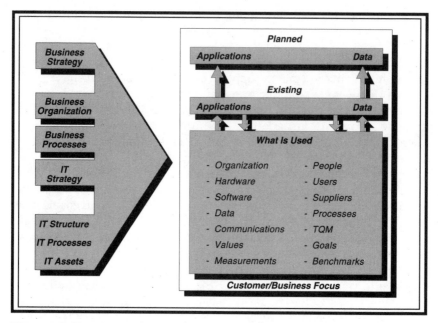

Figure 4.5 IT quality planning components.

Steps IS Can Take to Align with Business Strategies

The discussion so far sounds very academic and theoretical. However, a quality-driven IS organization considers these kinds of activities and issues as a basic part of their world. Boiled down to their simplest form, several actions are always taken:

1. Understand and be part of the overall business planning process of your company or agency.

2. If one does not exist, be the leader who introduces such an approach, and not just in IS but across the entire enterprise. It is a wonderful way to introduce the early stages of a quality-driven culture.

3. Make sure that your vision, goals, strategies, and action plans are consistent with those of the enterprise as a whole.

4. Identify your critical processes (as defined by what is important for the enterprise as a whole to achieve its objectives and deliver what customers really value).

5. Evaluate the effectiveness of your processes and participate in the assessment of those outside your organization that rely on IT or could benefit from such technology. Use any criteria you want (for example,

Baldrige or ISO 9000), but be consistent across the enterprise and from year to year.

6. Revisit constantly what your customers want and then how you are investing in IT.

7. Never build an IT plan that fails to address the critical processes of the entire enterprise, not just those of IS.

Many companies are increasingly applying these approaches to the implementation of quality-based strategic planning in IS. Roger Woolfe, in a recent article in *The Executive's Journal*, documented a rising concern in this topic by IS executives. He identified four stages of IS alignment with business plans:

1. functional automation

2. cross-functional integration

3. process automation

4. process transformation

The first two stages we are all familiar with: when IT is applied to the automation of existing business functions. Toward the end of phase two, however, one sees significant changes in the critical business processes of an organization, caused in large part by process reengineering and new applications of IT. Companies are beginning to see that not until the end of stage four do the kinds of strategic alignment spoken of by Henderson and Venkatraman exist. Quality practices are essential just to get through the second phase, and by the end of phase three are not seen as separate and apart from the normal day-to-day practices of the organization.

IT's changing role even affects measurements. For example, insurance companies are increasingly adding profit measurements to their activities instead of simply looking at market share, which was a more common measure. Both in Europe and in the United States, IS organizations and their companies as a whole are searching for faster and better ways to perform their work with a heavy emphasis on moving to paperless work flows to reduce cycle time, increase turnaround time, and improve productivity. The same thing is happening with health organizations, which, driven by competition, respond to consumer demand for cost controls and industry quality certification standards. The same has been true for nearly a decade with almost every automobile manufacturer. In case after case, successful operations revealed extensive IT application to process improvement or reengineering. In each instance, business strategy was developed with IS aligned in a formal manner, using strategic business planning methodologies to identify the required actions.

Linking IT Planning to Quality

Linking IT and quality within an enterprise, regardless of whether computers are controlled by an IS function or by end users, calls for some similar actions. Experience has shown that a combination of strategies and actions draw together the values and practices of quality principles and the functions and realities of computer applications. I suspect that the dialogue between many types of noncomputer technologists and quality proponents parallels what happens between IT personnel and quality proponents.

The key is in creating in the enterprise an environment in which strategic actions are undertaken that value continuous improvement of everything—and that also focus on reducing the amount of time it takes to do things well. Those two principles—continuous improvement and process reengineering activities—have been important hallmarks of all successful quality programs, and in most cases of fundamental cultural transformation.

1. Manage processes not results. Expect results, and be explicit on expectations, but spend your time managing the improvement of processes. Strategic plans should not simply speak to how big, by when, with what strategies, alone. Your plan should also identify what processes are required to get to your vision. This applies to a company-wide strategic plan as much as to any department's. In IS this means less attention on technology, for example, and more focus on architectures. The former will not change culture or organizations, the latter will. Architectural views also cause technical personnel to apply technology in support of processes more often than not. This approach makes it easier for individuals to look at technology as facilitators of cycle time reduction and process simplification.

2. Within IS, strategic planning should be business oriented, not IT or IS focused. If you look at the activities of an enterprise as a collection of processes, then you can let the process owner drive transformations of his or her process. IS can facilitate process improvements by being part of the team doing that work, but not by owning or dominating them. IS then becomes a tool, a facilitator. Spending your time creating IS plans tied to specific business processes gets you away from planning in isolation and perhaps doing things that are not adding value to the enterprise as a whole.

Now, quickly, you would want to argue that some activities are unique to IS, such as how a data center is run, a help desk is staffed, or software is designed and programmed. All of these are generic to business processes and would not appear to involve any end users in any extensive manner. In fact, by this point in this book, you should realize that end users are involved. The key point is that what appears to be unique IS functions can also be looked at as processes, where IS personnel may be the process owners, but whose process teams should include members from the end user communities, possibly customers and also suppliers. So the principle remains the same: Manage strategic planning as a vehicle for controlling and improving business processes.

3. In looking at technology, and particularly software in systems and applications, good strategic IS plans will incorporate increased capability to change technology. If the business is undergoing rapid change, the last thing you need say is "we cannot make the proposed business change because the system won't allow us." We have all made that terrible little speech. But in a world of continuous change and (hopefully) improvement, that's crazy. So good IS plans should answer the question of what you are doing to make it easier and faster to change your architectures, systems, applications, and hardware. I would add measures of your capability to change those things. Creating a systems environment capable of changing software, of using common and productive tools (for example, CASE), with standards for such things as data, programming, and documentation conventions all help. Tied to this approach is the notion that your staff should constantly be learning how to migrate software and applications and be students of that activity. Their expertise on programming or maintenance will not link your activities to the quality practices of the rest of the organization, but expanding the skills required for your operations to change faster will.

4. Your strategic planning and quality values should have the same look and feel as those of the rest of the enterprise. For example, if your corporation does vision-based strategic planning, so should you. If the company's planning horizon is five years, so should yours. If your agency's quality philosophy is Deming-based or Crosby-based, you should conform to the particular twist taken by the whole enterprise. That means applying the same values, working on the same issues, and using the same language, techniques, and format in your planning. These actions then make it possible for your vision, goals, strategies, and even some action plans, to be owned jointly by IS and other functions of the enterprise. By incorporating other stakeholders in your success, you create a system in which IS is constantly getting feedback on performance, on what is or is not needed, and on what has to improve in order to apply IT effectively.

5. Develop a process for acquiring and using tools that reduce the amount of time it takes to generate new applications. This is not a tactical imperative, it is a strategic one. It is another way of saying, build into your strategic plans the capability of cycle time reduction in all that you

do, from designing, to coding, to maintaining, to processing of all work. Some of the required tools and techniques should reside in IS, but you may find increasingly that they have to be in the hands of end users in PCs or shared in LANs. That transfer of use does not happen by accident. Since it requires many acquisitions, often new skills, and takes years, acquiring and applying cycle time reduction tools has to be a strategic IS imperative. Some systems will always take too long to develop, but you will need fast-path strategies that allow end users to apply technology quickly.

While we will discuss quality-based applications in more detail later, an example of producing applications faster suggests the impact. Suppose that you are an insurance company, and the marketing people decide that they need to offer a new feature in a life insurance product. The product is presented to salespeople and customers as a computer-printed document that is attached to a process that calculates costs and accrued benefits. Clearly, to provide a new product, the application that generated the policy needs to be rewritten. If marketing determined that competitive pressures dictated that they get a product change done and out the door in thirty days—not in the six months IS needed to reprogram the application—another way would have to be found.

This IS organization, driven by its quality values, had been continuously shortening programming time. In this case, it provided end users with word-processing capability and a spreadsheet tool that, in effect, made it possible for marketing to write text for a policy change, quickly define the arithmetic steps required to recalculate costs and payouts, have those changes incorporated into the existing application, and access the client data base. The changes were made in days, not months. The bulk of the work was performed by marketing, not by IS. IS, however, took note of the change, ensured that standards for software assurance and data base integrity were in place (all transparent to marketing), and tracked the speed of the change as part of its ongoing strategy for improving the effectiveness of application changes.

6. Incorporate into your strategic plans the capability of enjoying short-term benefits. Changes in architecture, software programming techniques, implementation of LANs and new applications, should not all be sitting out three to five years. Nor should the adoption of quality tools (such as the use of statistics, Pareto charts, and so forth). Look for short-term victories and results that encourage your staff while linking IS performance to the requirements of all your stakeholders. In a quality-driven organization, "quick hits" are just as important as long-term continuous improvement and transformation to a highly motivated customer-focused culture. Short-term results can come from creating process teams working

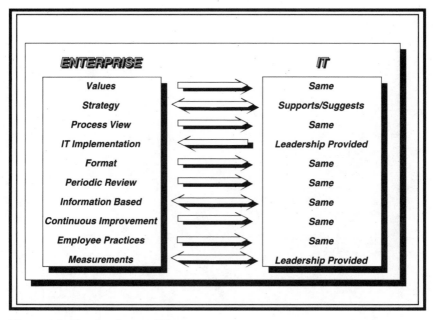

Figure 4.6 Planning characteristics.

with stakeholders on end-user problems and education, which are then applied immediately to measure or improve activities. As your organization becomes more comfortable with quality skills, you can expect, on a regular basis, shorter and shorter lead times to dramatic improvements in results. This is particularly the case in reengineering a process or in actually performing a repetitive task (for example, help desk functions).

Figure 4.6 pulls together the whole notion that your strategic planning effort should be aligned with that of the enterprise and lists the quality values it should display.

Again, your ideal model of how IS must perform should not be out of step with the rest of your corporation or agency. Figure 4.7 shows how your quality plan comes alive as a critical IT process.

Conclusions

I devoted this chapter to a discussion of strategic planning, a topic that does not usually come up in presentations about quality strategies. However, companies and government agencies that have been successful in implementing quality practices, and in transforming their organizations

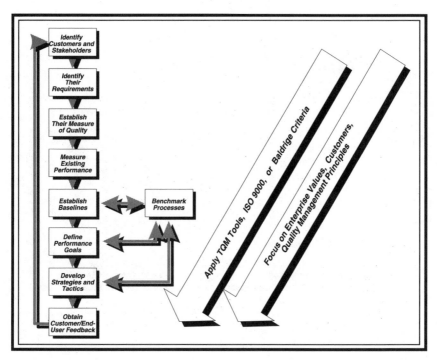

Figure 4.7 How an IT quality plan comes to life.

into what they wanted, all have an implemented business plan, not just a quality or TQM plan. They are focused, clear on what needs to be done, and demand conformance by all departments. They take into account their suppliers, their customers' requirements, and even (if appropriate) their customers' customers' needs. Successful IT organizations do the same.

For IS executives in particular, their role is personal. Listen to Roy Camblin, senior vice president at Wells Fargo: "My peers and I are businesspeople first and technologists second. The model of the business is foremost in my mind." It is the business perspective that drives the modern CIO, and to use Camblin's words, "that is the context in which your everyday work, and your work as a futurist for the business is set."

The keys to success are few but powerful:

- Align IS structure and resources to reflect what the entire organization wants to accomplish.
- Apply the tools of quality within the department, but also in conjunction with end users.

- Perform tasks and allocate resources that add value to what the entire enterprise is trying to do for customers and other stakeholders in your organization's success.

- View all work as a series of processes and all processes as shared activities between end users, suppliers, or customers and IS, with IT being applied as a lever, not necessarily as the cornerstone, of change.

Whether your company is attempting to obtain ISO 9000 registration, win a state quality award, or apply the Baldrige criteria to its operations, IS should conform to the overall shared approach. Participating in company-wide strategic planning is the easiest way to make that happen.

References

Henderson, J.C., and N. Venkatraman. "Strategic Alignment: Levering Information Technology for Transforming Organizations," *IBM Systems Journal* 32, no. 1 (1993): pp. 4–16.

King, W.R. "Strategic Planning for Management Information Systems," *MIS Quarterly* 2, no. 1 (1978): pp. 27–37.

Luftman, J.N., P.R. Lewis, and S.H. Oldach. "Transforming the Enterprise: The Alignment of Business and Information Technology Strategies," *IBM Systems Journal* 32, no. 1 (1993): pp. 198–221.

Parker, M.M., R.J. Benson, and H.E. Trainor. *Information Economics: Linking Business Performance to Information Technology.* Englewood Cliffs, NJ: Prentice-Hall, 1988.

Porter, Michael E. *Competitive Advantage.* New York: Free Press, 1985.

Prairie, Patti L. "Case Study: An American Express/IBM Consortium Benchmarks Information Technology," *Planning Review* (January-February 1993): pp. 22–27.

Pyburn, P.J. "Linking the MIS Plan with Corporate Strategy: An Exploratory Study," *MIS Quarterly* 7, no. 2 (1983): pp. 1–14.

Watson, Gregory H. *Strategic Benchmarking.* New York: John Wiley and Sons, 1993.

"What Is Our Business, Anyway?" *Open Systems Today* (January 18, 1993): S14.

Woolfe, Roger. "The Path to Strategic Alignment," *Information Strategy: The Executive's Journal* 9, no. 2 (Winter 1993): pp. 13–23.

5

Technology's Role in Quality Improvement

I never did anything worth doing by accident, nor did any of my inventions come by accident; they came by work.
                    THOMAS A. EDISON, 1923

Quality-driven IS organizations recognize that one of their major processes is the proper introduction of technology to an organization. In this chapter, I explore that concept in quality terms, discussing how to approach technology and processes, which technical trends to pay attention to, and the role IS plays.

Computer-based technologies have a profound effect on how organizations do their work. Many experts have made the case that the proper application of technology can have almost as much influence on the efficiency and effectiveness of operations as process improvements do. But two generations of IS managers can also attest that misapplication of technology can leave end users frustrated and senior management irritated at the enormous investment it has made. Since there no longer is any ques-

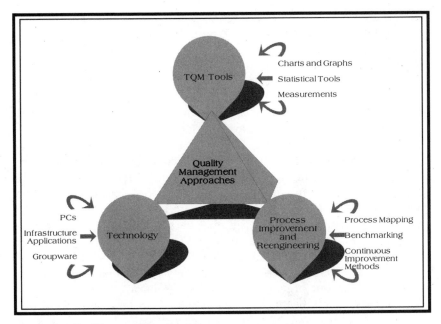

Figure 5.1 Facilitators of IS innovation.

tion about whether or not computers profoundly influence how organizations operate, the issue we face is how best to deploy such technology.

The purpose of this chapter is to explore those technologies and their use that most lend themselves to the effective application of IT in helping organizations improve continuously. TQM tools by themselves are not enough; nor are reengineering activities. Adding the third component of IT makes all three very powerful (Figure 5.1). As an IS manager or professional, therefore, you are responsible for identifying technologies that are suitable for process work and that improve operations, taking the initiative to tell end users, suppliers, and, where appropriate, customers what is available. The discussion that follows, however, is very select, limited only to the most important considerations, and does not reflect a complete survey of hardware. Greater attention to software will follow in the next two chapters.

The Case for Using IT in Quality Initiatives

The fact remains that in most organizations the way things get done has not changed fundamentally in years. In some cases, processes predate the introduction of computers (for example, how many state government regulations are implemented or how forms are treated within an office)! In other instances, old processes were simply automated, sped up. Where automation occurred, pieces of a process were computerized, still leaving others in manual form. For example, many of us continue to fill out our expense reports manually, but eventually they are aggregated in some computerized fashion and expense checks are typed or printed out for you. Partially automated processes, therefore, have time lags, gaps in communication, and new inefficiencies built into them.

Beginning in the 1980s, work done in many companies to improve processes has shown that incorporating technology while redesigning processes opened up new opportunities for improvement. An MIT study, for example, has illustrated that any normal process improvement effort should include a step in which IT levers are identified. Thus, instead of the usual cycle of process redesign that we all go through, we add the step. Figure 5.2 illustrates what process owners go through. However, note the addition of the extra step of looking at IT opportunities.

Historically, we have looked at technology by itself, asking how best we can use it in our organization, without seeing it in the context of a process. Existing applications were automated, or new tasks were performed due to the availability of some new piece of hardware. For example, a paper-based accounts receivable work flow would be relatively

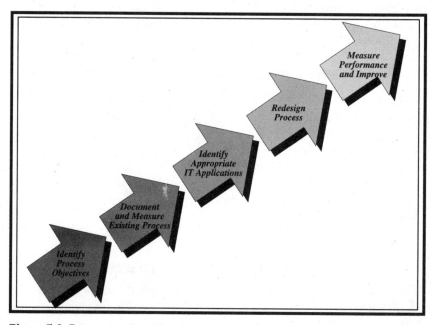

Figure 5.2 Process reengineering steps.

automated with a data base and CRTs. When bar codes came along, we started using this technology to track more closely flows of materials and products. But in neither case did we usually look at the entire accounts payable process or the logistics process to see how they could radically be improved using technology to influence the design of work flows.

When you look at process redesign by setting objectives for the redesign as your first step, then studying problems with existing processes that get in the way of achieving the objectives of the process, you have done a good job of positioning a team of employees to appreciate the potential improvements that can come from IT. Once you understand how your current process works and have a clear idea of what new objectives (or vision) you would like to achieve, then it is very powerful to expose process redesigners to IT. They will look at technology as a lever, asking very specific questions about IT. Then they can incorporate IT into a process as an act of continuous improvement or treat it as a central component of a new way of performing work. But it will always be treated in the context of a process to achieve predetermined goals.

I also frequently see process teams who, when they understand what they want to accomplish, may go back and revise their vision or goals after being exposed to various technologies. This happens when they realize that a particular technology gives them the capability of reducing costs even more or shrinking time not by a percent but by a factor. The same also occurs after a process has been designed, IT applied, and a pilot launched and studied. So the process of implementing IT within a process is also an iterative exercise, what you and I would call continuous improvement.

We know today that IT applied within the context of process improvement does lead to reduced cost of processes, to a significant reduction in the time to get work done, to improved output accuracy of a process, and to delegation of authority to do work lower in an organization. Thomas H. Davenport, in articles and in a book, documented many cases of this phenomenon, confirming these benefits derived from injecting IT into the redesign effort. My personal work with both companies and government agencies proved the same. It is a powerful lever and can have a profound influence on process redesign.

Exposing Process Teams to IT Leads to Useful Applications of Computers

How you achieve these benefits is a crucial step in process redesign. Most process teams know little or nothing about IT. Yet they must pick which technologies to use, incorporate them into the design of a process, implement the effort, and then test for results. So how is this done?

IS personnel can help in three crucial ways. First, by participating in a process team, they can suggest possible technologies all along the design process. As the team debates steps and functions, IS personnel can inject suggestions about how IT can be used in one step or another and begin to articulate why, sorting through various options. Second, they can identify technologies that the teams should be more knowledgeable about. They can arrange for the necessary briefings and demonstrations to facilitate teams appreciating the following characteristics of any technology:

- what it is
- what it does
- how it does it
- what it costs
- what it takes to use and maintain it
- how it might fit into the process
- how it supports the process objectives

One- to three-hour briefings by experts on particular technologies usually give process teams the level of detail they need to begin forming opinions about what to use.

IS personnel at this stage can help process teams sort through options and zero in on attractive alternatives. It is helpful for the teams to see these technologies in operation somewhere to visualize their application.

The third contribution IS experts can make is to facilitate the actual design of a technology's application within a process followed by its implementation. Experienced process teams will tell you that this kind of an approach makes sense. They also argue that the application of IT generally improves the communication of information from one end of a process to another, perhaps the greatest benefit of using IT in a process.

Many benefits are derived from applying technology to process improvements. Already mentioned is the benefit of improving or speeding up the flow of information from one end of a process to another. Closely tied to that is the accurate flow of information. If the data enters a process accurately, it can flow through a process accurately.

Second, some emerging technologies used to design software, called CASE tools, also can be applied to the design of processes. Just as you lay out the flow of command in programming, you do the same in processes. For example, many process teams use CASE tools to flowchart the steps of a process as it is being designed in a conference room, and behind each box in the flowchart add text describing the step. Such process models then can be programmed semiautomatically using CASE tools to hasten technical implementation. This is now a relatively common practice in many enterprises where CASE tools are in wide use. IS can provide that skill to the entire organization.

IS can improve the design work of a process team by teaching end users how to use prototyping and piloting techniques, which are in wide use within the IS community. This saves time, effort, and money before going live with a new and untested process.

Third, IT can link widely dispersed parts of an organization in an integrated fashion. For example, a streamlined order entry process in which actual processing of orders is centralized in a factory has to link salespeople all over the country to the plant. Placing an order from a laptop connected to a telephone line in a customer's office can fire the order to the plant or manufacturer, have a system there configure it correctly, check inventory, assign a delivery date, and trigger a build order, all in minutes. Folding the orders of many salespeople together can provide stable routine to the production processes at the plant as well, saving money, raising plant utilization, and providing fast feedback to salespeople and customers.

In this case, we also saw a fourth benefit: the ability of a system to displace human labor. In this instance, a software configurator can ensure that the order is properly placed, all needed facts are provided, and the correct price is quoted to the customer the first time.

Fifth, at each computerized step in a process, you can program in data gathering on the performance of that step. Such data then can be used to create in-process measurements of how the process is working. Data can include such information as error rates by salesperson and production; speed with which orders are placed, built, and delivered; speed and defects in the delivery process; and billing accuracy and collection times. Automation can eliminate one of the biggest headaches and complaints that all process owners have: their desire for in-process measurements on performance, but without having to go through the tedium of manually gathering that information. Such measurements also make it possible to assign costs to specific activities—the heart of ABC accounting methods!

Finally, IT can link all stakeholders in a process. As we move toward organizations whose lines of authority blur and as suppliers and customers participate more in an enterprise's processes, things like EDI and E-mail become crucial, even central to the execution of work flows. A decade ago, EDI was a convenient way to send an order to a supplier. Today, the supplier might have access to your forecast and hence use it to determine production runs at his or her end and use EDI to collect money for goods shipped and to assess customer satisfaction. Customers on Prodigy at home can order airline tickets and PC components. Very soon you will be able to order products directly from your television at home transmitted via telephone lines back to the source of manufacture for fulfillment. Fig-

Without EDI	With EDI
Postal mail (2-5 days) • slow	Electronic (seconds) • fast
Stand-alone enterprise • maintains inventory • pays bills • bills monthly	Linked to suppliers • maintains inventory for you • collects automatically • bills immediately
Independent vendor • seeks customers • postal mail • slow order taking • customer dependent • volumes of work based on staff size • limited partnerships • quality practices limited • quality practices internally focused	Customer's partner • relies on supplier • E-mail communications • fast order taking • customer dependent • based on MIPS/DASD • extensive partnerships • quality practices extensive • quality practices extended to suppliers and customers

Figure 5.3

ure 5.3 illustrates the profound effect EDI can have in shortening lines of communications between functions, within enterprises, and across stakeholders, all performing their work within processes.

In short, IS can present to process owners several classes of benefits derived from applying IT:

- reduced processing time
- precise management of a process
- accurate movement of data
- in-process measurements and cost accounting
- linked organizations
- IT-based decision making

Strategic Information Technologies of the 1990s

An enormous explosion is underway in the introduction of new technologies and in the improvement of existing hardware and software. The rate of change is continuing to speed up, the variety of change is expanding, and the significance of these changes is nothing less than profound. But this is not new to the IS community. However, users are seeing more articles in their business and industry press than ever before. You cannot read an airline magazine without seeing pages of advertisements for laptop and handheld (palm) computers and different kinds of pocket calculator/computers and telephone systems. We are very aware of significant amounts of technology being introduced into our lives.

Sources of change include a growing number of companies both within the computer industry and outside, in traditional national sources (the United States and Japan, for example), and also new places (India and Brazil, for example). Do they all contribute to continuous improvements in an organization? Are there some that are more important for process work? Which technologies support the management philosophies of Deming and Juran? These are all important questions. What can be said with some certainty is that some technologies facilitate quality efforts more than others. Their roles can be passive (for example, providing a utility function), invisible to end users (for example, IT architectures), or very proactive and obvious (for example, robots and PCs). For our purposes, I use the word *technologies* to refer to hardware devices, software, and sometimes base technologies (telecommunications, imaging, and so forth). While many, if not most, can contribute to improving the quality operations of any organization, some tend more than others. We will discuss the most obvious ones because they are the technologies your end users should be or are already exposed to through their industry and user organizations.

Networks will shorten communications and bring information to users faster. First there was mail, then the pony express, then the telegraph, followed by the telephone, and now fax. We went from sending a letter across the United States in three months to a fax in three seconds. How many of us can stand to operate today without fax? If nothing else, fax has reduced cycle time, created new levels of expectation, and made obvious to all that telecommunication is very important. It began for many with just the telephone, went to a CRT (often with E-mail), then was enhanced with a PC (later linked to others in LANs), and always with other concurrent applications of communications: video conferencing, EDI, and, of course, the fax machine. End users understand clearly the importance of having communications available on a demand basis, serving as a utility. They understand the benefits they receive:

- easy
- quick
- simple
- cheap

And they want more of it. They want their PCs linked together, they want access to data files, fax output from their PCs, and their copiers to be fax machines, too. They want real motion video conferencing, and they want more functions on their telephones. They also want these functions increasingly mobile in their automobiles, on their persons, and at home. This is not new news; however, the rate of demand is. Car phones are increasing in the United States by over 100,000 new subscribers a month. Data transfer over telephone lines is growing in double digits. In 1992, the FCC permitted telephone companies to transmit data over their lines into homes to TVs in the United States. That action alone triggered a massive effort to reconfigure the telephone companies, cable providers, and entertainment conglomerates into a new industry as yet unnamed. How far behind is transmission to home offices from businesses as a normal practice? Research that I have done on the "mobile work force" suggests that the demand for portable data processing and telecommunications that will need to be met in the mid- to late 1990s will be nothing less than massive, equal in volume to the proliferation of PCs in the late 1980s.

All of those elements can and do contribute to process improvements and process reengineering. However, as you sort through the complexity of delivering what end users want, what emerges as very strategic is the client/server model. In this model, work stations, PCs, departmental computers, mainframes, and other devices are all linked in miniature networks. Often these might consist of all the PCs in a department with one serving as a miniature host with extra data storage capability. The next step will be to make this all wireless so that we are not restricted to being physically in one or two places to use them.

More important than what type of network you have, is what it does. When you can link all the people who serve a customer or work on a process or problem together at the same time, you get two consequences. First, you foster teaming and sharing of work, ideas, and information. Second, you can focus the right resources on any issue quickly and effectively, thereby speeding up better quality work. The client/server model thus facilitates organizations moving toward a less hierarchical structure and toward a more decentralized configuration (Figure 5.4).

This kind of an organization is able to change more quickly by configuring itself into whatever group of people is needed to do something now. If a group of people needs to band together to improve the order fulfillment process (from order entry in a sales office to shipment from a warehouse), it can be done. If a problem has to be solved, all those required to accomplish the job can get together wherever they are, focus on problem resolution, and then disband electronically to reconfigure themselves to respond to some other issue. Probably no other technology will do more in the next few years to force organizations to become more

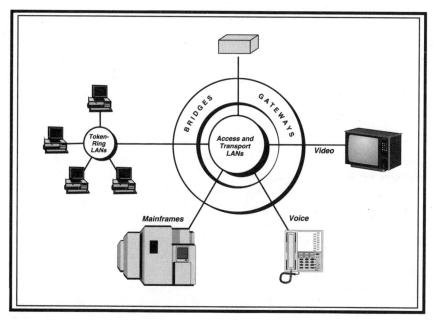

Figure 5.4 Client/server model.

aligned by process and function than telecommunications and, in particular, the client/server model. To facilitate the correct implementation of server/client technology requires more than simply understanding telecommunications.

It means educating end users and management about the implications of the client/server approach. What they need to understand, and to take advantage of, calls for filling several requirements:

1. to create well-defined roles for individuals and processes, since everyone can get to everyone else and thus everyone must understand their individual functions

2. to leverage a large variety of hardware, software, and applications that can increase specialization and skills within an enterprise

3. to take advantage of cost savings made possible when computer and telephonic technologies are merged in decentralized platforms instead of the traditional large mainframe-centralized approaches of the 1970s and 1980s

4. to reconfigure quickly an organization that needs to move people and functions, thus requiring networks that are utilities, with common architectures and systems, almost like plugging a light into an outlet for electricity

5. to facilitate technical portability and modularity in an organization, growing or shrinking quickly, working with corporate data files anywhere

Now all five needs are tied together with wire. Before this decade is out, the client/server model also will be enhanced with wireless communications. More than the car phone, this will include application of cordless PBX and LAN systems for interoffice and remote locations. Such applications of technology will further compress the time it takes for a process to work or for an individual to respond to customers and to get work done, all cost effectively. IBM, Federal Express, and others already use similar systems to dispatch maintenance personnel, communicate with customers, and track logistics. Major truckers in the United States use on-board computers with radio communications. Installations of these systems will increase for the same reasons as the client/server model will.

So if you thought IS's work with telecommunications was enormous in the 1980s, it will only get more complex and increase in volume because of increased end-user expectations and demands. Add to that workload a broadening of capability brought about by wireless, open systems, public and private bands, and you see that telecommunications becomes the source for a large number of operational processes within IS.

Desktop computing is already serving as a significant technological lever of process change. The PC took us by surprise in the late 1980s. We should have known it was coming; end users were buying them by the millions by the mid-1980s. Now desktop MIPS outnumber glasshouse cycles. Everyone seems to be an end user. In fact, well over 80 percent of the work force in the industrialized world in enterprises of over 50 employees depends on computers in one fashion or another to get its work done.

PCs are turning up in the strangest of places as technical interfaces to processes. In some states you can renew a driver's license in a shopping center at a PC-based kiosk with your old license and a VISA card. In many libraries and stores, you look up books and products and get directions by communicating with a PC. I look up library holdings at the local university from my home with the PC I used to write this book. People take driver's license tests at state departments of transportation via microcomputers, while others access municipal bulletin boards (as part of a city's communication process for its citizens) and national networks (as part of information-sharing processes of various organizations). Software allows you to do desktop publishing, communicate with anyone in the enterprise, and soon with anyone who has a telephone. The news is that affinities are developing that are not confined within an organization (like a traditional E-mail system) and are part of cross-functional processes.

The processor on the desk is rapidly acquiring far more power than the mainframes of yesteryear, and are becoming friendlier. Full motion cost-effective video for PCs is now widely available. Instead of looking up the text definition of a lion, you see that text with a video of a lion roaring. Instead of reading about Martin Luther King's "I Have a Dream" speech in an on-line encyclopedia, you also see video of him delivering it. My PC has more storage in it than perhaps IBM sold to all customers in the first few years of the existence of DASD!

The point of all this discussion is that desktop computing is making work faster and different and will play an increasing role in processes of the future. Your role is to make sense out of the chaos of technical incompatibilities and the need to link to wire and wireless networks, to provide data security and access, and so forth. Your challenge will be to provide processes and technologies with performance objectives and measures to ensure uptime, efficiencies, and in-process diagnostics.

Multimedia Technologies Simplify Use of IT, Changing the Way Users Communicate

Finally, coming into their own in the mid-1990s are multimedia technologies. They are a blend of various tools:

- touch-sensitive displays
- full-motion video
- still photographic-quality images
- outstanding quality voice and music audio
- graphics and text

They all mix use of computers, a variety of video and audio electronics, publishing software and printers, and telecommunications. Anytime you can use IT in a way that mimics how humans work, you present the organization with an opportunity to improve processes, reduce time to get things done, and simplify what workers do. That is the promise of multimedia because it tends to rely more on the natural senses of users (touch, image, sound, graphics), creating a more intuitive and spontaneous dialogue with the technology.

Quality-driven organizations need tools that allow employees to learn concurrently as they work. There is an old Chinese saying: "If you tell me, I will listen. If you show me, I will see. If you let me experience it, I will learn." That is the promise of multimedia. With products now on the market that integrate these various components of desktop computing and telecommunications in cost-effective configurations, multimedia has become very attractive.

Without engaging in a technical discussion of multimedia, suffice it to point out that the earliest applications were in the areas of training, public access to information, public transaction systems, and video desktop applications. All were highly portable: on an employee's desk, in a kiosk at a shopping center, and now with laptops. Video applications have been part of sales calls in which salespeople use portable PCs as powerful selling tools. Video conferencing has reduced the time it takes for teams to get together by eliminating the need to travel. The technology is becoming easier to offer because, like other aspects of IT, standards are being created to simplify installation and use. Standardization is very important because it simplifies your job in injecting IT into organizations. Standardization is taking place in the following broad areas of multimedia:

- video
- CD
- PCs
- networking
- storage
- strategic alliances (for example, IBM and Time Warner, TCI and AT&T)

Image Technology Is Becoming a Major Application in Process-Driven Organizations

Good process work requires more facts (data) in a more intelligible, timely fashion. By the early 1990s, according to *IMC Journal*, we were storing over 1.3 trillion documents in businesses alone and adding another 900 million daily. Those numbers seem very conservative to me. Yet the journal also estimated that 2.7 billion pieces of paper are shoved into file cabinets every day. The Association of Information and Image Management estimated that 95 percent of U.S. information is still stored on paper, another 4 percent on microfilm, and the remainder electronically. If your organization wants to compete by reducing the time it takes to do things, you can see that paper and microfilm approaches are just getting in the way.

Hence, the enormous interest in image technology. To clarify what I mean, application of image technology is the ability to capture, store, retrieve, display, process, distribute, and print information electronically that currently is not in digital form. We have seen this already with scanners in which whatever appears on a piece of paper is captured and digitized and, when played back, appears on your screen as it originally appeared on paper, complete with pictures, text, and hand scribblings.

Imaging has a number of benefits for quality-focused enterprises. Documents can be viewed simultaneously by many people across the entire organization. Security of the information remains at the document level. Routing can take place through a predesignated work flow or spontaneously at electronic speeds (no mail delivery). Such transmissions are pointing out where bottlenecks and inefficient processes exist involving preparation of documents. For example, proposal writing for many companies historically has been slow because it involves so many departments and sign-offs. Image processing is streamlining the effort, often through concurrent processing of steps and rapid movement of data through a process.

A document in this form takes less labor and time to handle. Filing, retrieval, copying, and distribution are done at electronic, not human, speeds. Availability is enhanced because you have fewer out-of-file or misfiled documents, and many people can look at the same data, retrieving and filing at electronic speeds. Today we know that image processing substantially reduces the time it takes to perform tasks that are dependent on working with documents. Many IS organizations, therefore, know they have an obligation to introduce this technology to process owners.

For those interested in new applications or services, use of this new technology is critical to their success. For example, if you want your customers to be able to order products themselves from their location, image processing can help. A kiosk at a shopping center equipped with a PC, image software, and a credit card reader allows a customer, for instance, to order clothing after viewing a video of various styles and colors.

Because this technology is now so important, where would you want to introduce it? Under what circumstances would end users be interested in applying it? Figure 5.5 catalogs some of the obvious candidates for this kind of technology.

Knowledge-based systems (KBS) are finally becoming practical tools in reengineered processes. Those who have been in IS for a long time have been promised that KBS is now here. In fact, practical tools began to appear in the late 1980s and early 1990s, but they are just now beginning to deliver on the promise. KBS is still very primitive when compared to what the artificial intelligence engineers and scientists of the human brain want, but it is here and working. We are learning that KBS can enhance better decision making by comparing data more accurately, by maintaining consistency of decisions across an organization, through more thorough analysis, and by faster execution. When KBS is used to train staff on how to perform tasks, organizations are finding that it does shorten training

---

Sample Image-Based Applications

Case Management	Insurance
	Welfare
	Criminal justice
	Team/Groupware
	Customer service
Product Demonstrations	Sales (all kinds)
	PC/TV advertising
	Kiosk order entry
Research	Students
	Marketing
	Scientists
	Doctors
	Stockbrokers
	Designers
GIS	Transportation
	Water works
	Highway departments

Figure 5.5

periods and streamline decision steps for new employees. KBS also can help filter out routine tasks by less skilled people.

In IS alone, applications are being implemented faster with the use of CASE and KBS tools than with more conventional programming languages. Some programs and applications that were too complex to develop in the past have now become easier to create and in shorter time. Prototyping can be done much faster as well. This is a critical strategic consideration for IS shops bent on reducing the amount of time they take to develop applications. For example, in traditional programming, the staff would document requirements, create an external design and then an internal design, write the software, validate it, install it, and then go live. In an expert systems environment, you still have to define the requirements, acquire data, design its use, develop the code, but then model its use to validate that it works. However, you do this all within a package. Once modeled, it can then be validated with users and finally go live. This description is classical prototyping, but with KBS the work is easier to modify, facilitates incremental software development, and gets done faster.

Three circumstances today lend themselves to the application of KBS and are worth pursuing aggressively:

1. Where many people are making similar decisions because, typically, that means there is a long training period for employees, an apprenticeship period, complicated decision-making rules, turnover, and lots of data to manage. This situation exists, for example, in insurance underwriting.

2. Where decision tree approaches are frequent and complicated. Situations that have many "but if," "except," and "unless" circumstances are examples. "We normally extend credit to young people, but if he or she has no credit history. . . ."; "We generally will do business except in Wisconsin, California, and New Jersey. . . ."; "We do not grant exceptions, unless that individual can provide a guarantee. . . ."

3. Where people do their work primarily on telephones. These include employees on help desks, 800 numbers, claims departments, or who take orders.

Role of Standards and Architectures

In the world of quality management practices, common standards are cherished as a technique for simplifying work. Making decisions easier, rooting out complexity, and facilitating access to information, communications, and processes are crucial. In the IS community, one of the most important strategic initiatives to implement quality-based processes is to rely heavily on standards and architectures. Also important is recognizing that these two strategic initiatives in themselves must provide insight on how to use standards and architectures more effectively. But first, let us begin with the obvious.

Standards Are Becoming an Important IS Tool to Facilitate Quality Use of IT

Technology vendors provide the networks, PCs, telephones, and other hardware and software to end users. IS increasingly has to ensure that all this equipment works together. Standards help facilitate flexibility in how organizations respond to their stakeholders and in the way you offer a utility function for IT. Applying many of the same disciplines found in Total Quality Management, you can define standards to support use of technology.

Open systems, a pipe dream just a few years ago, are rapidly becoming a reality as customers and governments around the world legislate them, and as vendors conform. Whether or not there will be open systems is no longer realistically debated, just how to implement them is. From the perspective of quality and continuous improvement, IS shops benefit by looking at standards across all their operations in a variety of areas:

- operating systems
- telecommunications
- systems management
- software development tools
- user interfaces
- data bases
- training

Each is important because you are looking for several key results:

- a set of technologies open enough to allow you to link up to suppliers and customers (for example, use of EDI), thereby facilitating the extension of your enterprise
- a system that feels like a utility to an end user—like electricity in a wall socket
- a system that does not get in the way of process changes, organizational restructuring, or redefinition of people's roles
- a system that is provided in ways that can be measured for performance and return on investment
- a system that adds value to what is important to customers

Because software drives most of the benefits sought after, more will be said about development and end-user tools below. However, just from an IS point of view, traditional benefits of open systems are:

- less dependency on a vendor
- market pressure for better quality technologies
- conformance to certification standards (for example, ISO 9000)

In addition, an IS organization can enjoy the benefits of exploiting process management techniques well by prizing stability and hence simplification of enterprise-wide change and maintenance. Also, open systems facilitate rapid acquisition of those technologies that make sense to the organization. For more on trends in technology, see references at the end of this chapter and in Appendix C.

vide relevant services that are measurable and manageable, and learn constructively from its experiences, your strategy requires the following attributes:

■ All departments and all terminals should be able to talk to each other. That requires total connectivity across the enterprise in a horizontal network independent of vertical organization charts.

■ Technical resources, particularly technical staff, should be leveraged across the entire enterprise. That means making them accessible to everyone.

■ Availability must reach 100 percent, which means zero defects in uptime with disaster recovery a real-time function. More than having reliable hardware and software, you need recovery processes in place within operations.

■ Data should conform to common definitions, have security features to protect data bases from attack or bad information, and be managed as a corporate asset. Data management must be a critical process of any IS shop.

■ Increasingly, emphasis must shift to I/O performance over computer performance. As computing horsepower increases at all points in an enterprise, due to increasing and less expensive chip performance, attention shifts to I/O transactions. I/O has to be more various and able to handle growing amounts of traffic. More than simply picking what laser printers to give end users, I/O must address such issues as speed of printers, volume printing by department, image data entry capacities, telephone bandwidths, and high-speed fax. Our industry has a terrible record of not paying attention to I/O. I suggest you treat the acquisition and deployment of all I/O functions as a major process within the whole area of IT acquisition.

■ Architectures and individual components should be managed and measured as one would any other major process. Taking a process or TQM view of all technology will force IS to link performance to end-user, supplier, or customer expectations. It also means that your stakeholders (end users, for example) will have to participate in selecting technology that they will have to live with as they perform or reengineer processes.

■ Architectures are introduced over time, not all at once. Therefore, your process for imposing standards is best served by (1) defining an architectural network consistent with what the business needs to accomplish; (2) assessing your current architecture map against what is needed to support the organization; (3) setting directions, timetables, and respon-

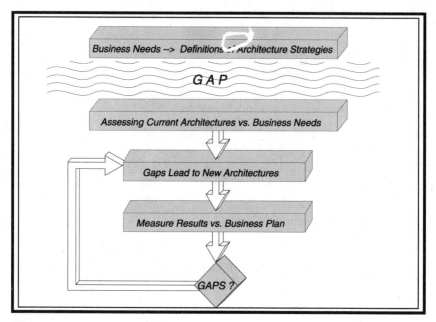

Figure 5.6 Aligning architecture to business plan.

sibilities for implementation of architectures; and (4) measuring results and revalidating that the original plan still makes sense given what your customers need to accomplish (see Figure 5.6). You will know that all the components are in place when your architectural plan takes into account:

- a work flow view
- an application view
- an information (data) view
- a technology view

Your strategy then can lead to specific implementation plans for major technology platforms for such things as distributed systems, networks, operating systems, and programming languages. Your plans can account for existing application and technology environments, recognizing that some are very good and will stay, a few are very bad but cannot go away, while others are ripe for reform.

We have gone through the architecture issue at warp speed for one simple reason: to call out its complexity so that IS can recognize it as a critical component of any effective IS quality program.

Conclusions

Implementation of quality practices throughout an enterprise requires the help of IS because technology can be applied in the redesign or improvement of many processes. The same applies to the IS organization itself, which is home to many processes ranging from production of reports to management of people. Not immune from the good habits required of other parts of the organization, IS has the added burden of linking three activities:

1. adaption of the businesswide strategic plan to that of IS

2. introduction of technology where it makes sense

3. application of TQM tools in its own operations

From a tactical point of view, IS historically was responsible for scouring the technological landscape for new devices and software, for identifying different applications, and then for convincing the rest of the enterprise to adopt them. In a world driven by the need to apply IS for strategic advantage, to reduce the time it takes to get things done, and to facilitate application of TQM tools, several approaches work well.

A variety of IT tools lend themselves to quality practices. Reviewed in this chapter were such things as CASE and KBS. Others will come along in the future (see Figure 5.7). The point is that an IS organization should study some technologies more than others if it is to support the quality efforts of the company.

It has long been clear that looking at the introduction of applications and IT through the implementation of strategically important architec-

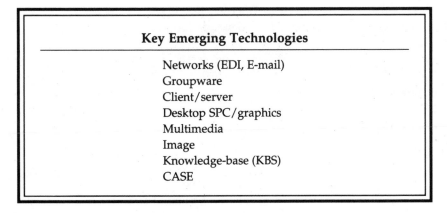

Key Emerging Technologies
Networks (EDI, E-mail)
Groupware
Client/server
Desktop SPC/graphics
Multimedia
Image
Knowledge-base (KBS)
CASE

Figure 5.7

tures (or platforms) makes sense. Laying in place infrastructures that reflect the culture and processes of an enterprise facilitates rapid application of technology. Architectures lead to utility functions, better communications, and faster implementation of IT within the context of processes. The same is true of the IS organization itself. Use of standards and internal client/server approaches, for example, leads to greater productivity in both small and large shops.

Your end users are requesting the same of you. For example, in a recent survey of insurance companies conducted by IBM, 104 executives said that among their top priorities was reengineering of key business processes. They needed strategic approaches from IS; 81 percent, for example, said EDI would be extensively used to process critical customer transactions. But most interesting of all, 87 percent said that client/server LAN technology represented an enormous opportunity for improving operations and competitive position. I could just as easily have cited similar surveys from other industries. The value of this one is that it comes from an industry that historically has not been viewed as heavily involved in quality practices, yet appreciates the value of IT. A stronger case for the application of IT with quality practices could have been presented from manufacturing. The point is that just as a strategic business plan is a critical element of effective implementation of quality-based approaches, so too is the need for a well thought out implementation of key technologies, standards, and architectures.

References

Branscomb, Lewis M. (ed). *Empowering Technology: Implementing a U.S. Strategy.* Cambridge, MA: MIT Press, 1993.

"Client/Server Computer Networks Aid Information Exchange," *Forbes* (March 29, 1993): S49.

Editors, Harvard Business Review. *Revolution in Real Time: Managing Information Technology in the 1990s.* Boston: Harvard Business Review Books, 1990.

Ferguson, Charles H., and Charles R. Morris. *Computer Wars.* New York: Times Books, 1993.

Gaynor, Gerard H. *Exploiting Cycle Time in Technology Management.* New York: McGraw-Hill, 1993.

Tapscott, Don, and Art Caston. *Paradigm Shift: The New Promise of Information Technology.* New York: McGraw-Hill, 1993.

Weizer, Norman, et al. *The Arthur D. Little Forecast on Information Technology and Productivity: Making the Integrated Enterprise Work.* New York: John Wiley & Sons, 1991.

6

World-Class Application Development

*Improve constantly and forever the system of
production and service.*
    W. EDWARDS DEMING, 1986

This chapter describes the role quality management practices play
in the development and maintenance of software. It introduces the
rationale for this discipline and describes how it is normally applied
at a high level and how it fits into an overall IT management process.
By the end of this chapter, you will understand how and why TQM
and software are very closely linked as important components of
MIS activities.

The aspect of quality management practices that has received the most
attention in the IT community is the application of TQM principles in the
development of software. Yet, as all the other chapters in this book suggest, quality management practices in IT span a much broader set of activities. The earliest application of TQM was in software development
because many of the activities performed in writing, testing, and maintaining programs easily lent themselves to this discipline. Because of this,

115

it is often IT management's first exposure to TQM with positive results. This is so much the case that management can introduce TQM to an IT organization easily through software development, experience the benefits of this disciplined approach, and then expand its application to the other areas as described throughout this book.

What Is TQM in Software?

It begins with the notion that application development can be continuously improved. That is to say that the quality of software rises increasingly as measured by its functionality and ability to satisfy the requirements of end users, and with decreasing amounts of resources needed to create and maintain it. Related to this concept is the notion that software development standards should be established and, over time, improved while keeping in mind that the elegance of a system is never as important as satisfying the needs of an end user in a timely fashion. Finally, there is the argument that investing in ever-better tools for system development is justified based on such ideas as cycle time reduction and elimination of errors and defects (otherwise known as waste) while delivering consistently better products to end users.

Quality management practices have built into them the concept that most software development problems are caused and solved by IT management. By understanding, for example, that we can learn from our mistakes without blaming programmers and project leaders, management can encourage self-inspection and learning at all levels of the organization, which will help development teams do the next project better. Management can also invest in training and tools in the spirit of enhancing the capabilities of its people.

Designing quality into software (as opposed to reworking software or just inspecting it after the fact) becomes a logical extension of the TQM approach. Closely tied to this is accepting the idea that development methodologies will constantly be improved or, put another way, be changed to increase the organization's ability to build in quality and pull out some of the need for post-coding audits. Such an approach increases your staff training costs, but if you insist on and get improvements in the quality of software, your savings in development time and maintenance more than cover the additional expense.

Many of the programming staffs' long-cherished values are reinforced by TQM. Three in particular are very common.

1. Programming today is generally a team-based activity. With systems just as complicated as ever, particularly the multimillion dollar projects, having groups of programmers and systems analysts work together in

teams to design, code, and test software increases the likelihood of getting the job done on time, on budget, and to the end user's satisfaction. This approach is not a radical departure from past practice. However, in applying quality practices, management also wants to reinforce the need to apply disciplined methodologies across all teams, demand that specific targets for completion of development steps are set and met by the teams, and respect end-user requirements to the same degree that your needs are respected by someone trying to sell you a product.

2. Training of teams in new tools and methodologies is very consistent with quality management practices, so long as you also add education in understanding what end users need. As managers, we have long known that leaving systems and programming staff isolated from end users was a bad practice. However, with the growing emphasis on understanding what end users want, the need to make sure that staff understands becomes crucial. The quality management approach calls for us to learn about customers (end users) by design, not by accident. This means formal presentations on their needs, thorough understanding of the environments in which they operate, and a deep appreciation of the business realities of the company or agency as a whole. It also means having common measures of performance that make sense to people within and outside the IT organization.

3. Developing partnerships with fewer suppliers of technical products and services—a quality management theme—is very similar to the idea of settling on some standard IT architectures. If you work closely with fewer and better suppliers, you reduce the cost of dealing with them and share the expense of maintaining the relationship and work efforts, while creating technical standards by which to make decisions. For example, while settling on an IBM operating system standard or LAN makes you more dependent on good relations with this vendor, it also allows you to have an architecture with which to guide software development.

Justification of TQM Practices in Software Development

TQM practices are very easy to cost justify. In fact, the areas of justification are now well understood in IT. Essentially, they mimic the same logic as those documented in manufacturing processes (which in many ways are similar to software production steps).

1. Cost of prevention. This is the idea of doing the right things correctly the first time. By avoiding rework (for example, recoding), you can avoid the cost of overtime and overruns. Since these expenses can represent as

much as 50 percent of the total cost of a project, avoiding them can be significant. Equally important, these costs are easy to identify and catalog.

2. Cost of internal failures. Simply put, these are expenses incurred in finding, testing, and correcting errors in programs before you go live. Careful use of effective methodologies and tools in programming can reduce these expenses. Not only do these costs represent salary dollars for staff, but also the lost economic benefits for an end user having a particular piece of software going into production late. For example, if you had a $50 million software project underway with expenses of $500,000 per month, and testing of code showed so many errors that the final delivery of the software had to be delayed by four months, you just added $2 million onto the cost of the project. The end user, who expected to save, say, $200,000 a month in salaries of people doing work manually, now has to plan on spending another $800,000 until your people get their work done. The same logic applies to very small projects.

3. Cycle time benefits. A reverse logic also applies when you can speed up the delivery of a software package. For example, if an insurance company has to get a new product on the market right away because of some changed law or market condition, there is significant competitive advantage in doing so before competitors. Since most insurance policies require extensive IT backroom support (to calculate terms and conditions, for example), your ability to compress development time is of specific bottom line value. Say the opportunity to sell a new policy represents $500,000 a month in sales. If a normal product introduction takes a year, but you and your end users can go to market with an insurance policy in six months, there is an opportunity to pull into the corporation an additional $3 million in revenue based primarily on your ability to deliver code faster than a competitor's IT shop.

Therefore, the value of quality can be quantified!

To a large extent, in software development, rooting out defects represents an extraordinarily fruitful area of cost justification. These have what is called "cost of quality," a term closely associated with the work of Philip Crosby, one of the early quality gurus. He argued that the Cost of Quality (COQ) was made up of the Price of NonConformance (PONC) to customer standards and the Price of Conformance (POC). PONC is usually defined as the expense of changes in schedules and costs due to uncovered defects in software. Since most software experts believe these are somewhere in the neighborhood of 30 to 50 percent of all expenses incurred in software development, it is a big number. This wasted rework can easily be defined. If your software development budget is $1 million per year, as much as

$500,000 could be waste. For our purposes, let's assume you are running a tight ship and, therefore, you come in at a lower rate—say 30 percent—this is still $300,000 of waste! POC is the expenses you incur in preventing defects: for example, systems assurances, tools, and testing. In most reasonably well run shops, that expense is normally about 20 percent of the total expense of software development. Now apply Crosby's approach and you understand the enormous value to you of rooting out defects:

$$COQ = PONC (30\%) + POC (20\%)$$

For your organization, therefore, here are the numbers:

$$COQ = \$300,000 + \$200,000 = \$500,000 \text{ per year}$$

The approach works. In industry after industry, in functional area after functional area for over two decades, the formula has held. As Crosby put it, quality is free because the expense of defect avoidance can be less than the cost of defects or waste. By investing in POC, you drive down PONC to levels below the cost of tools and techniques. And you have the added benefit of providing your end users with whatever value they had identified as coming from the software you delivered!

Experts on quality practices have proved that entire organizations can dramatically reduce their expenses by eliminating the wasted cost of defects. Depending on which expert you talk to, the opportunity to reduce expenses by eliminating defects in all that we do ranges from 15 to 30 percent. Put into an IT perspective, if your department's budget for everything (supplies, salaries, computers, software, telephone calls, and so forth) was $5 million per year, your opportunity to drive down budgeted expenses would be between $750,000 and $1.5 million.

Basic Components of Software Development

Three fundamental strategies can be applied to all software development: continuous improvement, prevention of defects, and measurement of all software development activities. Focusing on all three topics leads to overall improvements in how software is designed, written, tested, and maintained.

Continuous improvement is accomplished by applying a combination of methods and tools on a routine basis:

- use of formal software engineering techniques
- application of rigorous project management
- implementation of a quality assurance process

- use of written methodologies
- reliance on automated tools (CASE, for example)

Lois Zells has explained that the integration of these five sets of activities goes far toward creating an environment in which software is continuously improved. Thus, for her, software engineering involves the proper use of structured analysis, design, and programming (among other things), while rigorous project management is all the planning, estimating, and scheduling activities we normally think of in project management.

She has effectively argued that a quality assurance process must deal with a broad spectrum of issues: "verification and validation; requirements traceability; walkthroughs; inspections; phase reviews; independent testing; configuration management," among other things.

Having written procedures is one of the maxims of all quality experts. How things are done, documented, and managed are often far better controlled and guided if there is a paper trail. But closely tied to this idea is the need to use the very useful programming tools available—many of which assist in the documentation and discipline required—such as CASE tools, data bases, application generation tools, project management software, and programming languages. Rooting out defects before they occur drives down costs and speeds up production of new software.

Simply put, this is designing in quality before coding begins. Since we know that robust analysis and design can cause you to avoid between 40 and 65 percent of all software failures, time spent up front on these activities is how you design in quality and reduce costs of production. The idea is to ensure that every design step results in an error-free product.

How do software managers do that today? To a large extent the answer lies in careful planning and inspection of each design step to ensure clear work and the fact that your project team has considered the potential problems that a particular step might create for those working further down the software food chain. Rigorous documentation standards are imposed and rationale for designs written down. Inspect at this stage, not after you have started to code. An investment of 1 percent of additional work at the design stage can save you as much as 50 percent at coding phases.

As Figure 6.1 suggests, defect prevention should be viewed as a critical process within IS. By conducting regular analysis of problems and issues, you begin to understand patterns of defects, while also identifying specific problems. After conducting an analysis of these issues using such TQM tools as root cause analysis and application of statistical process control, an action team can recommend actions to fix these problems. But also look for recommendations that prevent future problems of a similar nature (hence the value of root cause analysis). By conducting regular feedback

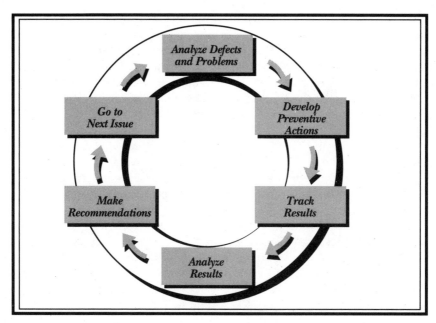

Figure 6.1 Defect prevention process.

sessions with developers and designers, the whole development team gains insight into sources of problems that they can anticipate and avoid. The key here is regular, routine feedback on all activities.

Tracking problems with rigorous documentation, measurements, and even such "soft" approaches as roundtables and interviews long before coding begins makes the analysis of problems more empirical and gets your staff away from operating in ignorance of real or perceived problems, root cause problems, and "gut feel." Analyzing results leads to specific recommendations for avoiding defects. It sounds simple, but so many project teams do not apply this approach. Engineers do it regularly, for example, when designing a car or an airplane, and it works! In short, quality management calls for software design and coding to move away from the black art approach and more toward that of the engineer. This discipline will cause your development process to have a heavy dose of defect prevention activities built into it.

IBM programming teams have reported that this approach has paid off enormously. They have documented that a 1 percent investment of time and resources in a defect prevention process has yielded a far greater return than any stock or money market account. They have cut defect rates in half at the component level design phase, by two thirds at the module level design phase, and in half during coding. Similar orders of declines in defects have occurred at unit test and functional verification test stages. With fewer problems, fire fighting declines as a normal activity in software development. That can be documented by the declining number of defects per programmer, calls from end users, and time and people spent fixing problems. Measurement of all software development activity replaces impressions with facts, gut feel with specifics.

Once you have a formal software development process, you must design a measurement system to tell you how things are going. As Edward Yourdon has so neatly put it, you have software metrics if there is "the desire to improve." A part of that measurement system is the collection of metrics that gives you insight about activities and results. Their purpose is simple: to identify opportunities for improving the quality of everything that is done.

Each major activity in software development—from design through final acceptance testing—should have measures of performance. By looking at each step, you can ask yourself several questions:

- What do I need to know about this activity?
- What constitutes a success or win with this activity?
- How will I know that my design, coding, or testing efforts are successful?
- What facts (data) do I have or need to collect?

Good metrics makes it possible for you to set goals for performance (also called targets). Goals tend to be statements of quality (for example, produce the best software at the lowest cost and as quickly as possible), while a target is usually numeric (for example, reduce coding defects by 10 percent every six months). Increasingly, software development teams are finding that goals have to be measurable. Having one that says "produce the best" does not do the trick; having one that says "produce code with 50 percent less defects coming out of the design phase than last year" gets closer to being actionable.

What are some categories of things that should be measured? The most common in well-run shops include the following:

- development process
- delivered software performance

Within the development process, one normally would measure the progress of various activities, their quality, number of people involved and their performance, and results of applying productivity tools (costs, time saved, lines of clean code written, and so forth). Delivered software measures tend to fall into two categories: size of software and utilization of computer power.

For very large projects (those costing tens of millions of dollars), a development team may actually have a software measurements staff that plans, collects and analyzes data, maintains data bases of this information, and reports results to the other hundreds of programmers and analysts in some organized manner. But even in a small shop, a microcosm of this sort of activity is highly beneficial.

Figure 6.2 illustrates a broad matrix of the kind of measures software developers can collect. While more will be said about measurements in Chapter 10, note that there are nine different categories of measures you can capture. Over time, you will want to fill in the gaps in this matrix as your software development process gains maturity and robustness.

Figure 6.3 shows how these various measures affect each other. Note that you can go from individual, discrete, even mundane, measures to a linked set up to a broader, higher purpose: end-user satisfaction or revenue for the corporation. The value of such a matrix (Figure 6.2) and an understanding of the interrelationships among measures (Figure 6.3) is that they are universal; that is to say, they can be applied across all of IS and the entire company, and not just in software development. In other words, you can begin to have common sets of measurements across the entire company that can be clearly understood by both technical staff and end users!

The variety of measures of software is endless; each organization seems to come up with its own twists. However, there are six good rules of thumb to follow:

1. Make sure that data is presented in numerical and graphical formats (for example, bar graphs and pie charts). It is easier for people to understand the relationships of data to actions.

2. Insist that the measures make sense; eliminate elegant and even trivial measures that add little to the elimination of defects.

3. A measure should be easy to calculate. If not, the cost in dollars and time may not be worth it, particularly at the data gathering phase where the lion's share of the expense can be. Ideally, capturing the necessary data should occur without interfering with the activity it is measuring.

4. These measurements should not be trivial. It is useless to measure something that only has the potential to improve performance fractionally. Go after big, high-leverage things; measure the basics, such as error rates or the time to get major steps completed.

5. Make the measurements timely. If a measure can be delivered to a software development team while this group is still working on the pro-

	Growth	Stakeholder and Customer Satisfaction	Productivity	Cycle Time	Waste	Reliability	Quality	Flexibility	Financial
System Requirements Analysis/Design	# Preventative Processes, Files Needed	% of End-User Involvement (FTEs) in Design	% of Total Project Spent on Design		# End-User Design Changes	Complaints	Actual vs. Planned ROI		Planned vs. Actual Cost
Software Requirements Analysis	# New Changes to Design	Enhancements by Module	# Interfaces with Existing Software	Time to Acquire Requirements	# of Changes Required	# Omissions Noted in Review of Objectives		Speed of Changes	Cost of Phase as % of Total
Preliminary Design		End-User Satisfaction	# Data Items Passed between Modules		# of Changes to Specifications Due to Design Requirement	# Changes to Project Plan, Test Plan after Review	# Changes to Design after Review Due to Error	# Screens/ # Required User Interfaces	Cost of Phase as % of Total
Coding and Testing	Modules or Lines of Code in Excess of Original Design	% Grade by User	% of Time Spent on Coding	Time to Code a Module & by Type	% of Code Changed Due to Reliability Errors	Errors/Module	Defect Rates (Improvement vs. Plan)	# Lines of Code Reused	Estimated Hours vs. Actual
Integration and Testing	# of Modifications by Type, Module	# User/Tester Mis-understandings	# PTF Steps Reduced	Time to Train User, Tester of Documentation	# of Recoded Modules	Problem Rate	Errors in Coding Problems/ Month	Rate of Speed to Change	Defect Fix Time
End-User Acceptance Testing	Growth in Customer Acceptance of End Product	Time Spent on Walkthroughs	% Features Tested at Alpha Sites	Time to Performance vs. Planned	# Defects Total	Complaints	% Grade from Usability Lab Testing	% Resolution of Defects	# of Delivered Errors
Overall		Complaints, Customer Satisfaction	Ratio of Work Days per System/Lines of Code/Module	Timeline of Finished Code	Defects by Program	% of Missed Deadlines	% Improvement in Inspection Effectiveness	% Changes Mode/Work Day of Effort	Cost of Executable Instructions

Figure 6.2 Samples of software development.

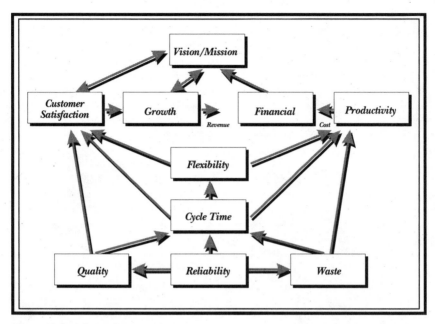

Figure 6.3 Relationship among measurements.

ject, the data can have a positive effect on subsequent work. Giving the team information six to nine months after the project is done may be of little or no interest to them; it certainly will not change the results of the last project.

6. Measure consistently across all projects to learn how to improve from one effort to another. A common example of good practice is use of function points. Do you count lines of reused code? Do you measure the use of INCLUDE statements (for example) as they are applied from application to application? Function points are practical in many shops since, increasingly, management wants a measurements process that looks at a broad variety of activities such as design, documentation, test cases, and user manuals.

Figure 6.4 is a hodgepodge catalog of common measures evident in well-run software development projects. It is not a complete list, simply a sampling to give you an idea of what often gets measured. However, some advice: Since software development always experiences more variation than manufacturing (where use of statistical process control first began), the use of SPC tools must be applied as aids to management rather than as technical inputs. By that I mean the measurements themselves can be used to suggest to management how to motivate programmers and

Type	Format	Why
Size (# of Lines, Modules)	Numbers	Size Drives Cost
#/Type of Defects	Sigma (Errors per Million)	Quality of Software, Performance of Developers
Error Density (Pages/Hour)	Logorithmic Chart	To Understand Quality of Review
Resource/Plan Expended	Bar Graphs	To Understand Effectiveness of Planned Application of Resource
Customer Feedback	Bar Graphs, Pie Charts	To Understand Types to Eliminate
Review Rate	Bar Graphs	To Understand Quality of Review Process, Speed of Work
Ranges of Errors	Control Charts	To Understand Pressure onWorkers to Speed Up Production
Inspection Effort, Intensity	Logorithmic Chart	To Understand Effect of Speed on Workers, Quality of Work
Customer Detected Defects	# and Type Bar Graphs	Quality, Level of Customer Satisfaction
Production Failures	# Control Chart	To Develop Predictability
Application Size at Time of Delivery	Lines of Code or Modules Control Charts/Bar Graphs	To Improve Project Predictability
Development Costs/Time	Tables, Trend Chart	To Improve Predictability of Costs and Effort
Trouble Spot Density	Scatter Diagram	Project Control
Actual vs. Planned Costs	Spider Diagrams, Variation Charts	Project Control
Size Growth in Relation to Control Limits	Bar Graphs	Process Control
Defect Removal Efficiency	Tables, Control Charts	Process Control
Reductions in Process Variance	Run Charts, Process Control Charts	Quality Management
Innovation Adaptation Rates	Run Charts, Trends Diagram	Quality Management
Rework as Percent of Total Effort	Pie Charts	Quality Management

Figure 6.4 Examples of software measures.

designers to perform more effectively, how to instill the basic beliefs in quality across an organization, and as a way of suggesting what investments in training and skills development are needed to create a quality-focused work environment. Some of the data will be very useful from a technical point of view to show, for example, trends in defect types and preventive actions, where problems are and how effective solutions prove to be, but these benefits are only half of the story. The other half is their ability to help managers create a quality work world.

Of all the things to measure, those with the greatest leverage are:

- *Size of software.* Fail to understand this, and all the tools in the world will not allow you to recover from blown budgets and schedules.

- *Number and type of defects.* Knowing the number, time, source, and type of problems is more useful than knowing their level of severity. This insight allows you to get rid of many "bugs" and not recreate them later.
- *Resources expended.* This includes people assigned, overtime expense, cost of consultants, and hardware acquired or used for the project.
- *Customer feedback.* Often this involves not only tracking defects in software, but also how fast problems were solved and how effectively from the end user's perspective.

Applying Quality Practices to Maintain Software

Probably only a few IS executives would argue that software maintenance is a small activity in their organizations. It is not uncommon to have shops spend up to 70 or 80 percent of their resources taking care of existing software. Old systems, in particular (now with their own trendy title— "legacy systems") are notorious. Old systems written in Assembler, flat files in an age of data bases, applications written in languages nobody knows or which are poorly or simply undocumented—all are chronic problems faced by every IS organization. If we could get rid of software maintenance or simply run what we have with fewer resources and headaches, what a wonderful job it would be to run an IS organization! We know that the reality is different. However, the same quality strategies applied to the development of software can also be used in assessing the performance of existing code. These tools can help classify patterns of performance, classes of defects, and results of modifications. The same nine factors presented in Figure 6.3 can be applied to existing code. That view of software leads to several important benefits:

1. Measurements tell you what to fix in one package and then across your entire portfolio of software.
2. They tell you what behavior is going on that either increases your costs of maintenance or could reduce them.
3. They help you decide when, from a business point of view, it is time to replace a piece of code, also giving you technical reasons that are specific and measurable.
4. They give you a much broader understanding of the sources of problems across all your assets: people, software, hardware, vendors, technologies, and users.

With such a comprehensive view of how your assets are deployed and where sources of problems exist, you can now make decisions about replacement with greater confidence. Essentially, you are led through a gap analysis that illustrates how older systems perform versus newer ones. Normally, in any gap analysis, you would look at six components:

1. organization (your and end users')

2. technologies (hardware, software, architectures)

3. applications and processes

4. end-user requirements (and those of the company)

5. financial and budgetary issues (your and the company's)

6. personnel (primarily skills, availability, cost)

Replacement is not as easy an option to exercise as one is led to believe; therefore, the six areas that you look at lead to specific areas to concentrate on in improving existing systems. They do not all have to be replaced; they frequently just need to be tuned and changed, but in an organized manner, just as you would any new piece of code.

Some common practices are evident in well-run shops, however, that reflect the application of quality management techniques. Each takes time to implement and improve, but all are necessary components in any maintenance strategy.

1. Performance measures are developed for existing software and are shared with technical and end-user staffs regularly. The most popular of the communication vehicles are graphical reports and staff meeting presentations done on a monthly basis, sometimes weekly if a highly unstable system is involved.

2. End users and technical support staff participate in the design of fixes, improvements, and formal assessments of performance. These same techniques are used in the design of new software, and for the same reasons.

3. Emphasis is placed on eliminating sources of problems and not just today's issues. Root cause analysis of common and specific sources of problems are routinely applied. Often the lack of documentation, training, and coordination among groups is the major source of problems.

4. People place emphasis on simplifying use of software. This is more than just GUI, it is reducing the number of word processing packages that you support, the variety of data bases that you maintain (the whole architecture discussion from Chapter 5), and tools deployed limiting yourself to those few critical ones and then insuring that they are used effec-

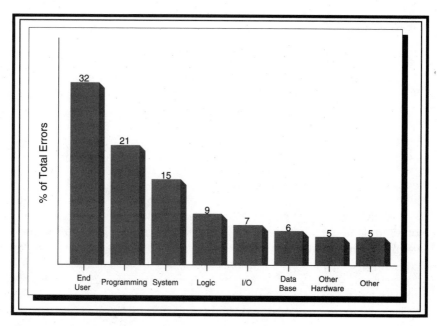

Figure 6.5 Pareto chart of causes of software errors—release 1.

tively. Another pattern is the attempt to simplify how support is provided to end users through more disciplined and organized help desk functions that incorporate better problem-reporting methods.

The key to helping operations staffs maintain existing software is a good set of measures.

As Figure 6.4 suggested, there are many ways of looking at software. Some common favorites among operations staffs, however, are applicable in all IS organizations.

Pareto charts display in descending order problems by package or system. Figure 6.5 is a simple example of software errors within one release of a particular software package. Figure 6.6 shows the errors in a subsequent release of the same software.

Run charts are of extraordinary value because they display what happens over time. In hardware, CPU utilization is a classic example. You can do the same for software, application by application over time. Figure 6.7 illustrates a common example.

A classic study by D.E. Knuth of a typesetting package over ten years (1978–88) showed that other things to measure to document trends included fifteen classes of changes and maintenance of software:

algorithms	language
blunders	mismatch
cleanup	portability
data	quality
efficiency	robustness
forgotten	surprise
generalitation	typo
interaction	

Some of the classifications represent errors in development (for example, blunder, cleanup, data, forgotten, language, mismatch, robustness, surprise, and typo), while others are simply improvements adopted over the years (for example, efficiency, generalization, interaction, portability, and quality). Knuth measured the number of work days to perform error correction and improvements over time and by type. That kind of information is very powerful because it tells management where to focus attention, how errors crop up and are fixed, what types of improvements are required, and at what cost—information that is also useful in the development of replacement systems.

Fishbone diagrams (also called cause and effect diagrams) are increasingly appearing along with more traditional graphical reporting. For ex-

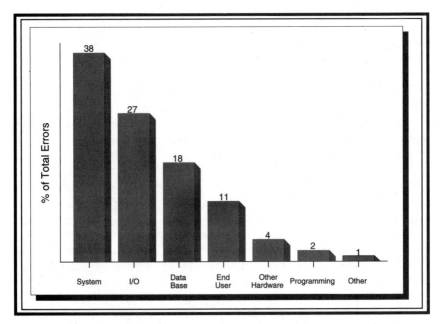

Figure 6.6 Pareto chart of causes of software errors—release 2.

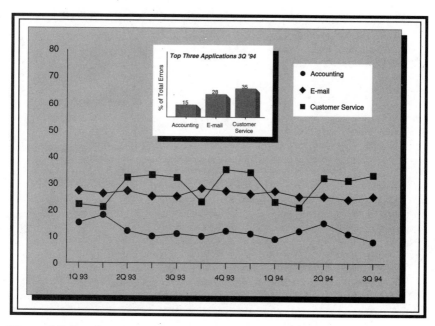

Figure 6.7 Run chart on CPU utilization by application.

ample, in many organizations today the top half of a sheet of paper will have a specific measurement in some graphical form (a bar chart, for example) that shows a problem. In the lower half of the sheet might be a fishbone diagram showing that the folks maintaining the software had identified the cause of the problem. Finally, at the bottom of the sheet might be short comments on what is being done to improve the situation. Figure 6.8 illustrates such a use of graphics.

Quality Assurance Strategies

Organizations that embrace the notion of quality practices frequently will point with pride to their quality assurance organization as testimony of management's commitment to quality. However, surveys conducted by the American Society for Quality Control (ASQC) suggest that the vast majority of these quality assurance groups do not know, let alone practice, basic quality improvement techniques (Pareto charts, error-prone analysis, etc.). Furthermore, many of the techniques used are ineffective—chasing "bugs" in software after the fact, using slogans, or improving testing methods. Surveys of effectiveness indicate that all these techniques add

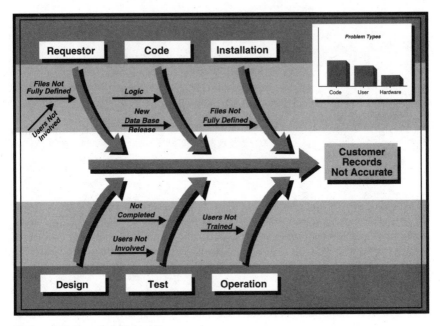

Figure 6.8 Sample fishbone diagram.

up to only about a 30 percent effectiveness rate in improving software quality.

So how do you make a quality assurance strategy effective?

First, such an approach should focus on reducing the number of defects in finished software, develop approaches to ensure costs and schedules are not violated by development and maintenance activities, ensure that the software can be used as committed to end users (e.g., features, functions, performance levels), and provide ways to ensure improved quality of software in subsequent releases.

Second, use this quality assurance strategy to inject quality practices throughout the development process. Attaching a quality assurance department onto an IS organization does not do it, as suggested by the surveys previously cited. You have to build quality into all of an IS organization's activities from the beginning of the cycle, through the quality of the programmers and analysts, the tools used, hardware deployed, and so forth. Richard Zultner and Edward Yourdon are correct when they argue that more than changing tools and techniques, you should change the culture of the enterprise (along the lines suggested throughout this book), not just at the point of software development.

Quality assurance can become a strategy that has, as its many tasks, to prioritize what gets worked on or fixed, to track the status of actions to be taken, to implement changes, to communicate feedback across all appropriate groups (including end users), to administer the causal analysis files or data bases, to offer generic analyses of patterns of software problems and work practices, and to promote the celebration of improvements.

Ultimately, it is the weaving of quality practices throughout the entire IS organization that provides the most effective way of enhancing the quality of software. Not that a quality assurance team does not fit in the process; indeed it does for the purpose of promoting the use of quality practices and then reporting results, not just inspecting code. This same group can help the entire IS department settle on a clearly understood definition of what quality software is—not an easy thing to do. Normally, such definitions include reliability, usability, usefulness, maintainability, and stability as components of any set of standards. They are all measurable and can be understood by programmers, analysts, IS management, and end users.

Conclusions

Software development and maintenance are two sides of a coin. In a quality-driven organization, they achieve improved levels of performance by the application of TQM tools, which are a natural fit for the kind of work done by IS professionals. Measurements of how things are accomplished, results, and how performance is perceived by end users are central elements of all management activities. Treating development and maintenance as collections of processes with the same discipline seen in any process management effort is the primary function of any software development effort. In short, quality management practices encourage the effort underway across the entire industry to move from an arts-and-crafts approach to software engineering. Structured tools become more valuable in this kind of an environment, as does the notion of continuously improving the ways in which software is designed, written, delivered, maintained, and replaced.

Richard Zultner, an expert on software engineering, has identified obstacles to software quality that need to be recognized because, as you implement quality management practices, they will get in your way. They are:

- hope for the quick fix
- belief that new software or hardware will transform MIS
- "our problems are different"
- obsolete training in software
- poor instruction in the use of statistical tools and techniques

- "that's good enough—we don't have time to do it better"
- quality-control people given the responsibility for quality
- false starts
- thinking you installed quality
- unmanaged computers
- only meeting specifications
- poor testing of prototypes
- demanding that outsiders know everything about your operations before listening to them

This is a real-world list; many of these problems even exist in non-IS parts of many organizations!

Implementing quality practices in the development and maintenance of software is a good place to start for any IS organization. Working out its implementation bugs here is easiest because the issues involved are very precise when compared to such topics as managing personnel practices and business planning. If you can make quality practices work in software development, you will also have specific measurable results that you can use to defend the move to quality management practices in the rest of your organization and then outside, where the end users live. Since end users believe that the only thing that you should do is to deliver software fast and keep it very reliable, quality implementation activities in this area give you a very strong story to tell the rest of your company or agency while you are meeting or exceeding expectations.

References

Arthur, Lowell Jay. *Improving Software Quality*. New York: John Wiley & Sons, 1993.

Cho, C.K. *Quality Programming: Developing and Testing Software with Statistical Quality Control*. New York: John Wiley & Sons, 1987.

Gibbs, W. Wayt. "Software's Chronic Crisis," *Scientific American* 271, no. 3 (September 1984): pp. 86–95.

Grady, R.B. *Practical Software Metrics for Project Management and Process Improvement*. Englewood Cliffs, NJ: Prentice-Hall, 1992.

Knuth, D.E. "The Errors of TeX," Report No. STAN-CS-88-1223, Department of Computer Science, Stanford University, Stanford, CA 94305.

Meyers, Glenford J. *The Art of Software Testing*. New York: John Wiley & Sons, 1979.

Rockart, John F., and J. Debra Hofman. "Systems Delivery: Evolving New Strategies," *Sloan Management Review* (Summer 1992): pp. 21–31.

Schulmeyer, G. Gordon, and James I. McManus, (eds). *Total Quality Management for Software.* New York: Van Nostrand Reinhold, 1992.

Walrad, C., and E. Moss. "Measurement: The Key to Application Development Quality," *IBM Systems Journal* 32, no. 3 (1993): pp. 445–460.

Yourdon, Edward. *Decline and Fall of the American Programmer.* Englewood Cliffs, NJ: Prentice-Hall, 1992.

Yourdon, Edward. *Structured Walk-Throughs.* Englewood Cliffs, NJ: Prentice-Hall, 1979.

Zultner, Richard. "The Deming Approach to Software Quality Engineering," *Quality Progress* (November 1988): pp. 58–64.

7

Applications That Support Quality in an Enterprise

The moral is that it is necessary to innovate, to predict needs of the customer, give him more. He that innovates and is lucky will take the market.
                    W. EDWARDS DEMING, 1986

This chapter is a guide for the general IT executive who wants to know what applications the IS organization should propose to the enterprise as a whole that facilitate use of quality management practices. Included are high-level strategic discussions of selection criteria, groupware, E-mail, and tools that get the enterprise closer to its customers.

A massive number of articles, books, and seminars are available today on how to make IT a competitive tool for the enterprise. IT executives are told how to deploy strategic initiatives, increase shareholder value, reduce costs, enhance global competitiveness, and facilitate downsizing or, in the elegant parlance of the mid-1990s, "streamline" the business, and all with a customer/market focus. But as Deming, Crosby, Juran, and other experts on quality have long argued, how the processes of a company are managed is how things can be done most effectively and continuously improved. It turns out that when some applications of technology are implemented, they facilitate quality management practices in other parts of the organization in a relatively dramatic fashion. Therefore, we will discuss the enterprise-wide actions that an IS organization can take in the spirit of facilitating quality management practices. Everything that follows is strategic, as have been most recommendations in this book. I also have included tactical discussions.

Just looking at quality practices provides a clean rifle-shot view through the enterprise because it is a process perspective. As Thomas H. Davenport has so effectively demonstrated, process innovation or reengineering is best done with a heavy dose of IT. However, the IS community can, in turn, offer a bag of tools that extend beyond the "computer department" as a technology infrastructure in support of the goals of the company or agency.

I have already addressed the importance of an IT architecture (Chapter 5), using the discipline of engineering in the development of software (Chapter 6), and later I will discuss how day-to-day operations are run in a quality manner in support of enterprise-wide applications (Chapter 8). But first we need a sense of which computer applications facilitate quality management practices. And a reminder of a point made in Chapter 5: The cost of technology continues to drop suggesting that more tools will be used than before and that even more effective leadership from IT will be needed to implement them (see Figure 7.1).

In addition, all the talk about IT being a strategic business partner that no longer operates in isolation or as a business within a business calls for IS to facilitate the exploitation of management practices and values in evidence across the rest of the company. In other words, if the company as a whole is implementing such quality management practices as TQM, process reengineering, and team-based work, then IS's recommendations concerning what applications to implement should also include suggestions regarding quality practices. In fact, those suggestions then become part of the definition of a company's strategic needs, and causes an even closer linkage between IT's actions and what is needed by the rest of the enterprise.

How to Select Enterprise-wide IT Applications

If IS has a responsibility to recommend to the rest of the enterprise applications that facilitate use of quality management practices, what criteria should be used? Business strategists tend to ignore this question, focusing instead on "big bang" applications that make companies competitive, change the rules of the game, or cause significant declines in expenses.

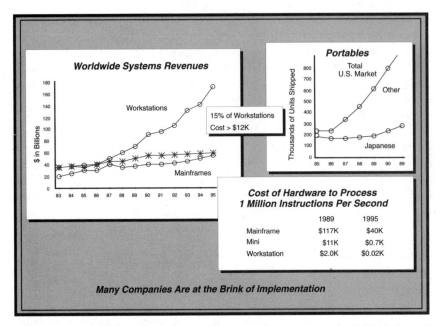

Figure 7.1 The decline in cost drives microtechnology to customers, individuals, and products.

All of these are good reasons for using IT, but we will explore them only as they enhance the practice of quality management principles. The question remains: Are there some applications that, if implemented, will encourage the use of such practices in general across the entire enterprise? The answer is definitely yes!

The selection process begins by establishing criteria for identifying applications. But first management should recognize that these applications in themselves facilitate competitive advantage. This is not new news. For example, in a survey of seventy-one health insurance company CEOs conducted in 1992, the top three business strategies for remaining competitive included better customer service, which means, from an IS point of view, applications that more closely link customers and vendors; containment of costs, which means facilitating process improvement and reengineering activities, which in turn calls for access to corporate data on processes; and better information, which requires different data, such as measures of performance of processes. Customers wanted more customized solutions and better controls over claim costs. Don Tapscott and Art Carson, in articles and now a book, have described in considerable detail how IT has broken down traditional walls between various organizations within a company and also serves as the glue holding the enterprise together.

The implication for quality management is that IT has to consider implementing applications that:

- cover the entire enterprise
- are accessible by all process teams
- are relevant to process teams
- speed up transformation of processes
- foster teamwork
- promote closer ties to customers
- make possible more customized services and products
- speed up work

Questions to ask are:

- To what extent will a project facilitate closer relations with customers such that they will buy more goods and services from us?
- To what extent will a project make it possible for the company to respond quicker and with greater effectiveness to changing market conditions (with more customized offerings)? Or cause these market conditions to change in favor of the company?
- To what extent will a project facilitate individuals and the organization as a whole to learn to sustain innovation and be capable of improving constantly?
- To what extent will a project speed up the activities of the organization?

But first let us recognize what features of IT help individuals change processes and apply quality management tools and techniques. Figure 7.2 catalogs a variety of the characteristics that facilitate improvement of any process. It is even better when IT can either focus these features on specific process improvement projects in the organization or provide applications that make it possible for others indirectly to do process improvement work. Essentially the requirement for IT initiatives outside of IS is supportive, even passive, but necessary to facilitate others to practice quality management. Therefore, any enterprise-wide process that has characteristics listed in Figure 7.2 becomes a candidate (for example, E-mail and EDI).

A second way to look at the selection criteria is to respond to business-driven architectures, suggesting to the IS community how it must respond. Figure 7.3 is a graphical representation of this approach. The business settles on a business strategy, which the firm implements by

Characteristic	What IT Does	Significance
\multicolumn{3}{c}{**Characteristics of IT That Facilitate Use of Quality Management Methods**}		
Transactional	Converts unstructured activities into routine ones	Drives down costs, errors, and waste
Geographical	Moves data fast to wherever it is needed	Improves effectiveness, lowers costs, speeds response to situations
Automational	Reduces labor content	Lowers costs, increases consistency, reliability
Analytical	Provides tools to facilitate fact-based decision making	Improves productivity, quality of decision making
Informational	Provides vast quantities of data in usable formats	Improves knowledge of teams, enhances fact-based management
Flexible	Can cause rapid changes in how tasks are performed	Mass customization allows for more effective response to customers
Linking	Connects together various people and organizations	Improves effectiveness, improves customer retention, drives down costs
Tracking	Will monitor and measure performance of processes, people, and resources	Improves performance, increases productivity of resources

Figure 7.2

designing processes and organizational structures that support the strategy. Simultaneously, IT is requested to develop applications that support both the business strategy and the processes required. In turn, the IT community marshalls its resources to meet the requirements of the business. As it does that, IS staff ask themselves what applications and data are needed both in and outside of IT and how these applications and information will be made available. Answers to those questions provide the linkage to the seven sets of activities normally evident in an IS organization (see bottom line of Figure 7.3) and that influence what applications are developed. At the same time, activities at these lower levels offer IS and planners an idea of what is technically relevant and possible for the entire enterprise to use in implementing quality practices.

The resulting list of possible applications can be enormous. For example, looking at the characteristics in Figure 7.2, it becomes very obvious that good backbone telecommunications capabilities are crucial to a quality-focused enterprise. Once the decision to put in such a TP backbone has been implemented, the number of possible applications is extraordinary. This is not a new idea; indeed, people have been exploiting it since at least the 1840s! Figure 7.4 suggests the actions that industry has taken and in what order.

A third way to look at establishing criteria for selecting applications is to mix IT characteristics with IT functions. Figure 7.5 catalogs some of the more obvious examples of this approach. You ask what IT can do (for example, provide modeling tools) and then determine what effect that should have (for example, helping to identify what processes to change), and what benefits should accrue (for example, lowering costs or making processes more effective to the customer). This list is arbitrary; your IS organization should develop its own based on its core competencies, business strategy of the corporation, and realities of existing IT. The list need not be any longer than the example.

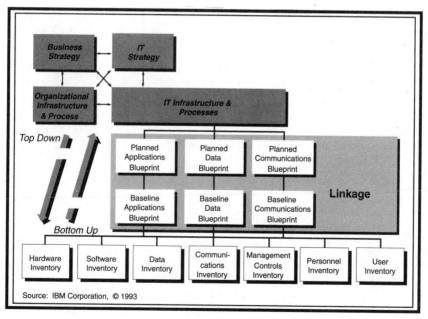

Figure 7.3 Business-driven architectures must drive the I/T process in the future.

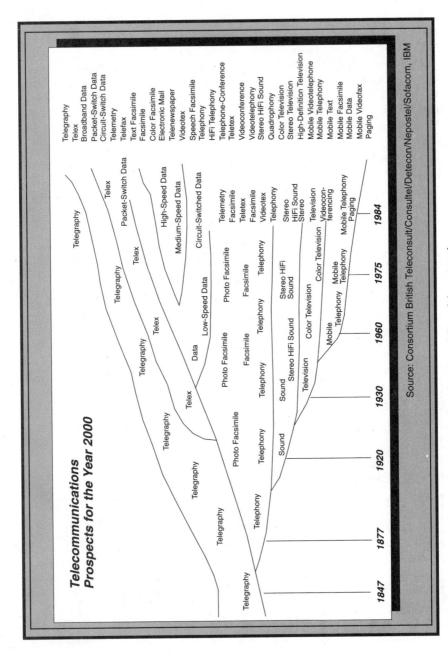

Figure 7.4 Telecommunication expands the functional capability of the network.

Framework for Exploiting IT as an Enabler of Quality Management		
IT Effort	Effect on Quality Processes	Anticipated Benefits
Laptops in sales	Makes work mobile	Faster response to customers
Modeling tools	Identify what processes to change	Lower costs, more effective processes
Automation	Reduced steps, reduced or augmented human labor	Accuracy, productivity
Networking	Teamwork, communications	More effective results, employees
Data bases	Fact-based decision making	Confidence, accuracy
Competitive/ Customer records	More knowledge of rivals and customer needs	Become more competitive, improve decision making
Decision analysis	Improves "what if" and "what happens" analysis	Less risk of big mistakes, better quality decisions
Data gathering	Performance monitoring, measurements	Accurate, fact-based, improved decision making

Figure 7.5

One expert, Thomas H. Davenport, has developed his own list of application types that support processes at a tactical level within a manufacturing operation (see Figure 7.6). The list fits most manufacturing companies and is a nice twist to the suggestions in Figure 7.5 because it takes the list of selection criteria down to the functional level.

Armed with a list of selection criteria, you can select applications that have the potential of serving the widest number of employees across the entire enterprise, not just within IS. The rest of this chapter is devoted to describing examples. However, each industry has its own unique opportunities that you should not ignore. For example, in the gas and electric utility business, reengineering manual meter reading efforts (a popular activity at the moment) is dependent on state-of-the-art customer information data bases with hooks into satellite communications and a billing system to which telecommunications can feed data. In the insurance in-

---

Examples of Generic Processes of IT

For Product Development Processes
- Automated design
- Simulation systems
- Tracking systems
- Decision analysis systems
- Interorganizational communications

For Order Fulfillment Processes
- Product choice systems
- Microanalysis and forecasting
- Voice communications
- Electronic marketing
- Interorganizational communications
- Textual composition

For Logistics Processes
- Locational systems
- Recognition systems
- Asset management systems
- Logistical planning
- Telemetry

Figure 7.6 *Source*: Adapted from Thomas H. Davenport, *Process Innovation: Reengineering Work Through Information Technology* (Boston: Harvard Business School Press, 1993): pp. 50–63.

dustry, it is the capability of doing rapidly "what if" analysis in order to bring new products to market. In the credit card business, it is mass mailings using extensive marketing/demographics data bases. IBM, with its far-flung development, manufacturing, and marketing activities in over 130 countries, needs the best E-mail and EDI systems, while Federal Express requires telemetric systems to track packages and trucks as they move around the world. All have in common the profound influence of base systems on such quality management practices as process reengineering, fact-based decision making, and process measurements.

Communicating and Sharing Information Faster and Better

No application over the past ten to fifteen years has affected the culture of large organizations as much as E-mail. It has facilitated rapid communications independent of geography and time. E-mail has made it possible to eliminate layers of management and bureaucracy. Work goes faster because, for example, people with E-mail no longer have to hand write a letter, have a secretary type it, proof it, have it retyped, and finally mailed. They just swing around to their terminal and bang out a note that is delivered instantaneously. At IBM, for example, secretaries are rare as hen's teeth, and the large word processing centers of the past have been replaced by small groups of subcontracted workers mostly focusing on PC-based graphical presentations, not narrative documents. The same is true in many other companies.

E-mail is fast. Instead of taking two days to write a document and four days to deliver it, the transaction takes seconds, leading to many iterations of communications. Mike Prince, director of IS at the Burlington Coat Factory, typifies the pattern. He was recently quoted in an interview as saying E-mail allowed him and others to stay in touch: "There's an awful lot of the business running across in E-mail discussions. And E-mail is a hell of a lot more effective than meetings."

This application encourages teaming and empowered employees. In the past decade, we have learned that E-mail made it possible for people to communicate with each other on projects or as teams. They also have not hesitated to communicate with whomever they needed to in the enterprise because it became increasingly difficult to block communications with, for example, executives by using administrative assistants and secretaries.

In the world of quality management, anything that makes it easier to disseminate internal information across any organization is attractive. In fact, it is so convenient that a problem exists: overuse. Some IS organizations are complaining about the enormous increase in disk space such systems use and increasingly are reporting that E-mail is taking up 5, 10, even 20 percent of their mainframes. However, the perceived problem of overuse is simply a reflection of this tool's convenience.

In a 1992 survey involving more than 17,000 managers, Datamation and the Business Research Group discovered that even during a recession, the major applications of IT involved sharing data using a backbone communications system. The most popular technologies were local area networks (46 percent), client/server architectures (43 percent), and GUIs/windowing (37 percent). The most attractive applications were LAN management (30 percent), electronic mail (27 percent), office automation (24 percent), and records management (23 percent)—all to save money, increase the speed with which things were done, and equip employees with practical tools.

E-mail Is Used for a Large Variety of Applications That Support Quality Initiatives

When E-mail first appeared, it typically was used for two purposes: to send and receive short notes and to keep track of appointments using an on-line calendar. Over time, organizations found they could use E-mail software to provide the backbone interface for a variety of other applications, which, it turns out today, supports a variety of quality practices. These spinoff applications include:

- *bulletin boards,* which can announce training classes in quality tools, achievements of various process teams, and performance of the company or processes, or can recruit volunteers to work on projects
- *best practices data bases,* which can house information on what process teams are doing around the enterprise or even outside the organization
- *conference applications,* in which people debate a topic of concern to the enterprise, with the dialogue stored in its own directory
- *statistical process control tools,* which can be accessed on-line through E-mail to measure the performance of a process
- *forms delivery,* which can be filled out and returned to the appropriate part of the organization, be tracked, studied, and its instructions carried out
- *on-line training* in a real-time environment, useful for teams acquiring specific skills needed right now to perform their work
- *news clipping services* accessing hundreds of commercially available data bases as a library on a desk, facilitating fact-based research on business issues and informal benchmarking

The list is endless. IS management has discovered that once an employee has signed on to the command screen in E-mail, that screen can serve as a convenient gateway to many other immediate applications. Most individuals who have access to E-mail from their terminals will sign on to this application when they first come to work, remain signed on most of the day, and turn to it periodically for news, to check their mail, and to perform applications. In short, E-mail is a fundamental component of how organizations are configured and operate.

E-mail Is Being Used as Part of Reengineered Processes

As process reengineering teams design new ways of doing tasks, they are increasingly turning to E-mail as an integral part of the process, but normally after E-mail has been installed because by then they understand its implications for a process. For this reason, IS should move quickly to introduce this application if it does not exist today.

Three new uses illustrate how E-mail is part of reengineered applications:

1. Employee suggestion processes. The old wooden box with the large padlock is out; it generated only about one suggestion per employee per lifetime and has been replaced with new processes that are gen-

erating up to three to four implemented suggestions per employee per year. Employees submit their ideas in E-mail forms and then send them to either their managers or a designated suggestion handler. Because subsequent communications with the suggester also is done via E-mail, ideas are acted upon quickly. Suggestion software tracks transactions and provides a wealth of data on the types of issues being addressed by "empowered" employees. In fact, suggestions serve as indicators of employee commitment to improvement and involvement.

2. Employee opinion surveys. Surveying employees on a large range of issues is one of the most useful things a management team can do for itself. Such a process tells them what is on employees' minds, documents their level of morale, and leads to conclusions about how to improve the overall efficiency and effectiveness of daily operations. The best survey processes today are done through E-mail, not with paper questionnaires. The benefits of using E-mail are:

   - Confidentiality—it is easier to preserve using software guards (passwords and access restrictions, for example).

   - Speed—a whole company can be surveyed in days and reports and analysis completed in hours.

   - Analysis—a critical success factor for such processes is the detailed numerical/statistical analysis that must be done to identify trends in changing opinions by topic, location, type of employee, and time, all of which can be done conveniently using software.

In the privacy of one's own workstation, an employee can access a survey right off the command line in E-mail, complete it, and then transmit it to the survey E-mail address conveniently and quickly.

3. On-line query and ordering by customers. Over the past decade, customers have increasingly been given access to their supplier's E-mail systems, making communication with a vendor as convenient as with a fellow employee. New twists added the capability of looking up specifications and prices for products and services and then the ability to order these by E-mail. As with the other two examples, this is done right off the command line. Companies also conduct customer surveys the same way they do employee surveys—as a subprocess within E-mail.

Implementing LANs and LAN Management Systems Allows Employees to Share Information Effectively

In addition to implementing E-mail systems, small and large organizations have found LANs to be of extraordinary value in supporting the flow of information across the enterprise and as a way of bringing employees together. In fact, implementation of LANs during the early to mid-1990s was the most popular new IT infrastructure application. In the 1992 survey previously cited, one third of the respondents said they had major LAN projects underway, almost as extensive an effort as the rapid expansion of E-mail systems. While more will be said later about groupware and teams, keep in mind that if you are interested in fostering open exchange of information, then LANs and servers nicely compliment E-mail. LANs tend to carry larger files, since these types of data are tied to specific projects and are extensively used by project and process teams. The third leg in this communications infrastructure, which we will deal with in more detail later, is EDI. All three can be linked to facilitate the rapid transfer of information back and forth from customer to vendor, from one employee to another, and from the top of the organization to the bottom and back up.

Communications Applications Fundamentally Support the Move to a Quality-Based Culture by Changing How People Think and Act

Transforming how a business operates cannot be done without the proactive involvement of IS. The application of IT is a crucial component of the change. A large number of researchers have now documented the importance of IS's involvement. They have learned what you can expect from using IT to facilitate your company's cultural change.

First, employees are beginning to challenge the limits of their authority. For example, if an employee has access to the same information as the accounting department has, why wait for accounting to prepare reports that arrive in the middle of the month when the employee can pull down the data, do the analysis, and apply the results earlier in the month? Employees who do not like a new policy announced by the human resources department can fire off a note to the CEO suggesting why it should be changed.

Second, employees are changing the way they perform their work. A simple example is the decline in travel since much more work can be done via E-mail, LANs, and telephone systems. But more subtle is the fact that things can be done more quickly, making it possible to do more and, from a customer's perspective, respond faster with a service. There is growing evidence that employee availability to each other also increases.

Third, employees access information at their convenience. Since most communications involve two or more people, eliminating the requirement of having them both together at the same time saves time and effort. Using E-mail, for example, you can send information needed by people when you want to and they can receive and use it when they need it. Unlike a telephone conversation, where both parties have to be together at the same time, voice mail and E-mail do not require that kind of coordination of calendars. So employees can perform increasing amounts of work when it makes ideal sense to them. In short, convenience becomes a productivity tool.

Fourth, employees are moving away from a "command and control" world to one more democratic in tone and style. If your company is interested in delegating authority and "empowering" employees, it is crucial that it move toward a more democratic environment where individuals take the initiative to express opinions, take charge of circumstances, and make decisions. Electronically, we face each other without the need for hierarchies that had always been in place to funnel information around an organization. People are no longer working through meetings to get things done, where the rank or status of individuals counted. In an electronic environment, status is disappearing as an important factor. A democracy of ideas and abilities is slowly appearing to replace status and personality, leading to a more open discussion of ideas and alternative actions. It does not completely root out politics, but it certainly is beginning to reduce its harsher features. We have very strong evidence that results of this new circumstance are better quality decisions, products, and solutions.

However, if your company is not interested in flattened structures, open communications up and down the organization, and empowered employees, then the kinds of backbone communication systems discussed here probably should not be implemented because they will change your culture. But if you do implement them, then four actions also should be taken to ensure success with the effort:

1. Make the backbone network (for example, E-mail) available to all employees.

2. Encourage an environment in which information is shared openly (don't blame people for bad news).

3. Build systems that attach to the network that facilitate dialogue and communications (for example, on-line forums and data bases).

4. Change your personnel practices to encourage open dialogue (for example, implement suggestion systems and bonuses for leadership activities).

How Teams Can Be Supported by Technology

Less understood than the effects of E-mail is the role IT can play in facilitating the effectiveness of teams. Most companies have just started to implement team-based work practices. Also, most research and literature on teams still discusses how they behave when they all get into the same room. For example, the most widely read book on team behavior, Joiner Associates' *Team Handbook* (which has sold over a half million copies) does not discuss the effects or even application of IT on teams.

Yet those who have implemented LANs and user friendly GUI applications have seen several effects on teams.

- They need not be geographically located in one spot; they can be scattered across the country and still be effective.

- The number of teams that are geographically dispersed is increasing.

- Reliance on larger quantities of data is increasing because these teams have the tools with which to handle information conveniently.

- Teams are being formed more frequently from cross-functional organizations.

The last trend is important for IS because, increasingly, experts from the technical community can join end users, both working on projects in the comfort of their own departments via E-mail, groupware, and so forth. This kind of cross-pollination is a way of facilitating use of IT, particularly in reengineering major processes outside of IS.

At the heart of the issue is sharing of information, which is why groupware is both convenient and controversial. It is convenient because it facilitates the exchange of ideas, documents, decisions, and analysis. This kind of software allows teams to come together quickly to perform a specific task (for example, fix a problem) or to work on some long-term project (for example, a long battle or a multiyear product design of a new airplane). It is a way to facilitate the democratization of work and to permit nontraditional linkages among workers based on needs, responsibilities, and abilities.

However, there still is the problem with sharing information. If people want to hoard data in the belief that information is power, then all the use of Lotus Notes will not facilitate teamwork. Clearly, this problem is a momentary one because so many organizations are investing heavily in converting their operations to team-based work. Groupware is a critical component of the effort. Today, almost every major software vendor is selling or developing software to facilitate this new environment. Your organization will, in all probability, be required to form an opinion about this software, set standards, and select and support packages.

Use of groupware fits nicely with quality management practices and is catching on very quickly. Lotus Notes, for example, is used by over 750,000 people, and that is only one software package! Microsoft and others are also in the market. Yet hiding information, or simply not sharing, is still a real problem compounded by the fear that some of the information could negatively affect individual employees.

The best way to encourage use of groupware is to create incentives for employees to share information. Specifically, sharing of data should be in their performance plans. Rewards and compensation should be tied to the degree they share, and the results of team activities serve as the basis of recognition.

Electronic brainstorming is one way of applying groupware that does not depend so heavily on sharing information in the more traditional ways. Brainstorming can facilitate cultural changes required to make groupware work. Traditional brainstorming is a group of people in a room putting up on a wall all the ideas about an issue, then assessing options and arriving at conclusions. We all have experienced mixed results; sometimes good ideas emerge, other times people are reluctant to share a thought for fear of being criticized. An electronic approach reduces the shyness factor and allows people to record their ideas as they occur (instead of waiting for their turn to talk). Research is showing that as a result more and better ideas are emerging. Participants also like electronic brainstorming over the more traditional approach.

The effort is very similar to oral brainstorming. Using a piece of software to manage the process, participants type in ideas at will during a session (which can hold as many people as you want); these ideas are categorized (the affinity technique, a TQM tool) by topic and redundant ideas are tossed out; then people rank the ideas by whatever criteria they want (importance, cost, and so forth); action steps are defined the same way with suggestions from all participants; finally, the plan is printed out. There are many pieces of software available to facilitate these exercises that the IS organization can explore and make available to the entire company. Some of the more popular packages are TeamFocus, GroupSystems, VisionQuest, and Software-Assisted Meeting Management.

Most applications of this kind of software are still done with all the participants in one room, each with a terminal, and a screen at the front of the room where results are posted. Conversations are held as in a normal brainstorming exercise, but instead of using cards (meta planning) or writing ideas on a flip chart, they are typed into the terminal. Video conferencing is just beginning to make it possible to conduct such efforts for multiple locations simultaneously. Research comparing electronic to oral brainstorming shows that you get more ideas by using terminals, can handle a larger group of people, work faster, and satisfy everyone more with the outcome. However, like any new software application it has some drawbacks: Everyone has to know how to type; senior people in the meeting experience some loss of power; there is a partial decline in social interaction; and it is expensive and can be oversold. Yet, the consensus among those who have used this approach is that its advantages outweigh its drawbacks.

Toward the end of this chapter, we will discuss kinds and availability of TQM software tools. IS can help teams understand what software tools exist today and make a group of these available to the entire organization on the mainframe, through LANs, or for use on individual PCs. Several actions can be taken to support end users this way.

First, monitor the availability of quality software tools the same way you would other emerging technologies. In other words, someone on your staff should pay attention to the various software packages emerging to handle brainstorming, statistical process control, data handling, and so forth, bringing forward recommendations to the entire enterprise on what they should be using. This individual can work with quality staffs in the enterprise to perform this review. The enormous amount of new software coming out now to facilitate Total Quality Management makes this an ongoing effort.

Second, select a set of software tools that your organization will support. Much as you would when selecting word processors, operating systems for PCs, and so forth, pick a group of packages that you will help end users install and use via help desks and training programs. You can add and subtract to this list over time as IS and end users find better tools or requirements change. Candidate packages that fall into this category include spreadsheets (like Lotus 1-2-3), the very popular Lotus Notes, such graphical tools as Freelance, and other windowing packages.

Third, link the selection and support of these TQM packages to your data base strategy so that they are compatible; end users will want to port machine-readable data into their TQM packages. Historically, there have been seven TQM techniques (cause-and-effect diagram, check sheet, control chart, flowchart, histogram, Pareto chart, and scatter diagram). But others are being proposed that are computer-based, presenting data in graphical form, typically in some 3-D format. Over the next few years, you will get considerable pressure from end users to support such tools; all require extensive access to data bases, hence the need to link your data base and TQM tool strategies together.

Fourth, insist that IS staffs use these tools themselves. In addition to their benefits to non-IS users that also accrue to IS is the advantage that the IS community will come to understand the issues associated with the use of such packages and techniques. These include the usability of such software, its effectiveness and relevance, support requirements, and functionality. Moreover, as the IS staff becomes more active as members of cross-functional process improvement or reengineering teams, it is imperative that they know how to use the same tools and techniques as other team members. Process teams find that the lack of any standardization of tool usage is a significant inhibitor to fast starts in dealing with issues because team members have to settle on a common set of tools and learn how to use them. Avoid the problem by encouraging standardization of tools and then use them yourself.

Increasing Productivity of the Entire Organization through Office Applications

Today, the majority of all workers perform their work in offices. Even in manufacturing companies, a small percent of workers are on the production floor. Workers are becoming more mobile, working at home, in their automobiles, in airplanes, and at customer locations. While the mobile work force has received an enormous amount of press coverage, the real observation is not so much that they are mobile but that they work with office applications, some in offices and others "on the road." The implications for IS and the enterprise as a whole are significant.

Work Flows Will Change Substantially in the Next Decade

An extraordinary push is going on now to supply every worker who is functioning outside the traditional plant environment with new tools; cellular phones, laptop computers, and portable fax machines are examples. It seems that every sales organization is rushing to provide its sales staffs with laptops equipped with modems so that they can demonstrate products at customer locations (for example, using video and imaging), take orders, and answer questions (for example, by accessing mainframe data bases). Guess who has to support these new uses of IT!

The economics of this move are very compelling. Take a sales force as an example. If a sales representative costs $100,000 (salary, benefits, and so forth) per year and you could replace that salesperson with a fully loaded PC at $20,000 (hardware, software, line charges, help desk expenses, and so forth), you begin to understand the dynamics at work. Some companies are giving PCs to customers, allowing them access to company files to place orders, inquire about on-order and billing issues, and learn about products and services. Underwriters in insurance companies are using such tools as Lotus Notes to perform work that has equally valuable returns on investments, while Federal Express allows its customers to query the status of packages. My stockbroker allows me to manage my own trades through his system, thereby avoiding the cost of a trader. This is the tip of the iceberg!

As has always been the case with new technologies, the acquisition of mobility-enhancing tools is coming first and most frequently from end users. However, right behind that wave of acquisitions, two other issues will emerge. First, IS will be asked to support all of these tools, which will require us to address the same kinds of issues of support and standardization that we faced with PCs in the 1980s. Second, and of greater significance, organizations will have to change the way work is done. In short, the implementation of so many new IT tools will cause profound changes in processes, calling for new ways to do traditional tasks. Obvious examples include increasing reliance on customers (rather than clerks or salespeople) to place their own orders all over the map, vendors accessing your forecasts for parts and understanding (and even affecting) production schedules in order to provide components in a timely fashion (JIT), a variety of new work methods to customize products and services to individual customer requirements. These are profound changes by anyone's standard, and IT will be in the middle of them.

Much of the Change Will Come in Traditional Office Processes

The key to understanding where to focus attention lies in traditional office activities because these functions are changing the most and becoming mobile first in many organizations. Already mentioned at the start of this chapter is the move to more sophisticated E-mail systems. Let's be more precise: The move is toward more LAN-based E-mail systems because they are more portable and team-focused. In a survey of U.S. companies, International Data Corporation found that the number of mailboxes in a LAN environment in 1991 was about 20 percent, but amounted to approximately 55 percent by the end of 1993. At the same time, mainframe mailboxes went from 35 percent of the total to just under 20 percent. The drama in the numbers lies in the volume: 6 million mailboxes in 1991 versus 35.5 million in 1993!

Variations suggest what new applications IT is being asked to supply or expand as office processes are reengineered. Some of the more obvious include:

- voice mail, which doubled in usage between 1991 and 1993
- traditional E-mail up one third
- LAN-based messaging up 25 percent
- EDI penetration at 42 percent in 1993 versus 28 percent in 1991
- fax up more than three-fold
- graphics in E-mail now is in about 60 percent of systems

In short, the process has started!

The more popular office applications in evidence today include expanded use of electronic funds transfer, electronic bulletin boards, and electronic reporting capability of rating services. Companies that move things, such as package delivery firms and trucking companies, are equipping their vehicles with on-board computers for inventory tracking, linked to host systems via satellites and cellular phone technologies. As early as 1991, *Quality Progress* was beginning to report the expanded use of electronic meeting systems (known as EMS). These can be stand-alone

PCs running software that includes data from other people, laptops and voting keypads for meeting participants, and the electronic brainstorming. Already, end users are subscribing to CD-ROM versions of *Newsweek* (called *Newsweek Interactive*), the *Wall Street Journal,* and the *New York Times* by fax.

One challenge you will face is to provide process teams insight on how to merge telephonic and traditional IT. Woody Ritchey, a marketing manager at AT&T, was quoted in *Industry Week* (January 17, 1994): "Down the road it will be difficult to define what is a phone and what is a PC. On your desk will be a hybrid, an information appliance that will eventually deliver full-motion multiscreen video, still images, voice, data, text, facsimile, and E-mail." Wallet-sized telephones are now available with PC and fax capabilities causing some people to work away from their offices 100 percent of the time. That technology is expected to become commonplace by the end of the decade.

AI Tools Are Beginning to Appear in Office Settings

Those of us who grew up in the information processing industry are very wary about forecasting use of artificial intelligence (AI) tools; it has been the most oversold, most underperforming IT technology of the past forty years. However, AI is now coming into its own and increasingly in office settings. Its most primitive forms are the automated work flow programs just beginning to appear that compare tasks to be performed with the performance plans and skills of individuals and then assign out the work. It is geographically independent in that work can be sent out electronically to people across many states. An earlier variation of this function was dispatching systems in which software had available workers and skills in a data base, knew their schedules, and could automatically route work to them. Your IBM field engineers have been dispatched to fix machines that way for over a decade. Today, the use of AI in E-mail systems is still theory, but under development at universities (such as MIT) and in software houses (such as Dun & Bradstreet's Software Services, Inc.). AI is also being injected into EDI applications for such uses as determining what parts to ship, judging basic issues associated with billing (for example, is the bill paid in full, if not what should be done), and actually paying bills upon receipt of goods and services. We are also already using fuzzy logic in simple applications, such as looking up names in on-line telephone directories without spelling the name correctly.

Given the enormous changes underway in the office, one way that IS can help foster quality management practices is by applying IT to reengineered office processes. Taking the trends just cited, applying IS's knowledge of IT, and participating in process improvement teams, IS can ensure that the disciplines it uses internally can be shared with end users.

The heart of the issue from IS's point of view is ensuring that technical standards are set and supported that facilitate quality management practices:

- secure and accessible data relevant to processes
- end-user satisfaction with the ability to use tools effectively
- cost-effective exploitation of IT at the right time
- faster performance of tasks with fewer resources
- quick change of processes and tools

Given the major changes happening at the IT level, this is a good time for IS management to take the initiative in going to communities of end users in office settings and proposing examination of existing office processes to see how better to perform them. We can avoid the problem faced in the early to mid-1980s when end users acquired PCs despite resistance of the IS community in many companies. This time, because of the high IT content of revised processes, IS has to participate as the transformation leader or changes will be made without the benefit of IS's insight and help.

Implementing Applications That Reduce Cycle Time

Managers were electrified by the concept of reducing the amount of time to do things with the publication of *Competing Against Time* by George Stalk, Jr., and Thomas M. Hout in 1990. The concept had been around for a long time, but the case for using cycle time reduction as a strategy was new and never so compellingly described before. Since then, cycle time reduction has become a major component of quality management practices, especially in improving or reengineering processes. Never has a new business perspective come along that so perfectly exploits IT. Anytime you can do something at the speed of electricity, versus the speed of a human being, there is the potential for cycle time reduction and new justification for IT.

The logic is simple. Surveys show that customers will pay more for goods and services provided sooner rather than later, so provide it more quickly. Second, the less time that exists between when something is needed and when it is available, the more the cost of carrying inventory or parts is reduced. Third, by designing in speed, you often have to root out redundancy and steps, which simplifies work and thereby reduces resources required to perform a task. Cycle time reduction has become a boon to those who want to reengineer processes.

Examples abound everywhere in which processes have been developed that reduce time to do things by relying heavily on computers. Car designs

---

IS Example of Cycle Time Reduction for
Obtaining Telephone Directories

Subject: Print your own phone directory. Up to date Version.

1. Type BRPHONE on the main menu of PROFS.

2. Type the printer to send printout to.

3. Choose option T for tie line.

4. Type in 744 633 665 586 (tie lines for Wisconsin).

Hit enter, and it will print a wonderful 4 page directory sorted alphabetically.

Figure 7.7 This note was sent by an IBM employee to fellow workers in Wisconsin. PROFS is the name of the internal IBM E-mail system.

in the 1970s took up to seven years, five years by the late 1980s, and now less than three years. Package delivery companies came into existence to compete against U.S. and European postal services because they could deliver faster, later, cheaper, and more reliably, creating a multibillion dollar industry. At IBM, instead of printing telephone directories and then shipping them out to tens of thousands of employees, IBMers print them out whenever they want a new one. Figure 7.7 shows how one organization performed the task. It is a simple example, but one that nonetheless shows how IT can play. In fact, this is a function that comes right off the command line in IBM's E-mail system.

Focus on Cycle Time Reduction in All That IS Designs and Does

The first step in applying cycle time reduction techniques is to decide that no new application or service will be designed and offered that cannot be done faster than its predecessor. Tied to that decision should be the commitment that improved cycle time will be documented both as part of the cost justification of the new project and, second, measured against the performance of the previous system or service. This is not the place to engage in a detailed discussion of how cycle time reduction is justified; it is sufficient to say that major sources of justification include making money sooner rather than later, reducing the content of human labor, and avoiding the carrying costs of parts and inventory.

A good example of all three at work is book publishing. It used to take a year or more to produce a book once the author had a draft of the manuscript. The actual production work took only several weeks; the rest of the time the manuscript or page proofs sat on desks waiting to have the next steps done to it. Publishers began to eliminate that dead time between tasks in the 1980s, driving down production times by almost a third through this simple expedient. They also began to eliminate steps that took time, for example, going from manuscript to galley sheets and then to page proofs, now moving from manuscript on a diskette directly to page proofs. That use of technology and elimination of a long-standing step (galleys), saved another one to two months.

Today, we can produce a book on average in six to seven months. Some publishers are attempting to get down to less than thirty days. In fact, the U.S. Government Printing Office and some internal publishing operations within corporations can do it in less than a week. If a publisher can get a book out sooner, the product sells earlier. If a publisher can have the flexibility of introducing a book at the ideal marketing time, greater sales are possible. For example, introducing a biography of President Nixon the week after his death is a far more attractive marketing gesture than bringing it out six months later. The difference is simplified production processes and a heavy dose of technology.

Understand the Different Types of Cycle Time Reduction Possible in an Organization or Process to Make Sure All Your Bases Are Covered

By understanding the various types of time burners, you can make sure that you are constantly working on the reduction of all types, and not leaning in the direction of just one type. Figure 7.8 lists the more obvious types. By identifying activities within processes, organizations, and industries that match the types, you can quickly have some idea about where the real opportunities for improvement exist applying IT.

Another typology of cycle time is classes of time. Figure 7.9 illustrates the more obvious ones.

Finally, there is the issue of improving overall effectiveness, particularly of processes and systems. That is done by looking at time, timing, and duration of a cycle. All three elements interact and affect one another. Understanding and measuring the interaction between the three is critical. These speak to the speed with which organizations apply their resources to improve efficiencies, effectiveness, and economic value (what is cost justifiable).

- Time should be treated as a finite business resource and managed accordingly.

Types of Cycle Time	
System	Length of time to get something through a system. Examples: product design, customer orders, major reorganizations.
Product, Service, Process	Length of time from when a concept is announced to when it is implemented. Examples: product design steps, entering an order on a screen, preparing closing documents for a mortgage.
Project or Task	Length of time to move from activity A to activity B. Examples: building a house or factory, replacing an IS application.

Figure 7.8

Classes of Cycle Time	
Predecision	Time spent getting an idea to go/no-go decision. Examples: R&D, cost justification.
Decision	Time to make a decision. Examples: signoffs, paper work, corporate politics, regulatory requirements.
From decision to activity	Time needed to marshall resources to do something. Examples: ordering equipment, hiring or training people, paper work.
Activity	Time to do the tasks. Examples: order entry, data transfer, process steps.
From activity to implementation	Time for a process or system to go live. Examples: elapse time to assigning people, installing software on a PC, taking delivery of needed hardware.

Figure 7.9

- Timing is the management of opportunity and resources such that, for example, the biography of Nixon appears during the month of his death, not six months later.

- Cycle duration is the time it takes to get something done regardless of size, scope, characteristics, and so forth.

Hunt Down and Root Out Activities That Waste Time

We all can think of many ways that time is wasted. But if you can catalog time wasted by type within your organization and across the enterprise, you have another view of what to apply IT to and what issues to resolve. Time is wasted in many ways:

- systems and cultures

- policies and strategies

- management and people

- processes and functions

Managers lose time through poor planning, lack of innovation (particularly in systems), inadequate transfer of data and information, overuse of human interfaces (such as coordinators and administrative assistants), changed priorities, poor feedback or none, lack of direction, and ignorance of better ways. Employees are guilty of the same set of time wasters. There are also unique time wasters by function (manufacturing, sales, accounting, and so forth). IT loses time by adhering to its own schedules and not to those of customers or end users, poor deployment of people and tools, and downtime due to bad equipment or sloppy management. Customers and suppliers waste time for the same reasons your own organization does.

Identifying categories of lost time by type makes it possible to measure the extent of the problems and then to propose, project-by-project, their elimination. For example, suppose that a chronic problem in your company is the time lost because of changing priorities due to fad and fixation with the quick fix. As a member of an IS organization, you might encourage more formal planning disciplines and even provide quality management tools to facilitate the transformation. Use of electronic brainstorming, application of systems design disciplines to strategic business planning, and exploitation of E-mail to communicate goals and objectives can contribute to the elimination of undirected, wasted time.

The role of IS in implementing time-based quality management practices is a relatively new subject, with little documented best practices or research. However, it is an area of great promise and contributes directly to the bottom line performance of any enterprise. Indeed, it is rapidly appearing as one of the most attractive reasons to deploy IT today—so much so that strategic business planners are encouraging general managers to seize leadership from IS in determining how best to deploy IT as a strategic weapon.

Getting Closer to Your Customers

At the heart of all quality management principles is the notion of meeting or exceeding customer needs and requirements. How an organization does that is greatly influenced by the role of IS. It is not enough to wait until end users come to you with suggestions. IS, too, has an obligation to come forward with ideas, based on its knowledge of the technical capabilities of IT and IS. While a number of ways to accomplish this have already been discussed (for example, laptops for sales representatives, on-line order entry, E-mail), the overall strategy has not been. Effective strategies for deploying quality managed processes that are customer focused generally have three characteristics about them:

1. They tend to make organizations accessible to customers. Everything reasonable is done to make it easy for customers to find people and information and to do business with an organization. This is most frequently done by use of 800 telephone numbers, telephone systems that get a caller quickly to a warm body or a knowledgeable person, and even by giving customer access to your E-mail.

2. Information is shared conveniently with customers and suppliers. This is accomplished by implementation of on-line systems that quickly give employees data that customers want or by actually granting customers and suppliers access to your data bases. The combined roles of EDI and effective data base management are crucial to the success of this strategy. Once implemented, customers find them just too convenient to use other vendors; they come to you.

3. Systems are developed that make it possible for companies to implement strategies of mass customization. For example, instead of offering a standard set of products, items are produced for customers made to order but with the economies of scale of mass production, hence the term *mass customization.*

The key skills required of IS are the abilities to collect, store, manipulate, retrieve, and categorize data, especially customer information. Manage this information with the disciplines of TQM and best practices in data base administration and you have the makings of a world-class, highly competitive, customer friendly set of applications and processes.

Nowhere has this truth been proven more than in the retail industry where the customer and product data bases are often the most valuable nonhuman resource of the enterprise. Using IT, retailers today have a greater understanding of what customers want and are responding with stock inventory of the right kind faster and better than at any time in history. The number of employees and warehouse space used is also the lowest ever per sale. Mechanically, they track and provide merchandise with systems, catalog types of sales and by whom (all real time), and determine how customers pay for their acquisitions (through verification of credit, use of credit cards and checks, and cash). Today, tracking sales and merchandise is done primarily through computer-based applications by half the retailers in the United States. Besides 800 numbers, retailers have also installed PC-equipped kiosks and video-equipped monitors in stores to explain merchandise to customers, and use scanner-read coupons. More innovative applications include check-writing terminals and equipping sales personnel with lightweight computer pads that they can use to assist customers anywhere in a store. Kmart monitors customer traffic in the store and uses kiosks as its latest IT innovation. Wal-Mart uses kiosks to inform customers about fishing reels and to match batteries to a customer's car, for example. ShopKo uses kiosks to inform customers about drugs, warning them about side effects.

A second key skill is the ability to link electronically with suppliers and customers. Providing such a link makes it possible for the rest of the enterprise to build new processes that bring customers and suppliers closer faster and more effectively, while making both customers and suppliers dependent on your organization as the traffic cop for information—a significant competitive advantage. EDI has come a long way in the past decade, facilitated by positive experiences, expanded use, and better management procedures for ensuring its effectiveness, not the least of which has been the application of TQM principles. Several recent surveys suggest the reasons for EDI's popularity:

- provides more accurate data
- has enhanced customer service
- leads to competitive advantages
- leads to reduced expenses

In a survey reported by *InformationWEEK* (March 29, 1993), three-quarters of the participants agreed that EDI met their expectations. In the retail industry, it is not uncommon today to see 50 to 100 percent of all orders being transmitted to suppliers via EDI. Overall across American industry, over 30,000 companies use EDI; this application grew at a compounded growth rate of 25 percent between 1989 and the end of 1993.

EDI links organizations, pointing out obvious areas for improvement in how work is done on both sides of the line, causing fundamental reengineering of processes (like letting your supplier manage inventory and product forecasting). Speeding transactions and changing plans to meet customer requirements (otherwise known as market demands) has proven equally successful. Inventory modeling has led to more inventory turns, sped up the rush of products to shelves, improved intelligence about customers and the marketplace, and reduced the risk of guesswork in marketing programs.

The virtual organization, in which activities are outsourced either because they are not critical to your core mission or are critical and you cannot do them as well as others, is largely made possible by EDI. Until an organization has EDI that allows it to link up with possible business partners, suppliers, and customers, the potential of the virtual organization remains too remote and abstract. With EDI, companies have been able to experiment and slowly, but effectively, take steps that led them toward the virtual organization. Increasingly, such firms are customer focused and concentrate on quality management (to keep EDI up and relevant). EDI caused these organizations and their business activities to change faster than at any time since World War II.

More than simply a quality issue, EDI has become central to many companies because it upsets the status quo (good for building competitive advantages), reestablishes new orders on terms favorable to those who have invested correctly in data and networking, and builds impregnable links to both customers and suppliers that endure for years and lead to the intercompany partnerships that were the original promise of EDI.

But now EDI is actually going further because some companies have sufficient confidence in their networking and customer processes to extend EDI to individuals doing business with them. MasterCard International is now experimenting with a variant of EDI to individual customers. It currently plans to allow its U.S. banking affiliates to offer consumers the capability of performing a variety of banking activities using MasterCard's networking. One early application will be a customer's ability to pay bills electronically to any merchant or provider of services, even if the merchant today does not accept payments electronically. Customers can pick any technology or PCs with which to link into the network. Called MasterBanking, this will also create a demand for a new generation of home banking and telecommunications software.

IS as a Source of Quality Software

Thousands of software packages are now available that deal with quality management. It is inevitable and logical that employees throughout the enterprise would turn to the IS organization for guidance on what is avail-

Subjects for Which Quality Management Software Is Available	
Calibration	Quality costs
Capability studies	Reliability
Data acquisition	Sampling
Gauge respectability and	Simulation
reproducibility	Statistical methods
Inspection	Statistical process control
Management	Supplier quality
Problem solving	Assurance
Quality assurance for	Taguchi techniques
software development	Training

Figure 7.10 *Source*: Adapted from "Quality Progress, Tenth Annual QA/QC Software Delivery," *Quality Progress* 26, no. 3 (March 1993): pp. 21–84.

able and how to use it. Let's make this easy. Every spring *Quality Progress*, the most widely read magazine on quality management issues (over 135,000 subscribers), publishes a listing of recently available software tools. For a decade, it has provided information on the name of the package, its functions and features, what it runs on, price, and address where you can get it. The listing is huge; today nearly 250 companies' products are described. Chances are there is a copy of this widely subscribed to magazine floating around your building. If you are serious about quality management practices, you already subscribe to it.

This is the most useful source of information available on software tools. In addition to covering a great deal of software alphabetically by name of company, it lists the packages by function. Figure 7.10 lists the subject categories for two reasons: to suggest what is out there and also to hint at the various topics in the world of quality now serviced by software. In addition to this source, every quality management magazine carries advertisements from major software vendors.

Conclusions

Quality begins at home, first in your department and then, later, across the entire enterprise you serve. As we have moved across a number of activities necessary for quality management to function in IS, it should now be evident that a core competence in quality within IS is a prerequisite for helping the rest of the organization with such practices. As suggested by Figure 7.11, the twin guiding principles are meeting customer

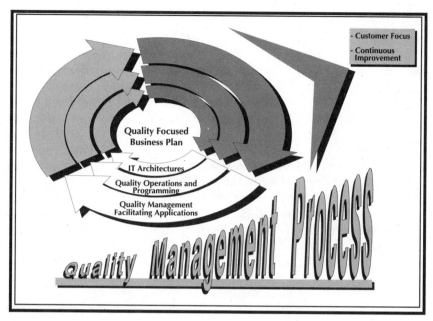

Figure 7.11 Guiding principles for quality management.

and end-user requirements on the one hand, and on the other doing things continuously better across the entire IS organization. Beginning with a plan moving outward, you build an IT architecture that supports your intent, perform well yourself, and finally lay in place tools that support the entire enterprise.

To a large extent, what infrastructure and support you create will consist of four pieces:

1. relevant data bases easy to get to and use
2. backbone network accessible by customers, suppliers, and employees
3. well-understood, reliable IS operations
4. tools, skills, and leadership in quality management

An end user stated best what the end game should be. Karen Wetherell, vice president of customer service at the Connecticut Mutual Life Insurance Company described what IS had done for her:

> We have set standards to which others in the financial services industry can aspire. And, we have changed the way in which information technology is used to provide world-class service.

Not a bad vision for what IS's quality purpose should be!

References

Anonymous. "The Smart Office," *Industry Week* (January 17, 1994): pp. 31–39.

Benjamin, Robert I., and Eliot Levinson. "A Framework for Managing IT-Enabled Change," *Sloan Management Review* 34, no. 4 (Summer 1993): pp. 23–33.

Cole, Christopher C., Michael L. Clark, and Carol Nemec. "Reengineering Information Systems at Cincinnati Milacron," *Planning Review* 14, no. 3 (May/June 1993): pp. 22–26, 48.

Davenport, Thomas H. *Process Innovation; Reengineering Work Through Information Technology.* Boston: Harvard Business School Press, 1993.

Filipzcak, Bob. "The Ripple Effect of Computer Networking," *Training* 31, no. 3 (March 1994): pp. 40–47.

Finkelstein, Marvin S., Edward J. Harrick, and Paul E. Sultan. "Sharing Information Spawns Trust, Productivity, and Quality," *National Productivity Review* 10, no. 3 (Summer 1991): pp. 295–298.

Gallupe, R. Brent, and William H. Cooper. "Brainstorming Electronically," *Sloan Management Review* 35, no. 1 (Fall 1993): pp. 27–36.

Gaynor, Gerard H. *Exploiting Cycle Time in Technology Management.* New York: McGraw-Hill, 1993.

International Data Corporation. *White Paper: Electronic Mail: the New Corporate Backbone.* Boston: IDC, undated.

Liberty, Jack. "Quality Data Collection," *Quality* 31, no. 2 (February, 1992): pp. 44–47.

Mathieson, Kieran, and T.J. Wharton. "Are Information Systems a Barrier to Total Quality Management?" *Journal of Systems Management* 44, no. 9 (September 1993): pp. 34–38.

Quality Progress. "Quality Progress, Tenth Annual QA/QC Software Delivery," *Quality Progress* 26, no. 3 (March 1993): pp. 21–84 (and annual).

Stalk, Jr., George, and Thomas M. Hout. *Competing Against Time.* New York: Free Press, 1990.

8

Applying Quality Practices to IT Operations

Coming together is a beginning. Keeping together is progress. Working together is success. HENRY FORD, 1900s

In this chapter I describe quality practices found in IT operations. Included are discussions about successful operations strategies, case studies of help desks and network management, role of a data center, and effective measurements. I emphasize the twin requirements of good IT operations: a focus on end-user/customer needs and continuous improvement.

Instilling a Customer Focus

It is easy, particularly in large IS organizations, for the operations staff members to be caught up in their own efforts. Often, the bulk of their time is taken up by the care and feeding of large systems in "glasshouses" surrounded by extraordinary security measures such as badged entry and armed guards. In such a world, they could be expected to focus on the efficiency of the equipment and software, as measured by "uptime." Help desks by their nature are an exception since they are staffed with people who spend a great deal of time with end users and possibly even customers, if their companies are linked electronically to suppliers and customers.

However, quality management practices in operations calls for the entire staff to remember, first, that they serve end users by providing services at a level satisfactory to the end user, not to themselves. Second, they also must take the initiative in feeding back into the IS organization the needs and wants of their end users. This second responsibility is increasingly becoming difficult as the people making up end users include fellow employees, suppliers, customers, and occasional users (such as consultants working on a project in your company for a few months). Effective operations meets its responsibilities the same way as other organizations do. This part of IS develops, communicates, and updates its:

- vision of service levels
- mission
- strategies for fulfilling its responsibilities
- processes for end-user feedback
- measurements of performance

Normally in a quality-focused organization, several effective activities are often present. They have a process for collecting customer feedback on operations. End-user feedback processes are very similar to customer feedback processes. In fact, if your IS organization does not routinely survey end users and use that information to improve performance, go to a part of the same company or government department that does and learn how to develop such a process. Other data centers in your community also can help. The easiest way to find out who is doing this kind of survey is to ask other IS managers either by calling them or by asking them at the next meeting of the local chapter of the Data Processing Management Association (DPMA).

But all these processes are very similar. For every major service provided to end users, good processes assess how effective they are from the end-user's perspective. Since requirements keep changing, the polling must be ongoing. So monitoring, measuring, and assessment activities must go on all the time by application and service, and then be collected for the entire department.

Traditional IS measurements do not always tell you how end users feel about your services; so often IS organizations must create new ways of understanding end users. For example, any computer operating system will tell you what percent of the time the computer was up, but probably will not tell you what percent of the time E-mail was up at the end-user's terminal. For that, you must measure different things: line availability, application performance, LAN activity, even performance of individual terminals. You and I know that the closer you get to an end user (and, conversely, the further away you get from the mainframe) the greater the degradation of uptime. By measuring from the end-user's point of view, operations can go back up through the terminal, the LAN, the network, the application software, and finally, to the CPU, to see where performance (availability, speed, and so forth) can be improved.

Since end users rely on IT to help them fulfill their business objectives, increasingly IS organizations are looking for ways to link their own measures of end-user service to business objectives. For example, at Xerox, IS management routinely seeks out a better understanding of what end users and customers want from its IS operations. Xerox's IS measures, which were historically inward focused and typical of what most shops have, now sport a set of measures that are customer oriented. At Corning Inc., end users are surveyed once a quarter to gather similar types of information. With such data, normal TQM tools can be used to improve performance of processes critical to customer service.

Successful IS Organizations Use a Variety of Survey Techniques to Understand Their Customers

Figure 8.1 lists commonly used survey and data source techniques employed by IS. As it suggests, the data today do not exist in traditional IS measurement schemes. Gathering and using this data require new and different efforts as well as normal process management techniques.

What Kinds of Questions Would You Want to Ask an End User?

Typically, these questions involve overall assessments of IS performance and questions concerning specific services. Gathering both numerical and narrative data is useful. Effective questions to ask continuously include:

- In general, how satisfied are you with the services you use from MIS?
- How satisfied are you with the availability of applications (or systems, or whatever other service provided to end users)?
- How satisfied are you with response time?
- How satisfied are you with the applications and other software tools provided to you by IS?

Sources of Customer Opinion Data	
Type	Frequency
End-user survey	Quarterly
Employee opinion survey	Annual
End-user feedback sessions	Ongoing
End-user help desk contacts	Ongoing
On-line comments	Daily
Project surveys	Ongoing
Project status meetings	Ongoing
Problem determination meetings	As needed
End-user suggestions	Ongoing
Advisory council	Quarterly

Figure 8.1

Usually, it is also helpful to define terms widely used by MIS, but not necessarily by end users. For example, with the question on availability, you might add parenthetically (your software is available when you need it) or for the query about response time (your computer handles requests for information in a timely manner). Settle on several core questions to ask every time so that, over the years, you can see how end users judge your operations. In case you are saying to yourself "over the years?!!," if you ever apply for a real quality award like the Baldrige or Deming, the judges are going to look for data over the years, at least three to be precise! So you have to think strategically and long term. Ideal things to ask about are overall performance, availability, response time, and quality of IS tools provided. Obviously you can add other questions that are important this year but may not be in five years. These would include questions about specific pieces of hardware (PCs and printers, for example), tools (Lotus 1-2-3 and E-mail, for example), applications (billing and expense reporting, for example), and about your people (to what extent do they understand what you need? how responsive are they?).

But with the data on the core questions, you can quickly see how you are doing. The information is very understandable to both your staff and end users, and should be shared. Figure 8.2 illustrates the kind of reporting that is possible.

Since not all end users will be happy, you can expect to find enough dissatisfaction to track that as well. Why do you care? Data on dissatisfaction, more than simply a negative, is the source of a great deal of insight on what needs to be improved. That kind of data should also be presented in terms that are understandable to all. Figure 8.3 illustrates such a report.

IS shops increasingly are sharing customer (end-user) feedback information with staff and users. Post the reports either individually or as part of the department's report card (if it has one); also ship copies to end users to tell them what you have learned and what you are going to do about better service. The challenge you will face in using that data is that, once published, you change your culture; you do not have an option, it happens. If end users find fault with some specific aspect of operations, you

End User Satisfaction (% Satisfied)				
Satisfaction Category	1991	1992	1993	1994
Overall	70	69	71	74
Availability	80	80	82	86
Response time	71	69	73	77
Tools provided	60	64	68	69

Figure 8.2

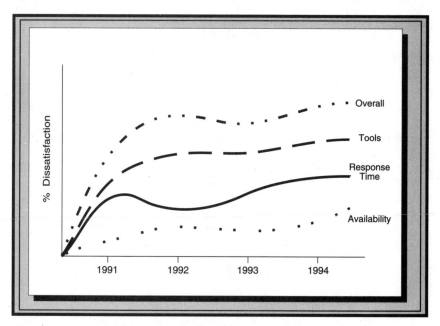

Figure 8.3 Trends in end-user dissatisfaction.

must resist blaming your people. Rather, you will want to encourage them to use the data to improve their operations. That is very hard for many MIS directors to do. However, once you have created a culture in which continuous improvement exists, driven by customer requirements, then problems can be handled in an entirely different way. For example, when a problem occurs, you can admit it, discuss the source and fix openly, and report quickly to end users about what will be done. Figure 8.4 is a letter sent by a CIO to all of his end users. Take a minute to read it.

Notice a couple of things that are different from what might have occurred ten years ago in MIS. First, this CIO's obsession with customer service led him to write the letter instead of ducking the issue or letting someone lower in the organization issue it. This CIO took personal responsibility for improving performance. Second, he explained what was going on, how he was going to address the problem, and what help was needed from end users (in this case, patience).

Chief Information Officer
IBM Corporation
One IBM Plaza
Chicago, Ill 60611

February 16, 1993

MEMORANDUM TO: Midwestern Area End Users
SUBJECT: Unacceptable System Availability

The purpose of this document is to provide information regarding the disappointing performance of our OfficeVision systems as we continue our move from the Area Information Center in Chicago to Lexington.

Unfortunately, our hopes for transparency while relocating have not been achieved. The disruptions you have experienced are as unacceptable to us as they are to you, and we are working through this unexpectedly difficult time. Please continue to report problems to the Help Desk at 653-6966.

Attached is a brief summary of our current status, unique problems we have encountered since relocation on February 5, and our action plans to avoid similar problems in the future. [See Figure 8.5].

My team and I are working to ensure we receive quality service. It is our plan to further sensitize our suppliers to the impact their outages create. We are holding them accountable for process verification and root cause analysis on these problems.

Again, thank you for your patience.

Howard A. Fields

Figure 8.4

Current Status

On Monday, February 15, our VM system software failed six times. We isolated the cause of these failures to the RACF security facility. The problem was evidenced by RACF not properly releasing storage. We have identified five fixes to address this problem. The first fix was applied during the sixth failure at approximately 4:00 p.m. on Monday. The system software has been stable since that time. With the exception of the MSPVMIC1 print subsystem move this weekend, it is our intent to avoid making any other changes to the system until March 4, as this is our next change management milestone. We will consult with the Trading Area CIOs to determine the acceptability of this plan.

Problem Summary/Action Plan

We are in agreement with our suppliers of service that each of the problems described below are supplier quality issues which must not occur.

1. Lexington Network Capacity Problem: On Monday, February 8, at 9:45 a.m. CST our network connections failed due to Network Control Program capacity problems. Upon investigation we learned that Lexington had ignored the network configuration recommendations of our area telecommunications team. In doing so, they created a data traffic bottleneck both into and out of Lexington. Response times quickly degraded for both interactive and print functions. At 2:00 p.m. CST Lexington recycled the system and two additional NCPs were added which addressed these problems.

2. Application Access Problems: On Tuesday, February 9, table definitions for CH1 and MSP were dropped from the system. These definitions had to be changed due to our move to Lexington. Quite simply, the Change Management Process failed and many of our users were unable to log on. These problems were not completely resolved until Thursday afternoon, February 11.

3. Dial Access Problems: Beginning Monday, February 8, and continuing through Sunday, February 14, Boca had similar table definition problems which intermittently prevented dial access. Corrections were made to permanent VTAM tables on Sunday, February 14.

4. Print Delay: Print processing was moved to Lexington on Sunday, February 14. New network configurations were installed to support this change. Delays caused by network routing problems were identified by Lexington and Boca and were resolved at 11:00 a.m. CST on Monday, February 15.

Figure 8.5

Third, this CIO made it clear that this MIS organization does hold its staff and suppliers accountable for customer service. This CIO could have been forgiven for the problems encountered, since two data centers were being merged into one and physically moved—not a trivial operation—and he had some 4,500 end users within the organization he supported linked to over 200,000 other people in the company and to thousands outside. Nonetheless, he wrote that letter. End-user reaction was predictable: They provided patience and, in the next opinion survey, did not lambast the IS organization because they understood what was happening.

What kind of reporting went on behind the scenes? Within MIS, everyone saw the letter reprinted here. Operations met to understand the problems and submitted to the CIO a report outlining what was being done to fix them. That report (Figure 8.5) shows no blame and illustrates classical IS problem definition techniques at work, but also reflects concern for end users. Even the language is that of quality management practices: "cause of failures," "change management," and "suppliers of service" (fellow employees elsewhere in the company).

Roles and Responsibilities within an IS Organization

As the values of an organization change to accommodate more aggressively such concepts as customer focus, continuous improvement, and greater accountability and empowerment of employees in operations, it becomes imperative for management to help its people by working with staffs to define more precisely than ever the roles and responsibilities of each employee. Organizations that have undergone enormous change find that employees who in earlier times were confident and knowledgeable about their roles and responsibilities, became confused, lost, and demoralized. This was particularly true of organizations that downsized their staffs because now people did not know the "rules of the game" that would ensure their survival on the payroll. Often, members of management are in the same predicament and, because the culture that they are creating is also new to them, they do not know what the new roles and responsibilities should be. However, it is imperative that, sooner rather than later, an attempt be made to define clearly in writing what people should do and what is expected of them. The benefits are:

- reduces anxiety level for all concerned
- helps everyone define what the roles and responsibilities should be in the changing culture, thereby facilitating the new order

- points out gaps in management's thinking about service levels
- helps focus attention on what changes need to be made to personnel practices involving pay for performance, appraisals, reward systems and strategies, and hiring criteria

Often management will wait until the second or third year of major change before attempting to document and communicate the new roles for two reasons: They did not know what to write or they did not realize that even very bright and otherwise effective employees needed such descriptions. But once realized, the most effective approach involves gathering together groups of employees operating either as task forces or as process teams, to hammer out drafts of roles and responsibilities, to discuss these with fellow employees and management, and to link these back to the vision of service, mission, and strategies of the IS organization. Ultimately, the best run organizations can point to their vision, followed by a mission statement, a set of policies and strategies that answer the question of how they intend to implement their vision, and finally to defined roles and responsibilities consistent with strategies and vision (see Figure 8.6).

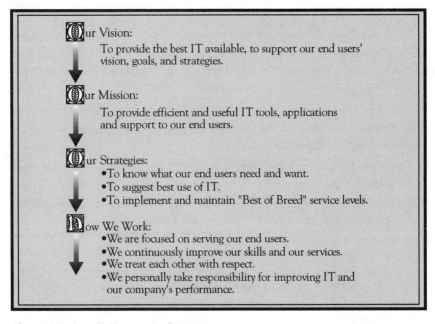

Figure 8.6 Sample IT strategic plan.

Job Definitions Need Not Look Like Human Resources Performance Plans

Before writing a performance plan for a particular function, which you would use if your organization conducts formal appraisals and still ties performance evaluations to salary increases, you should think in clear terms about what the job must be and the expected benefits of that function. From this thinking, you can derive a performance plan that would make any human resources manager happy. For example, you can describe a telecommunications architect's position like this:

Job Activities

1. Creates enterprise-wide telecommunications strategy.

2. Defines telecommunications architecture.

3. Advises application programmers concerning telecommunications issues and considerations.

4. Designs and evaluates telecommunications architectures.

5. Designs and communicates telecommunications standards.

6. Evaluates effectiveness of telecommunications technologies.

Notice that there is none of the usual human resources language here; that can be added later (for example, develop skills, be a team player).

Begin first with the key business issues with your people. Next articulate in the same manner the expected benefits from the job so that you minimize misunderstandings about the role of, in this case, the telecommunications architect. In this instance, these might be:

Expected Benefits

1. Increased user satisfaction through more effective implementation of telecommunications standards.

2. Controlled telecommunications infrastructures to increase service level targets.

3. Advice to IT management while it performs its strategic planning responsibilities.

4. Advice to those responsible for day-to-day operations.

Again, with such a simple approach, you define and communicate expectations. This method can be used for all functions and can be shared with everyone in the IT organization.

One more case illustrates how to define clearly someone's role. Using the example of a project manager, such as you might employ in the delivery of a solution, (for example, an application), reinforces the notion that this approach works with any job.

Job Activities

1. Lead and assist end users in defining their requirements, project objectives, and scope of work.

2. Develop and manage the schedule and budget of the project.

3. Define and articulate the roles of members of the project team.

4. Participate in defining what evaluation parameters will be used to assess the work of each team member.

5. Define jointly with all concerned the quality assurance standards and techniques for the project.

6. Staff the project.

7. Recruit and work with an executive sponsor.

8. Communicate with all involved throughout the project to resolve issues, report progress, and develop contingency plans.

9. Get the team educated in those skills needed to complete the work and obtain necessary tools.

Expected Benefits

1. Assures consistently applied system development processes for all projects (for example, TQM in software development).

2. Assures end-user expectations are met and that project objectives are realized.

3. Increases and improves quality and level of communications among IT, end users, and project team members.

4. Improves the quality of IT's management of project, process, and operational activities.

You might say these descriptions are not new news. Indeed, the first two examples are drawn from an IT organization in the utility industry. However, look again. First, in both examples, there is an emphasis on end-user satisfaction that must be achieved, not simply aspired to. Second, these two job descriptions stress the application of a process for performing the work (use of TQM tools, looking at the work as a process, and so forth). Third, the twin values of end-user satisfaction and process management are consistently applied across all jobs. Over time, that evolves into an organization that has a shared set of values and expectations that are woven deeply into the fabric of daily activities. That is why such an approach is used.

As you define jobs in more quality-focused ways, you may find that new functions and titles are required. For example, it is increasingly evident in large IT organizations in particular that internal expertise is needed in the area of measurements. Such an expertise, let's say in the form of a measurements manager, would have a specific set of responsibilities:

- Defines the measurements by which the IT organization assesses its own performance in meeting end-user needs and continuous improvement.

- Performs assessments of key activities such as defining the value of legacy systems, new applications, data sharing, cost accounting, and so forth.

- Institutionalizes a measurement architecture across the IT organization.

- Conducts quality audits (using Baldrige or ISO criteria, for example).

Roles and Responsibilities Can Then Be Matched to the Collection of Processes of an IT Organization

Most employees like to know how their work fits into the "big picture." Providing them with a map of your major processes helps them take their job descriptions and determine where and how they contribute to improve the efficiency and effectiveness of the organization, along the lines discussed in Chapter 7. A process map for IT does the same thing for an IT organization that a description of the role of individuals does. Figure 8.7 illustrates a map that is in use today.

Finally, you can then impose on this map a set of processes that integrate three activities:

1. Plan-Do-Check-Act cycle of quality management process

2. roles of individuals

3. key processes

Figure 8.8 illustrates such a map. Note that the centerpiece is Figure 8.7, pulling things together. This kind of graphic is very useful in helping to explain to end users what your organization does for a living and also its style of management.

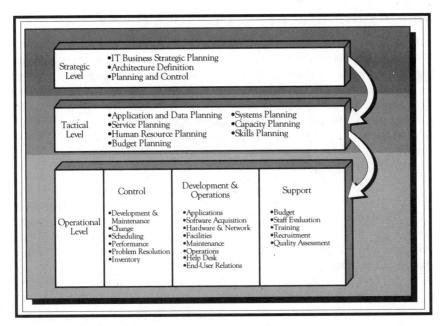

Figure 8.7 IT key management processes.

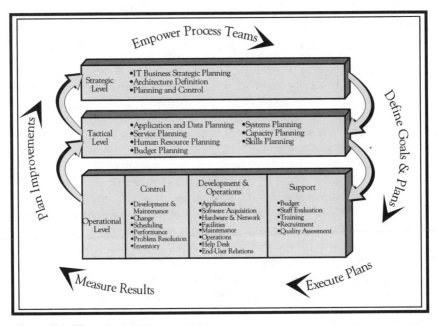

Figure 8.8 IT continuous improvement process.

Role of Governance of IT Operations

Armed with job responsibilities and an understanding of what major processes are performed is not enough. Structure and vision are required to link the two to ensure that the right services are being provided to end users. The strategy that has been employed most effectively for decades has been the use of some sort of steering committee. That approach still makes sense if the group's function is treated like a process—subject to the same quality management rigors as any other process. That means setting specific goals and objectives, measuring its effectiveness, and making changes to improve it.

Defining roles and responsibilities this way helps end users as much as IT people. For example, describing in writing that senior management owns the responsibility for governing all its major functions (including IT) is a first step. Taking that to the next level by articulating what that responsibility means helps senior management, too. In this case, their required actions are:

- to prioritize what IT does

- to assign ownership to major projects involving IT (for example, major application development)

- to embrace and enforce enterprise-wide IT standards, policies, and procedures

In short, senior management should know what their role is at the top of the pyramid in the area of strategic management. The IT community then functions immediately below that first tier in tactical management and, finally, at the operations level. Figure 8.9 illustrates the steering committee's role as a process. This function should then be communicated to end users and IT employees so they understand how major IT strategic initiatives are selected and controlled.

So how are the steering committee's role and that of an IT organization integrated? What should an IT organization look like in a quality-focused world? The answer is, it depends. It depends on what you think of your organization's effectiveness today, what your end users want from you, and what works to improve quality management practices.

There is a growing trend to reconfigure IT organizations to reflect a more process or end-user oriented view of operations. Traditional functional structures are giving way to more fluid ones that rise and fall rapidly as teams come together for projects and then reconfigure themselves when one job is completed and another started. However, some tasks are done in a repeatable manner day in and day out, that have more stability

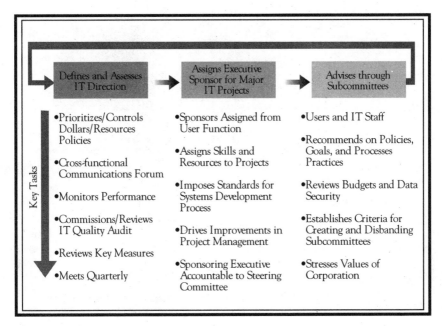

Figure 8.9 Steering committee process.

(for example, data center functions). Figure 8.10 illustrates an organization chart that suggests what increasingly is becoming an attractive model, particularly for large IT organizations. This is not necessarily the ideal model, nor is it the worst. What it does illustrate, however, is a blending of end-user views of IT with more traditional IS functions. If you read the chart from left to right, first there is the IT organization's response to end-user requirements and supporting relations with IS's critical stakeholders. Second, toward the center of the chart, is the development mission designed to deliver to end users what is required, and finally, on the far right, are the backroom support functions that must be performed within IT in order to support end users.

Thus, you bring together an alignment of many operational considerations: governance, organization, processes, and roles and responsibilities. As Figure 8.11 suggests, such an alignment makes clear how all the various activities link together. Armed with that process view of the IT community, you can then inject into it an IT vision, a set of values, defined end-user expectations, prioritized activities, and a way of measuring results, all using quality management tools and techniques. Such a graphical representation of this alignment is a proven way of communicating

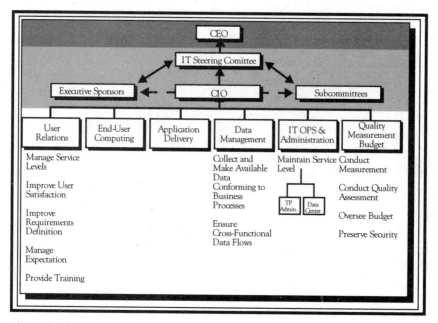

Figure 8.10 Process-focused IT organization chart.

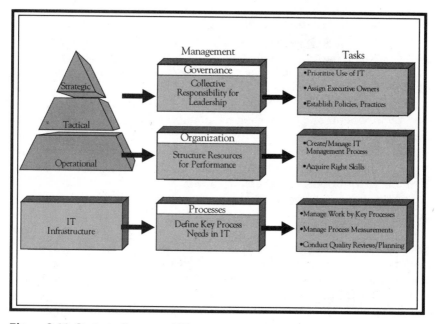

Figure 8.11 Strategic alignment of IT.

what IT is doing while facilitating the coordination of its daily affairs. I am hammering on this point because IT organizations rarely use graphical representations of their activities other than to flowchart software, organizational structures, and some processes. Increase your use of graphical representations because your end users understand those more frequently than simple bullets on a chart or narrated descriptions of activities.

Applied Quality Practices: Cases in Networking Management and Help Desks

End users and IT communities meet most frequently on two fronts: application development and help desk functions. From an end-user's perspective, IT either is building a new application or system for them or is supporting existing ones. Since we devote other parts of this book to applications and software development, using the example of networking and help desks illustrates how quality practices can be implemented in day-to-day interactions with end users. Given the sea change that has occurred over the past decade in computing, as it moved from a glasshouse dominated function to the desktop, looking at networking and help desks gets to the heart of many end-user support activities.

Network management activities involve the establishment of networks that allow end users and their customers or suppliers to communicate electronically with each other and to share information. Your role is to ensure that the most effective technology is installed, kept running, usable, and improved. Another role is to explain to end users how to use this technology and then help them resolve any difficulties they encounter. In a quality-focused organization, you would study how you performed these functions in order to improve their effectiveness while reducing the amount of labor and effort involved. This kind of quality assurance frequently involves understanding and eliminating defects. Typically, that requires understanding the work flows, sources of errors, and end-user issues. In quality-focused organizations, there is the constant analysis of the root cause of performance issues as one of the primary strategies for improving service. By understanding root causes of problems, help operations can:

- improve deployment of resources within technical support functions
- improve deliverables to end users, such as help functions in systems, manuals, and training
- communicate issues, problems, and suggestions for improvements to other parts of IT, end-user departments, and vendors of hardware and software

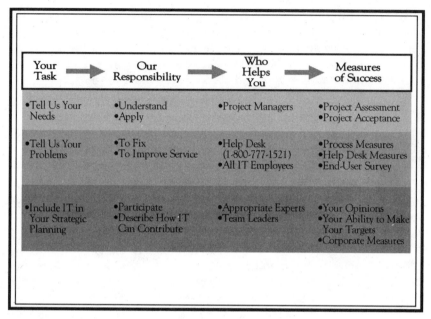

Figure 8.12 Role of your IT support organization.

As you strive to reduce defects, step one is to describe in clearly understood terms the role of the support organization. Figure 8.12 illustrates an example that can be used within IT and with end users. Normally, such a function can aspire to reduce end-user concerns (sometimes measured by the number of end-user complaints). A second widely seen measure of quality is the number of questions answered the first time, or within a period of time (for example, one business day). Now we are seeing support functions go the extra step to understand the types of questions raised by end users to see if an 80/20 rule applies. Such a view allows an organization to change some function, documentation, or training to reduce a large body of questions or problems.

The premium here is on capturing information accurately (usually in real time) about end-user issues, cataloging them by type, and then reviewing these regularly (weekly or monthly) to understand patterns and trends. Some shops will also rank incidents and defects by type or severity. Examples of types include:

- capability
- usability
- reliability

- performance
- documentation
- maintainability
- other

This approach, for example, exists in many of IBM's technical support centers. This kind of data is reflected in monthly reports to management providing item counts, time to respond, and other quality-focused evaluations. A similar cataloging of responses to these issues and subsequent reporting to the technical support team is also possible. Five types of resolutions are commonly applied:

1. corrective maintenance
2. explanations/training
3. preventive services
4. hardware replacement
5. end-user meetings

As data is collected concerning end-user support issues, managers are in a position to ask some basic questions that are tied to daily activities. They then can find answers that lead to improved support. Typical questions are:

- To what extent are problems caused by software or hardware installation activities?
- How many are systems-integration oriented?
- How many are sourced from network problems?
- Which ones are a result of defects in applications?
- To what extent are problems tied to client/server technology?
- How do architecture and standards affect service levels?
- To what extent is poor training of end users a cause of problems?

In managing such a support function, the notion of continuous improvement is currently offering the best results.

Such a never-ending cycle of support, measuring results, taking improvement steps, gaining feedback, and then planning new actions, is working. This is a four-step process:

1. Define and analyze problems, issues, and performance.
2. Identify the causes of problems and develop plans to correct these.

3. Implement changes and then confirm that results conform to expected performance through measurement.

4. Standardize the changes (if they work) and maintain them until they no longer are relevant.

This approach seems simple enough and has been well articulated by the gurus of Kaizen (Deming, Crosby, and others). The key is to do it in that order and regularly. Increasingly, IT organizations are finding that a critical success factor for a continuous improvement strategy involves building a detailed quality assurance library that tracks incidents and other relevant data over time.

Jim Whitmore, of IBM's Networking Systems Center in Gaithersburg, Maryland, has proposed a model of the kinds of data that should be gathered and reported, which embraces the spirit of providing facts upon which to make decisions on how to improve operations. Figures 8.13 through 8.15 illustrate the kinds of data and their presentation. They are simple, obvious, and effective because such data make knowledgeable decision making for changes possible. With such data, one can expect to improve efficiency of support and understand what new systems must incorporate to make them more usable from an end user's perspective and what resources would be required to maintain them.

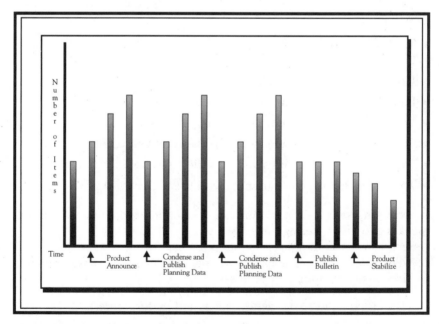

Figure 8.13 Size of on-line technical Q&A library.

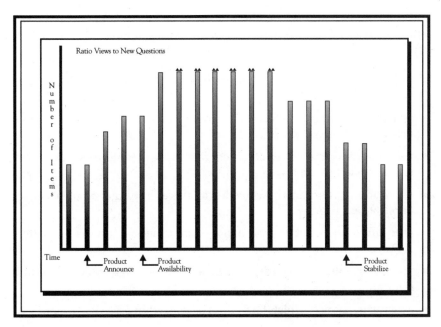

Figure 8.14 Model chart for ratio of views of existing documentation per new item.

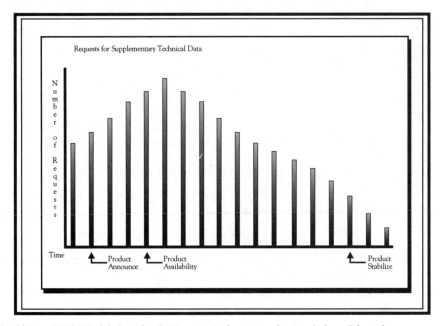

Figure 8.15 Model chart for Q&A requests during production/release life cycle.

Whitmore has studied the kinds of issues end users bring to help desks and, as a result, has compiled a list of categories of issues that should be tracked to help in continuous improvement. His general categories are:

- product environment, which he defines as something specific to a software or hardware item

- system environment, which he defines as product-to-product or product-to-hardware platform

- network environment, which he defines as system-to-network or system-to-system via network

- application environment, which he defines as application subsystem or application program

- user environment, which he defines as end-user interfaces (usually a command entry)

- architecture and standards, which he defines as an interpretation of standards

- general assistance, which he defines as everything else or "other"

Besides coding all incidents by category with a tag (a letter or number), he has proposed that one can also break down the data in a finer manner into ten categories (see Figure 8.16). In testing his approach in one time period, Whitmore discovered that 50 percent of the items related to product environment, 42 percent to systems or networking environment, and 17 percent to operations and usage issues.

These kinds of data, when gathered and used over time, make it possible for an end-user support function to know how good it is, to set standards for performance, and to appreciate how well IT performs in comparison to similar functions in other companies (benchmarking). Goals that can emerge from these kinds of efforts are, for example:

- speeding up response time from x hours to y minutes

- reducing recurring support costs by x percent by eliminating rediscovered problems or redundant activities

- reducing or eliminating specific classes of problems, thus avoiding specific types of activities and issues

- increasing the incidence of "first-time fix" by x percent

- improving end-user satisfaction ratings by x percent in y period of time (for example, within a year or a quarter)

Suggested Categories for Usage-Oriented Analysis	
Type	Description
1. Requirements	Future capabilities
2. Prerequisites/pricing	What to buy, how, how much
3. Install/customize/ configure	How to install, working
4. Maintenance/defects	Why broken, what is needed
5. Usage/operation	How do I use or operate it
6. Function/capability/ design	What it does, how it fits
7. Performance/availability	How fast does it go, how to tune it
8. Management/security/ administration	How do I manage, administer
9. Documentation	Where is this information located
10. Application interface/ coding	How do I connect to, how do I code

Figure 8.16 *Source*: Modified from James Whitmore, "Quality Improvements for the Networking Systems Center. Application of TQM Concepts for a Q&A Information Service." (Gaithersburg, MD: IBM Corporation, 1993): 16.

Use Customer Surveys to Determine Overall Effectiveness of Help Desk Support Functions

Everything just described relates to capturing information about incidents and reacting to that data. But that addresses efficiency and only partially provides feedback on effectiveness. To complete the understanding of performance, you still have to ask the end user, "How did we do?" Surveying end users can be done in several ways. First, if the company has an annual opinion survey, add a question about "to what extent are you satisfied with the IT Help Desk service." Second, to keep a pulse on perceptions, conduct quarterly surveys of samples of end users, transmitting the surveys over the network or on paper. These surveys can include a number of questions that address overall satisfaction, can probe issues that your data on incidents and problems suggest are growing issues, or test ideas for future changes. One piece of advice: Do not survey an individual more than once or twice a year and make sure that the survey effort requires less than fifteen minutes to complete, ideally five minutes. That advice will insure a higher level of participation in the survey process.

With a surveying process in place, you can set targets for improved end-user satisfaction that are based on your capabilities to improve. You can then report back (as you should) to end users about what you heard them tell you and how you intend to improve operations. You also gain the right to recruit end users for task forces and process improvement teams, if needed, to help resolve their support issues. Internal studies of various support functions within IBM showed a clear correlation between the ability of an IT organization to fix problems and improve services and customer surveys. Those that did not use surveys frequently or effectively simply did not perform as well in the minds of the end users as did those who implemented a survey process.

Encourage Bad News and Experimentation with Improvement

When you gather information and survey end users, it is inevitable that more bad than good news will be unearthed. It is easier to complain than to compliment. While the data you get are useful for improving operations, experience indicates that you must separate the information received from any judgment about the performance of help desk personnel. In other words, the data gathered belong to the processes of the support function, to be used to improve them. If bad news comes in, it should be interpreted as meaning a particular process has problems, not the people who execute the process. Letting process teams gather, interpret, and use data by applying standard fact-based TQM principles will cause your processes and, hence, your end-user support to improve. This means that you judge your people more on how they improve processes or on how end users perceive their performance over a long period of time. People then get away from feeling defensive about gathering, exposing, and addressing performance problems. Morale among IT professionals improves as does their confidence, ownership, and pride in improving services.

Communicate with your end users on a regular basis. While you need to get back to your end users after every major surveying effort to report results and how you are going to improve operations, there should also be an ongoing process for communicating regularly about operations. I suggest a three-tier strategy.

1. Put together a formal ten- to twenty-minute presentation that explains what the IT organization does, how it is organized, its major processes and projects, and include your measures of performance. Have various members of the IT organization present this message at end-user department or team meetings throughout the year, attempting to reach each department at least once annually. You may have to assign someone staff responsibility to keep lists of which end-user communities have been reached and which need this presentation.

2. From time to time, send an E-mail message to your users keeping them abreast of problems, fixes to problems, and changes being implemented. For example, if you are upgrading some software and will need to take down the system over the weekend, let your users know by Wednesday so they won't plan to come in on Saturday only to be disappointed.

3. Use newsletters or electronic bulletin boards. I like the idea of a quarterly four-page IT newsletter. A good example is *In Sights,* published by the IT organization at Appleton Papers Inc. An issue I randomly picked up had fifty to 200 word articles on "PC Support Update," "Teamwork Results in Cost Reduction," another announcing that help desk calls were up 11.8 percent over the previous year, but that incompleted calls were down 20.3 percent ("Special Recognition For A Job Well Done!"), "Applications Disaster Recovery Test," "Sheet Printer Survey Data," "Christmas Outage," and "Meet I.S. Team Members." What is particularly nice about this newsletter is that all articles were written by IT employees, not some communications expert, and they carried the author's byline, giving them ownership and pride in their stories while personalizing IT to the end-user community.

Measuring Glasshouse Operations

Measurements of central site operations benefit from a large repository of data captured by large systems control programs (SCPs) and other software designed to manage data bases, telecommunications, DASD, printers, and major software applications. Much of this data has been available for decades. Its great advantage is that it is the sort of data that operations staffs need to determine capacity, speed of operation, and errors in functionality. In short, they measure efficiency from the point of view of the IT organization and its technology. Organizations that are attempting to migrate toward continuous improvement and customer-focused operations recognize that this kind of data is useful in improving operations, but that it must be used in conjunction with heavy doses of customer-satisfaction measures discussed earlier in this chapter. Useful measures of glasshouse operations to quality management of processes and operations include:

- abandoned telephone call reports
- application problems resolved by department
- average response times
- peak average response times

- network response times
- average transactions
- primary CPU utilization
- primary workload—paging rates
- DASD forecasts
- DASD percent growth/year
- production rates/week

The format and presentation of this data are changing. Increasingly, two trends are evident: moving to graphical rather than merely statistical representations of the data and providing the data for multiple periods of time (for example, for the last twelve weeks, ten months, three years). Bar graphs and line graphs are proving to be the most popular. Figures 8.17 and 8.18 illustrate these types. Another trend has been to post these charts and graphs on bulletin boards within the IT facility for all to see. This is done on a regular basis (daily, weekly, and monthly), and the information is reviewed as a "package" at IT staff meetings also on a regular basis.

When central site operations do end-user surveys, they typically find a core set of issues they must probe in order to link performance of the type measured previously to results required by end users.

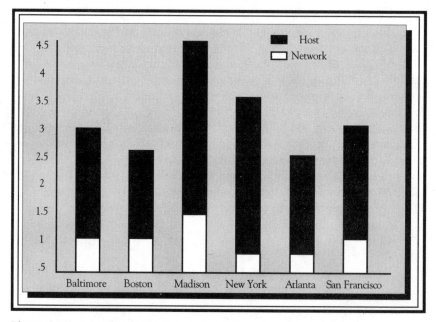

Figure 8.17 Average response time peak periods.

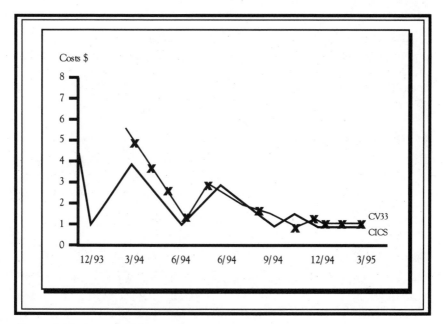

Figure 8.18 Average peak response time.

Frequently, these end-user-related issues boil down to five items concerning the effectiveness of IT:

1. performance
2. timeliness
3. service attitude
4. communications
5. overall satisfaction

Each of these elements can be measured statistically and over time by simply surveying end users, then presenting the material graphically.

Performance

This is a perception issue concerning the availability and competence of an IT organization. Typically, as with the other effectiveness measures, you are looking for an assessment of performance in three categories: exceeded, met, or did not meet by a percentage of the surveyed community. If the data is presented by month, you can quickly see the ebb and flow of end-user opinions.

Timeliness

The issue is how quickly the IT community responds to problems, returns phone calls, supplies new applications, and so forth. Using a similar format as with the performance measure, you can look at exceeding, meeting, or not meeting expectations.

Service Attitude

This addresses the level of courtesy of members of your staff, their display of understanding and empathy toward the concerns of end users, and also reflects similar issues addressed by questions concerning performance and timeliness.

Communications

Depending on what questions you ask, this can mean teleprocessing (TP) availability or, more relevantly, the effectiveness of the dialogue between IT and its end users. The better the dialogue, the more each party understands the needs of end users and capabilities of IT, thereby setting everyone's expectations such that neither is disappointed in the others' performance. That is why such a quality indicator is so important to an IT community.

Overall Satisfaction

This answers the question, "When you put it all together, what do you think of the value of the services provided by IT?" Emphasis is on two issues:

- perception of IT
- value added by IT

The first deals with your reputation, which you can influence through communications and attitudes, while the second is more tangible and gets to the issue of what value have you added to the end-users' ability to do their jobs well.

Quality-focused IT operations create an end-user quality report card. To insure that various operational considerations do not dominate the most important emphasis—providing end users with quality service that they deem valuable—IT organizations are publishing quality report cards separate from other measures. These are distributed to all IS personnel, are posted on bulletin boards, and are communicated back to end users. Figure 8.19 is a model of such a report card taken from an IT data center.

It is simple to understand, quick to read, consistent from month to month, and comprehensive. Data from one chart can be compared to signals received from end users in another, leading to the kinds of probing questions that get IT staffs focusing on issues important to end users. You can correlate data from such a report card to other reports to identify problem areas. For example, if the performance rating declined in a particular month, checking the telephone log and problem types that came to the help desk that month will probably lead you to understand why end users were disappointed. The report card would, in this instance, tell you how much they were disappointed and, hence, the degree of importance that an end user places on particular issues! Fixes to problems identified by the help desk can then be checked for effectiveness through subsequent surveys of this type.

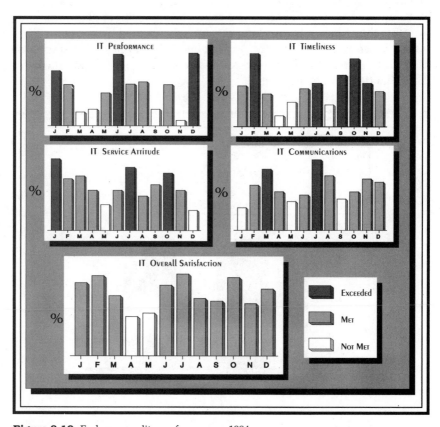

Figure 8.19 End-user quality performance—1994.

Measuring End-User Satisfaction Does Not Mean You Don't Measure Productivity

In their enthusiasm to promote customer focus and quality management practices, many advocates of TQM and quality improvement (QI) forget that you are running a business. Not every user demand can be met; it just does not make good business sense. So how do you balance the two? While there is no cookbook answer to that question—since it all depends—you can and should measure productivity much like any other part of the enterprise does. Figure 8.20 illustrates the cost per end user of IT services as compared to two other data centers. This is calculated by taking the IT budget and dividing it by the number of end users serviced. This kind of data allows you to measure your relative costs and costs of performing batch and on-line operations, and to set targets for percent reduction in costs and percent of headcount needed to perform specific functions.

Another popular measure is the cost of a data center in dollars per unit of computer resource. If you have a chargeback system in place, you want to know the quantity of computer resources consumed by your end users. But you also want to know the rate per charge unit billed to end users so that you can find ways to reduce those charges. Figure 8.21 illustrates how that data can be presented.

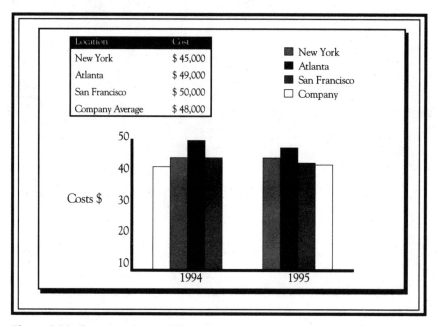

Figure 8.20 Cost per end user of IT services.

A whole series of measurements can be taken to determine the utilization of DASD and MIPS. You want to know what the ratio of DASD to MIPS utilization is for your shop and then compared to other data centers as a way of judging whether you have too much or too little DASD. You can measure gigabytes per MIPS by time and in comparison to other data centers. Figure 8.22 illustrates a simple example of this kind of report.

Understanding the ratios of IT people to MIPS can indicate productivity. You can measure, for example, cost of IT per MIPS, comparing data

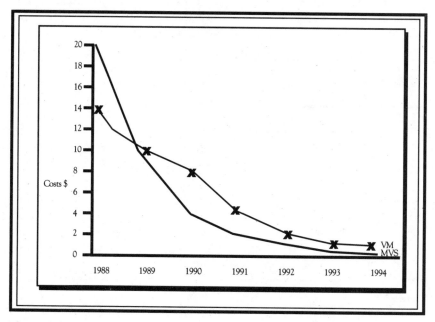

Figure 8.21 Data center costs per unit of computer resource.

Gigabytes per MIPS				
	Ratio			
Location	1991	1992	1993	1994
New York	3.0	2.8	2.6	2.0
Atlanta	3.2	3.2	3.0	2.6
San Francisco	3.2	3.3	3.1	2.6
Company average	3.1	3.1	2.9	2.4

Figure 8.22

Cost per MIPS			
		Cost	
Location	1992	1993	1994
Data center	$50K	$51K	$48K
Our company	$59K	$58K	$58K
Company #1	$50K	$52K	$48K
Company #2	$48K	$47K	$46K
Company #3	$47K	$49K	$48K

Figure 8.23

MIPS per IT Employee				
Location	1991	1992	1993	1994
Data center	9.5	12.2	13.0	13.0
Our company	7.2	9.4	9.4	11.0
Company #1	—	—	10.4	11.2
Company #2	—	—	11.6	14.4
Company #3	—	—	—	13.2

Figure 8.24

MIPS per Programmer				
Location	1991	1992	1993	1994
Data center	30.3	32.4	34.4	34.4
Our company	19.6	21.4	24.8	26.0
Company #1	—	—	28.6	28.0
Company #2	—	—	35.0	36.0
Company #3	—	—	—	32.0

Figure 8.25

center number of employees with computer capacity or by type of employee. Figures 8.23 through 8.25 illustrate these kinds of reports. While more elegant reporting schemes can be developed, these simple reports help to answer the question, "Am I getting my money's worth of IT?" This kind of data is particularly useful when reviewing overall IT performance with senior management. When tied to end-user survey data, you get a pretty good picture of the value of IT to the organization as a whole.

Conclusions

This chapter has emphasized several points. First, all the traditional activities of operations in IT can be treated as a collection of processes subject to the disciplined application of quality tools and practices. Second, increasing the "voice of the customer" in what services are offered, how, and to what level of performance should be profoundly influenced by the desires of the community of end users you service. This must occur whether they are fellow employees, suppliers, or customers of your company. Both strategies are just now beginning to be adopted by IT organizations. However, where they have been, the reports of increased productivity, strategic value of IT, and end-user satisfaction represent powerful arguments for everyone else to get on with adopting these approaches.

Developing a clearly understood set of measurements and communicating these well to fellow IT colleagues and end users are essential to the effective operation of an IT organization. Not only do they ensure that you are working on the right things, but also that a governance process can be effective in providing direction and support for IT operations. Since 70 to 80 percent of all the activities of an IT organization still involve maintaining and using existing systems—the heart of what data centers and operations departments do—it would be difficult to understate the importance of using quality management practices. Most TQM literature on IT focuses on implementing quality practices in the development and change of software—a natural and obvious target—but operations is equally a candidate. High-quality software alone will not make end users happy nor ensure the viability of any IT organization because it is to operations that end users and senior executives look for service and leadership, not to pieces of code.

References

Boynston, Andrew C., Gerry C. Jacobs, and Robert W. Zmud. "Whose Responsibility Is IT Management?" *Sloan Management Review* 33, no. 4 (Summer 1992): pp. 32–38.

Flanagan, Patrick. "Managing Networking Technologies," *Management Review* (October 1993): pp. 10–16.

Marr, J. "Help Desk System Project Tackles Customer Service Issues," *Texas Instruments Technical Journal* 11, no. 5 (May–June 1994): pp. 60–62.

O'Connor, Tom. "Get It Together," *Computerworld* (June 21, 1993): pp. 101, 103.

"Reengineering Top Challenge For IS Execs in '94," *National Underwriter Life & Health* (March 7, 1994): p. 36.

Whitmore, James. "Quality Improvements for the Networking Systems Center. Application of TQM Concepts for a Q&A Information Service." Gaithersburg, MD: IBM Corporation, 1993.

9

Personnel Practices in a Quality World

*Competent [people] in every position, if
they are doing their best, know all that there
is to know about their work except how to
improve it.*

W. EDWARDS DEMING, 1986

> In this chapter, I describe how information processing personnel practices change in a quality-focused world. Topics include functions and performance of teams, performance expectations and evaluations, development of skills and training, employee suggestion and feedback processes, the role of management, and what to measure.

A World of Teams

Departments committed to improving operations on a continuous basis find that deploying people in teams is a critical strategic step. Many corporations are finding this approach effective. But why team building? As projects and services become more complex, no one individual has all the skills to accomplish a task. But a group of people focused on one objective can have all the required skills. Operating a telecommunications network, for example, requires the services of a TP expert, another knowledgeable about LANs and PCs, a project leader for managing changes to the network, and someone conversant with particular pieces of software. Teams responsible for delivering services to end users are increasingly cross-functional in composition because they include end users and IS personnel.

A second reason for using teams is that it becomes easier to improve processes if a group works together, combining various activities into an organized process. For instance, a programming team cannot be effective unless programmers can work efficiently with systems analysts and users of the new software. The purpose here would be to ensure that the right software is developed in a timely manner and implemented correctly.

Frequently, management will call out a third reason, arguing that the ratio of managers to employees decreases in a team environment. It becomes easier to allow employees to self-appraise, peer-appraise, and to develop their own priorities linked to specific processes. As circumstances change more quickly and the knowledge required to react to them grows, only those closest to the situation can determine what needs to happen next. They know how to execute the change; frequently, managers do not. This reality requires more peer cooperation and communication. Furthermore, there is a cost savings in operations because you have fewer managers on the payroll.

How IT Teams Work

Before we discuss how such teams operate, some definitions are in order. A very common phrase in use today is "self-directed work teams." These are made up of highly trained employees given complete responsibility and authority to perform specific sets of tasks. They are granted authority, given training, and permitted freedom of action, and they are held accountable for the results of their work. I see teams ranging in size from as few as five or six to as many as eighteen; however, experience suggests that less than twelve but more than five is optimal. In IT, a self-directed team might consist of machine room operators, an administrative clerk, and a scheduling supervisor. A help desk team might be made up of three or four software/hardware experts (reflecting the skills in greatest demand as measured by questions from users), others from operations, and a quality coach.

Self-directed teams tend to look at themselves as responsible for one or two broad categories of activities, while more conventional task forces have a very narrow focus. Self-directed teams have a long life, possibly years, while task forces end when their project is over. Self-directed teams, not their supervisors or managers, make decisions by consensus and control their own activities and calendars. In more traditional environments, individual performance is rewarded; in self-directed teams, rewards are tied to how the team as a whole performs. In a conventional world, managers cherish the lone cowboy and seniority; in self-directed teams, skills and ability to work with others are more important.

Teams in business can be as different in style and mission as they are in sports. Baseball teams function differently than football teams, and so it is with IT. Once your people are on a team, their performance, appraisals, and rewards must be dependent on their new roles; the old personnel processes—which probably focused on individuals—simply inhibit the use of teams.

The need to ensure that teams work effectively is supported by the benefits possible. Evidence shows that teams are generally more productive than individuals. They streamline functions and respond to user needs, drive up the quality in all that gets done, commit to the team's objectives ahead of anybody else's, and result in greater customer satisfaction as they respond faster and with better quality.

Success stories from the world of MIS are becoming common knowledge. For example, Dana Computer Services of Dana Corporation uses self-directed work teams to achieve very high levels of service. The department moved away from over-management to self-directed teams, based on the suggestions of staff who said such an approach would improve their efficiency. Teams are assigned to specific customers (users of IS) within the company. Teams consist of five to eight volunteer members. They also have been given some structure: They must meet the financial objectives of MIS; changes must make good business sense, be legal, and moral; and changes must cause improvements, not degradations in service. Staff and management coach and support the teams. From an organizational point of view, internal customers are at the top, their support teams (made up of IS personnel) are next on the chart, and everyone else is below that.

Problem solving occurred at the team level between teams and with users, with little management interception. Results came very quickly. For one thing, problems were resolved faster and more effectively by those who knew what to do. For another, they measured performance (for example, errors, time to do things, costs per hour) using quality improvement methods and were able to identify quickly opportunities for improvement. Examples of improvements included:

- PC hardware problems going from twenty-one to one per month
- batch errors down 73 percent within one year
- job streams completed 25 percent faster
- staff reduced by 17 percent
- floor space reduced by 19 percent

Other teams in many companies report that errors decline and repeated activities become more stable and predictable. IBM's operations in Houston reflected a common pattern when it reported an increase in introspective analysis of problems and mistakes, which caused blame for problems to convert into opportunities for improvement. Team creativity also rose, leading to a more rapid implementation of new tools and automation, more research and benchmarking, and the application of more rigorous methodologies, particularly in programming.

How to Make IT Teams Successful

Because use of teams is a strategic imperative in the successful implementation of a quality-driven IT organization, some well-understood keys to success should be called out. Fortunately, useful studies have identified what is really important. The body of literature on how to make teams effective is now vast. However, one of the more useful sets of advice for IT organizations comes from a book by Carl E. Larson and Frank M.J. LaFasto, *TeamWork*:

1. Set clear goals. Successful teams spend a great deal of time planning and working with both process owners and their customers to ensure they have clear goals for what must happen. They appreciate that the set goals are important and worth working toward. Some teams even describe what they are doing with such language as "sense of mission." The old story about the bricklayers being asked what they were doing illustrates the point. The first answered that he was laying bricks, the second responded that he was constructing a wall, the third announced that he was building a cathedral. Are programmers writing code, building a system, or helping users serve customers? Clarity and elevation are critical components of successfully defined goals because they help teams ensure focus and concentration—two key requirements in effective delivery of services.

2. Make teams results-driven. Larson and LaFasto discovered that how teams are organized influences whether they are successful or not. They should be organized to facilitate communications among team members and, most important, to perform efficiently those tasks for which they were set up. Different structures are required depending on the tasks to be performed. For example, creative teams that must develop new processes need to be organized to optimize autonomy. Tactical team structures are employed when you want to execute a plan. This latter type is seen most frequently when MIS is installing equipment or software, or training users. Such teams have self-defined roles for each individual that, when performed according to some plan, result in a task being completed ef-

fectively and in a timely fashion. A third team configuration is required to maintain and improve an existing process, such as running a help desk. But in all teams, important success factors are clear definitions of roles and responsibility, accountability for results, effective communications, checks on individual and group performance, and judgments based on facts. The facts should be measurable and, ideally, quantifiable and empirical.

We are learning that we cannot have an unlimited number of teams because they are a finite and an expensive resource. Therefore, when your organization commits to creating a team, make sure that you establish a clear understanding of objectives before or soon after its creation, with buy-in from the team. Also make sure the team spends an adequate amount of time planning how its work is to be performed and what is to be done. Seeing the team spend a week or two getting "its act together" is normal and reasonable and, more important, improves efficiency by controlling project scope and building the team's personality and work habits.

3. Ensure teams have qualified members. The term *qualified employees* suggests people with skills. Skills are continuously developed and improved in organizations that focus on process management and use teams effectively. Productive teams are also made up of competent members, people who have both the technical knowledge required to contribute to the team's work and the personal characteristics required to get along with fellow team members. These are the kinds of interpersonal skills that we have always looked for in employees: compatible personalities, communication skills, intelligence, organized behavior, attention to detail, results-oriented, ethics, honesty, and so forth. They must also be able to sublimate their desire for individual achievement to team accomplishment; the team before self.

Because more MIS employees are joining cross-functional teams responsible for either solving immediate problems or managing customer-related processes, team members must display loyalty, be committed to the team, be action-oriented, and understand the need for urgency of results and responsiveness to big C and little c customers.

4. Implement unified commitment. Effective teams comprise members who are committed to the success of the team. Difficult to define, that spirit brings out a sense of urgency and desire for success in ways not otherwise possible. In IT we can see it in an implementation team's desire to plug hundreds of locations into a network before year-end, or to help a user department solve a problem by deploying IT.

5. Foster a spirit of collaboration. If you are an MIS executive using teams and transforming your business into a process-focused operation,

you have already learned how important it is to bring everyone along in accepting new values and working in collaborative ways. Executives often use the term "team speed" to describe how fast their organizations must evolve. That means it is more important to change at a speed that brings along the entire organization rather than at a speed that brings along individuals alone. Teams require collaboration of many people to work well. In sports, we understand the concept; in IT, it is everyone in operations doing their work well to ensure that all on-line systems remain up, and that end users have access to qualified MIS experts to answer their questions and can count on MIS team members who join cross-functional teams to share the same values and use the same process skills as deployed in other departments.

Trust and confidence are crucial in this kind of environment. Close behind these environmental conditions is respect. If you create a working environment in which employees trust and respect each other, whether they are managers or peers, there is less hesitancy to take risks, learn new things, improve processes, and make decisions. Getting caught doing something right is more effective than being blamed for doing something wrong. Successful teams typically share a set of values:

- honesty and truth
- openness and sharing
- consistency and predictability
- respect for all members

Collaboration fosters trust and confidence, and both can be lost quickly through the slightest errors by management, and hardly ever regained. Thus, it is imperative that from the start, as managers, we create an environment of openness and support. That is why the spirit of continuous improvement and investment in skills are so crucial in celebrating little and big victories and milestones along the way. W. Edwards Deming stated what most people secretly believe: that work can be fun and that nobody goes to work with the idea of doing a poor job. Increasingly, managers are capitalizing on his insight by creating environments where employees can "go public" with their optimism.

6. Make excellence of prime value. Every well-run successful organization values excellence in its culture because only then can it do more than before. Because MIS organizations are increasingly being asked to deliver results, often as participants in significant business transformation projects critical to the success of the entire corporation or government agency, excellence has to be cherished almost as a religion. The hunt for excellence naturally leads to bolder goals, particularly for more significant improvements in processes. Excellence gives purpose to work while inspiring loyalty to mission. Breakthrough improvements—far less frequent

than we are led to believe by quality gurus—nonetheless do come only when there exists boldness of purpose, and that requires a culture of excellence. Well-defined and aggressive goals, a commitment to excellence, and clarity of vision all in turn lead to standards of performance that are benchmarks against which to measure subsequent achievements.

7. Support and recognize team accomplishments. Support can come in many forms: giving teams resources needed to do their work (for example, office space, laptops), political protection from those who would resist their innovations, and investments in teams (training, team facilitators, and your attention). You can also offer recognition for effective performance by celebrating team results and articulating the significance of their work.

Protection is particularly important in the early stages of implementing teams within departments or across an enterprise. Since employees judge management's true values by what it supports, giving teams resources, protection, and recognition becomes a critical signal to others about what management really values. Lack of tangible support is usually one of the great failings of management. "Walking the talk" by modeling prized behavior is so crucial for management that it would be difficult to overemphasize the importance of such behavior.

8. Require principled leadership. Larson and LaFasto, like all experts on teaming or personal development (for example, Stephen R. Covey), argue that team leaders need very specific attributes and attitudes. Briefly put, they are:

- consistent goals and messages
- clear perspectives on expectations
- supportive decision making
- suppression of personal ego
- creativity

This has been a very brief overview of teaming and management of employees in a team-based environment, and it is no substitute for more detailed study. However, my central message is that many MIS organizations have been successful in achieving quality improvement by deploying teaming as a strategic imperative. We know that significant quality improvement efforts can be achieved because of equally successful implementation of teams. Yet, teaming is an effective way of organizing the work force to focus on tasks or processes. Ironically, MIS organizations have a great deal of experience using teams for programming. Now they are learning that teams can also be used in other parts of MIS: operations, user contacts, in cross-functional projects, and in strategic and administrative management.

Within the Information Services Division (ISD) at Corning, Inc., management learned what so many other MIS organizations are now realizing: that empowered employees working in self-directed teams produce results. In ISD about 90 percent of the MIS work force now works within teams. The management structure in ISD has flattened, and managers have become more facilitators of change rather than commanders. They have learned that for teams to work well, the managers (themselves organized as a team) must set clear goals based on a communicated vision; preserve their commitment to teams, visibly support them, and take risks; ensure that all levels of management share the same values; involve teams in all major activities of the division; communicate extensively to all levels; pay attention to the company's business issues and activities; invest in training for all employees; and support a reward process that recognizes individual and team achievements. One of the biggest problems the management team faced was learning new management skills and adopting new patterns of behavior to carry out these eight objectives. They have discovered the truth of Jim Lundy's comment in his book, *Lead, Follow, Or Get Out Of The Way* (1986): "For optimal success of the organization, however, a spirit of teamwork is absolutely essential!!"

Performance Expectations and Evaluations

Flattened organizations, self-directed teams, and empowered employees do not mean you are supporting anarchy and chaos. Quite to the contrary, by defining an organizational vision, defining strategies well, and assigning owners to key processes, you lead all to greater coordination of activities far in excess of what was practiced in the 1970s or 1980s. It also means, however, that individual expectations need to be well understood and personal accountability accepted for achieving these.

As organizations change, employees become confused and nervous about what they should do, how they will be rewarded and punished, and worry about the possibility of loosing their jobs. Management teams that have gone through significant corporate changes and adopted quality management practices will tell you that it is very critical that the new values, roles, and responsibilities of each individual be developed, documented and, more than communicated, they must be sold to employees. What are some ways to do this?

1. Use small teams of employees in similar positions to help think through what these new roles and responsibilities should be. Programmers working with fellow programmers, operations staff working to-

gether, and managers with fellow managers can, in a task force mode, develop performance plans and other explanatory documentation that incorporates the goals, values, and objectives of the enterprise at the individual level. Figure 9.1 illustrates such a performance plan.

2. Communicate to these teams the values, strategies, and goals of the enterprise as you see them and ask that they work in support of these

---

Sample Performance Plan: Data Center Manager

As we have agreed, your performance plan is based on the following components. Consideration for bonuses and appraisals will be given to quality, quantity, complexity, and relative importance of your contribution to the IS Department. The success of the Corporation will also be a factor.

Operations Management

- Maximize use of your resources (people, equipment, software, facilities, and budget) to provide the Corporation the highest quality of service and efficiency.
- Improve performance in key measurement areas over last year consistent with Corporate and Department business targets.
- Optimize expense recovery through expansion of EDI, E-mail and other network services.

Customer, Supplier, and End-User Satisfaction

- Develop and implement processes that result in improved overall customer, supplier, and end-user satisfaction with IT support over last year's.
- Increase end-user involvement, commitment, and support for your department's services.
- Consult with your stakeholders and be responsive to their business needs and concerns.

Technology Management

- Develop, maintain, and exploit a hardware and software architecture consistent with IS Department's strategic objectives.
- Remain current about emerging technologies, bringing forward recommendations for the use of these new tools.
- Benchmark your operations with at least three other IS Operations Departments.
- Maintain close ties to key technology providers to your department.

(continued)

Figure 9.1

Teamwork/Leadership

- Work effectively in a team environment with all Corporate and IS functions.
- Develop and use team-like management practices within your own organization. Demonstrate effective use of quality team practices.
- Ensure each employee has a skills development plan that is implemented, that every team receives skills development and is measured on results.
- In appraisals of teams and individuals 25 percent of weighting should be directed toward customer and end-user satisfaction, 50 percent on operational performance, 10 percent on skills development, 15 percent on role as team player.
- Demonstrate team player and leadership skills throughout the IS Department and with end users.

Professional Responsibilities

- Develop, document, and execute a plan to grow your skills that results in increasing your value to your stakeholders and to the Corporation. Skills should include an in-depth knowledge of teaming and SPC.
- Assume ownership of situations and accelerate their resolution and elimination of root causes of problems.
- Demonstrate sound business judgment in all situations.
- Communicate with other departments, peer IS managers, and other operations managers in the Corporation.
- Participate actively in DPMA and in at least one other IS national organization.
- Demonstrate an understanding of the Corporate and IS business strategy and assume ownership for your role in contributing to the IS Department's and Corporation's success.
- Assume personal responsibility to ensure an environment of continual improvement in all of your activities.
- Improve all processes under your control.

Figure 9.1 Continued.

intents. This is important because there are institutional constraints that they have to live within. Common boundaries to their activities include:

- budgets
- corporate personnel practices
- tolerance for change in your organization
- resistance to change by your employees
- union contracts that define job responsibilities

3. Leave to employees and their teams considerable room in which to define how they will carry out their responsibilities. They are in a better position than others to define the daily tasks once they understand the intent of the organization. Let them, for example, have a greater voice in defining what technologies or programming languages are needed in order to serve their end users better. Let operations have a greater voice in setting performance objectives for the glasshouse, the network, response times, returned calls from the help desk, and so forth, so long as they are consistent with the goals and objectives of the organization.

4. Ensure that performance plans and job descriptions have both continuous improvement and skills development provisions. Continuous improvement activities can include participating in process teams and contributing to their success as judged by their team members or process owner. Skills development means that all employees, from the head of MIS on down, must improve and upgrade their skills continuously. To a manager, it might be improving process and team management skills. To a programmer, it could be learning how to use additional CASE tools. To someone in operations, it might be acquiring knowledge of statistical process control. The point is, each employee should understand that an important part of his or her job, central to his or her success in your organization, is continued skills enhancement that makes him or her valuable both to fellow team members and to the end users who he or she ultimately serves, adding value to both communities.

Well-defined roles and responsibilities, jointly arrived at by both employees and their managers (or teams), make appraisals still possible. While an enormous debate is underway on whether appraisals should or should not be conducted in this brave new team-based world, the fact remains that most organizations still require them, and in many countries, labor practices and union contracts make them virtually mandatory. They are debated because appraisals go to the heart of management's role, the values of the organization, and the culture of the society in which a firm operates. Like teaming, appraisals have a vast literature of their own.

Deming, for example, believed employees normally want to do well. When they do not, it is usually management's fault because either it created an environment that failed to bring out the best in people or it measured them incorrectly. Others would argue that there should be no measurable targets of performance. However, looking at what the quality community thinks of employees can help you decide how to appraise your staff and measure the degree of its contributions. Increasingly, quality experts are discovering that variation in performance is more a function of the process or work than of the personal characteristics of the individual. But they accept the premise that people want to work, like doing it well, and are prepared to accept responsibility. Those three premises require us to make it possible for people to do the work they are skilled to perform and to reward behavior that models what you want (for example, good team performance, skills development, and acceptance of responsibility). In this model, managers concentrate an enormous amount of their time on eliminating obstacles to good work, instead of monitoring employees to make sure they perform. While personal blame may be appropriate for irresponsibility, an important managerial task is to work with employees to identify how to improve processes and how to eliminate problems within processes rather than to look for ways to place blame.

At one extreme end of the appraisal pendulum is the Deming view that annual merit ratings or management by objectives destroy pride in workmanship. We know, for example, how programmers resent targets, but accept the necessity for knowing how much tested code they develop and how important it is to make their drop dates on completed software. Appraisals, therefore, require an environment in which you control more through team and organizational goals and less through direct issuing of orders. Focus shifts away from tasks performed to results achieved by a process or team. Individual evaluations become more feedback in form, and the discussions shift increasingly toward how to improve.

Brian Joiner, a disciple of Deming and an outspoken critic of individual performance evaluations, argues:

1. Appraisals ignore the reality that employees do work within groups or teams. Individual evaluations, therefore, undermine teamwork.

2. Appraisals ignore the fact that employees work within systems or processes, not as individuals acting as masters of their own destiny.

3. Appraisals ignore the reality that employees work with variability and instability. Put in nonstatistical terms, workers perform differently on different days and appraisals usually do not take into account that variability. Take a systems analyst who does an outstanding job in the first half of this year working on an accounting application, then does a relatively poor job in the second half of the year working on an ABC accounting project, but is appraised on the second half only. Does that person get a favorable appraisal? Simplistic, yes, but the example challenges how we view people. As managers, we also know that we appraise frequently without knowing as much as is necessary to do the job accurately!

4. Appraisals ignore the reality that appraisal systems are biased and inconsistent. Managers are frequently asked to skew statistically how

many workers are appraised high and low, and yet we are arguing that all workers should continuously improve and be outstanding! There are biases on the part of the manager doing the appraisal and variations in his or her philosophy on whether or not to socialize earnings, treat all employees equally, and so forth. The result often is that appraisals are either extremely lax or too harsh. Bottom line: They are not as effective in motivating employees as once thought. So what do you do?

Shift Emphasis Away from People and to Process Performance

We still want to measure results, so move to an approach that looks at the results from a process. Improving processes, rather than controlling people, to achieve output avoids attacking someone (through criticisms in appraisals) and gets blame out of the way of improving the work—which is what you really are after. In fact, this approach is appearing in MIS organizations at a relatively rapid pace because of the project nature of most MIS work. Actual experience by such organizations shows that it is more effective to measure and study processes, which are then improved by employees, and then to measure the results of processes to gauge how additional progress can be made. This strategy offers management the benefits traditionally attributed to appraisal systems (ability to direct employees, give useful feedback, determine training needs, communication, and so forth), but without the negatives identified by Deming and others.

What Quality-Based Performance Plans Value

Appraisals of processes that are grounded in statistical or hard evidence rather than just on the performance of individuals make sense and lead to changes in positive terms. In that kind of environment, performance plans focus on how to make people do better work. Teams are valued because they optimize use of an organization's resources by focusing on customer-oriented tasks rather than on inward-looking bureaucracies. Leaders help craft visions and set goals so that individuals can frame their personnel or team-related activities in a manner consistent with what the enterprise needs to accomplish. The objective is to have employees make decisions that optimize implementation of visions and plans and then to execute the decisions with increasing skill and efficiency. In this world, managers understand the reality of variation in performance, accept it as normal, and use it to improve processes and hence performance of individuals. They value the concept that everything can and must be continuously improved.

The values cherished in performance and personnel development plans for individuals are:

- continuous improvement
- continuous learning and skill development
- learning in depth
- measuring all types of performance statistically
- interpersonal skills
- joy in work
- excellence

Good managers have long understood that happy, confident workers outperform disgruntled, paranoid employees. Catching people doing things right is well understood to be a far more effective strategy than blaming them for the inevitable problems that will arise. By translating the positive into the language of team, process, and individual performance plans, the values of a quality-focused organization are converted into action.

However, it is not enough to have performance understandings with employees that call for the implementation of continuous improvement in all that they do or in process improvements. Other processes also must be in place to help employees achieve these objectives. These processes should include skills development, employee feedback, recognition, suggestions, and so forth. Investing in one's employees is one of the first and most important tasks for a manager.

Skills Development Process

No organization that has changed from an old-line command and control culture to the kind described in this book did so without treating people as its main asset to be invested in with training and skills development. Organizations improve their ability to change and respond to changing conditions effectively if their people continuously improve their skills.

Large institutions such as governments (the United States and Japan, for example) and major corporations (Xerox, IBM, and Toyota, for example) have established training facilities, while smaller organizations spend as much as 4 percent of their budgets on consultants and community colleges. All these organizations have found it cost effective to do a certain amount of training on technical knowledge (for example, use of CASE tools and network management), general business topics (for example, accounting and business administration), quality management (for example, process improvement techniques), and interpersonal skills (for example, communication).

Most organizations still train in an ad hoc manner with little structure to the effort, thereby ensuring that not all the money spent on skills development is productive. But organizations that do it well recognize that skills development is a process, not a program. They also share three common elements:

1. Every employee has a written development plan that states what skills that individual will develop and how. Some of those skills will be learned in classroom settings, others through on-the-job experiences.

2. The development plan is owned by both the employee and his or her manager or team; they review it periodically just as one might monitor a business plan, and they implement it step-by-step.

3. The best skills development plans are tied to the needs of the business, not just to the department. These needs are related to the outcomes of processes the employee is involved with; weighted against anticipated turnover of availability of personnel; measured by the cost of hiring necessary skills versus developing these in-house; and defined by customer needs.

Quality-focused organizations provide training in leadership, on how to work on teams—communicate, conduct meetings, negotiate—empowerment, process reengineering techniques, statistical management, TQM, and strategic planning. MIS organizations increasingly track how many employees have received such training and measure results through employee opinion surveys on attitudes, results of process work, and through use of development plans to ensure application of newly learned skills.

How to Use Training to Build Skills

Because the primary tool companies use to change their organizations initially is training, a pattern develops. In the first year, everyone is run through one to several days of training on quality and cultural transformation. The second year, very specific skills seem to be the thing to study (such as statistical process control) and, in the third and fourth years, employees are more interested in specific training (two hours on root cause analysis) and would rather spend time in staff meetings discussing how to improve quality. It is a natural evolution from teaching employees, to employees sharing knowledge with each other, and finally to employees sharing with their customers and colleagues in other companies.

When employees are trained on quality disciplines, the normal cycle of instruction first involves running seminars on why the firm, along with the industry and economy at large, has to change. What typically follows is some detailed training on process improvement involving looking at tasks as processes, doing root cause analysis, and then improvements to all laced with a heavy dose of skills transfer on statistical measurements.

In many ways, skills development on quality topics follows the same pattern as technical skills development, and it is treated just as seriously, with equal value. The difference is that employees must tie their technical and quality knowledge together through a more common and more disciplined focus on the enterprise. To do that, they must learn to work increasingly in teams and to create visions, missions, goals, and plans for improving.

So how are skills considered a process? Figure 9.2 illustrates a high-level flowchart for one skills process. In this example, data are gathered and stored in machine readable form to facilitate the process of comparing needs to availability of skills, and then tracking who has what skills or who needs more training. In some cases, these data bases are parts of other processes (such as end-user customer satisfaction tracking), but they are linked through programming to provide insights into the organization not otherwise available.

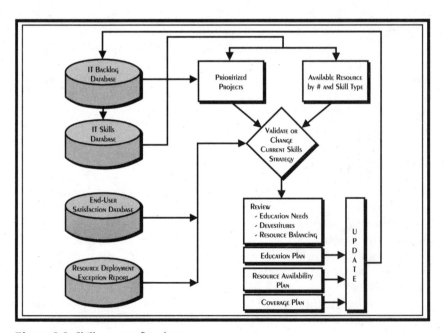

Figure 9.2 Skills process flowchart.

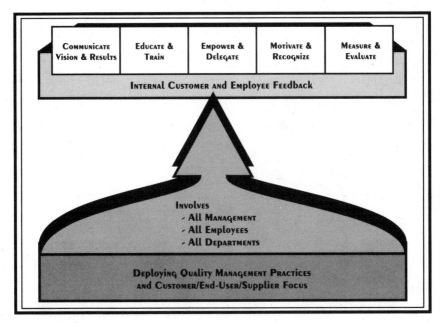

Figure 9.3 Quality, people, and skills.

In the model in Figure 9.2, all aspects of an MIS organization are involved. Managers offer training and computer facilities, and employees participate in the training and improvement of their skills. They are responsible for keeping their personal skills data file up to date. Figure 9.3 illustrates a model of how all these elements integrate to ensure that quality is built into the daily activities of each process.

Applying the Concept of Skills Data Bases

Standards for skills have to be set along with goals for improvement. For example, some organizations have defined skill levels from one to five in a number of predefined subject areas. Each employee's skill level is assigned a number. Someone can look at a skills data base and see how many skill level-one or -three or -five people there are for a particular assignment or type of opportunity.

In my organization, I might want to know how many skill level-five (the highest) people we have who can code in C so that I can look at a dispatching software package for field engineers that is coded in that language. If I do not have enough people to support that application, I then can begin making business decisions about whether to train programmers,

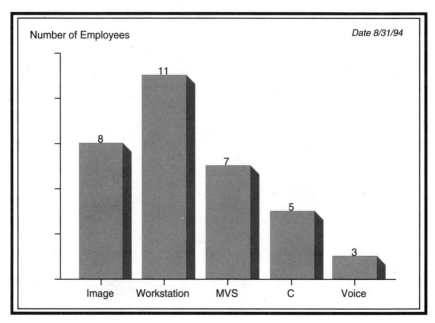

Figure 9.4 Information graphed from a skills data base.

contract out the work, or not look at a package written in C. Figure 9.4 suggests the kind of data such a skills data base can produce to help MIS management. Such a report can be produced regularly or as needed. The skills process owner would look at such data on a regular basis to understand trends in skills development and would identify changes in anticipated areas of need.

In our example, we can go further and even see what percentage of our employees have updated the skills data base within the past six months (as illustrated in Figure 9.5). In this particular example, the organization also set targets for improvement: Everyone is to update their skills file within six months, and all personnel must acquire a minimum of one level-five skill per year. Such a skills process also can be used to determine what kinds of people to hire, another way of improving the quality of your human resource pool.

The skills process has not yet received the same level of attention as other human resource topics such as quality education or recognition. However, MIS organizations have had to deal with skills development issues for decades. Applying the same techniques used to ensure an adequate supply of technical skills for the development of quality management capabilities works. MIS departments that function within organi-

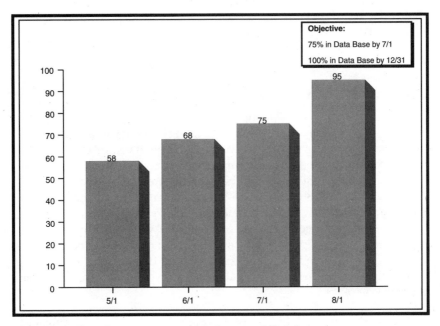

Figure 9.5 Chart showing progress toward current skills information.

zations applying the Baldrige criteria, for example, quickly and early-on develop formal skills processes because the pieces are there.

For example, the IBM MIS organization at its Rochester, Minnesota, plant (winner of a Baldrige Award) can tell you, by year, how many hours of training in quality skills each employee received and what skills they have acquired (both technical and quality) through the use of a personnel data base that includes an education record containing lists of courses taken, when, and length of each class. Other companies track who has been through various formal training programs, ideally the same ones that employees in non-MIS departments also receive to ensure common experiences and language across the entire enterprise.

Tracking participation in teams and what kinds of teams also becomes a useful tool for management. One MIS organization reported to me that by looking at patterns of team behavior, it noticed that over several years more teams were created to work on business and managerial issues than on more traditional project work, "with emphasis on including staff from areas not otherwise primarily involved in project work." In this particular organization, teams increasingly moved from project or task orientation (which leads to a final report with recommendations for management's action) to process ownership behavior in which the teams also carry out their own recommendations, measure results, and plot additional improvements.

Employee Feedback Process

It is not enough just to train employees and let them go about their work. Since they have skills and know what is going on in the organization, why not exploit their insight? Why not understand what concerns them so that their work environment can be further optimized? To carry out this objective efficiently requires a number of strategies—empowerment, team participation, process ownership—but also a way of capturing their opinions on personal and broad business issues. For that you need an employee feedback process. The use of a feedback process (often also called employee opinion survey) is not as widespread as it should be, and yet it can provide valuable intelligence on how the MIS organization is doing.

Widely used approaches for gathering employee feedback exist with the purpose of:

- determining how well they understand company and MIS business strategies
- defining the extent to which they endorse and understand the philosophy and concepts of quality management
- learning what they think of their managers and peers
- assessing how customer-oriented they think the firm is
- determining to what extent what the enterprise does meets the needs of customers and end users
- understanding what they think of the tools and practices of either the MIS department or the enterprise as a whole
- seeing how well they are being treated, paid, and rewarded
- determining the extent of their capabilities to serve the MIS department and enterprise as a whole
- learning their views on specific departmental and company issues and strategies
- assessing their morale in general

The last point is very important because happy employees work well with end users; poor morale is reflected in declining performance and a reluctance to take initiative and ownership for improving conditions.

What Good Surveys Have in Common

While there are many ways to gather information about employee opinions, one of the most effective is the formal survey. The best of these are increasingly done on-line, although paper surveys still exist. In fact, the MIS department can take the initiative with personnel departments to develop on-line versions for the entire enterprise, using MIS as the pilot. The best practices for such surveys include the following characteristics:

- absolute confidentiality
- taken once or twice yearly
- participation mandatory for all employees
- results reported to all employees within sixty days
- management required to implement plans to improve morale and other problems in a spirit of continuous improvement
- employees required to do the same, taking ownership for problems and opportunities to improve
- progress on issues regularly reported to employees
- data gathered statistically over many years to understand trends
- basic questions asked year in and year out to appreciate trends
- write-in comments encouraged, not just yes/no or multiple-choice answers

Today, many such processes also develop a morale index, which is a statistical average of a half dozen questions asked each year to provide a "sniff" test for management. These questions relate to whether employees like their jobs, to what extent they think the company or MIS organization is successful, if they are paid fairly, have opportunity for advancement, and are treated well.

It would be difficult to exaggerate the importance of confidentiality. Without it, you cannot expect to get truthful answers. So it must be in place from day one. The best way to ensure confidentiality is to use a computer-based on-line survey, report results by organizations no smaller than seven people (otherwise withhold the data), and have the personnel department or a third party "sanitize" write-in comments to make it impossible to determine who specifically wrote them.

When surveying MIS personnel, you can elicit additional feedback on the quality of the IT tools used, how competitive its pay and benefits are, and what new applications and technologies should be employed. If your staff is working closely with end users, particularly as members of functional process teams working in other parts of the organization or on large programming projects, they will have realistic and substantive input that can be gathered partially through the opinion survey. However, because they know little about the company's products and services outside of the enterprise, questioning them on these issues is far less productive.

Share Findings with Employees and Seek Their Feedback

As important as the actual survey is the process that you go through to give employees feedback. They want to know what their associates thought about the various questions so that they can compare where they sit on the issues. They also want to know that problems identified in the survey will be addressed and not be ignored. Managers want to resolve problems, but need employees to give them additional insight on issues and also to participate and even take ownership for addressing concerns. The best way to handle all these requirements is to report back quickly the results of the survey. With such feedback, I have seen groups of employees set numeric targets for improvements for the following year to be measured by the results of the next survey!

Generally, written comments have to be kept from employees because it might be possible to detect who wrote them. However, someone still has to read these, digest the essence of their messages, and make sure immediate action is taken if a critical problem is occurring right now (for example, an employee complaining about sexual harassment or ongoing criminal activity). It is amazing what you will get in write-in comments!

On the other hand, sample comments from the survey provide life for the statistical data. Use the surveys in feedback sessions with groups of employees to ask questions about how much they buy in on quality practices, what they think the progress has been so far, what needs to happen next, and so forth. Use the comments to flush out details concerning their opinions. Written comments are usually very blunt and often contain specific suggestions for improvement.

Roundtable discussions are very useful for gaining feedback regardless of whether or not opinion surveys are also conducted. Six to twelve employees gather around a conference table to meet with a manager or executive to talk about preestablished topics or about what is on their minds. Using executives and managers from non-IT organizations in the roundtable is an effective way to enhance communications and understanding across functions. Executives use these meetings to perform core drilling on specific issues within the organization.

The roundtable approach is also a good method for extracting lessons learning from teams that have been effective in implementing a new process. Roundtables can be enhanced by having a process team make a formal presentation on their process to other groups of employees, managers, and executives. Since teams working on a process may stay together for several years, their continuing learning about a process can be extremely valuable. For instance, a local team that developed a skills improvement process at one data center—long before the other MIS organizations in the company—can provide the entire MIS organization with insight on how to build a company-wide process based on its experience and through benchmarking. Since process teams usually do not go out of their way to offer advice, you will have to create situations that draw this information out (for example, holding roundtable discussions). That is why a proactive method has to be in place, such as Xerox's team rallies or Milliken's sharing rallies, in which teams are brought together to describe their successes and insights.

Suggestion Processes

In addition to surveys and roundtables, another method that can be used to get opinions and insight from employees is a suggestion process. Suggestion systems work on the assumption that employees have good ideas about how to improve the business. We also know that most suggestion programs are highly ineffective since employees make very little use of them. Quality-focused enterprises think in terms of continuous improvement processes or of ideas generating improvements. Looking at how to collect good ideas from employees is a different way of leveraging the most precious resource at your disposal: people. They happen to know a great deal about how things work well and poorly, and often rattling around in their brains are ideas for improvement. Your challenge is to collect those thoughts in a way that makes them actionable. But first you must understand why good ideas are not collected today on a regular basis.

Why Suggestion Systems Are Useless

Suggestion programs normally do not work for four reasons:

1. Little wooden boxes and stacks of suggestion forms are ignored. The boxes are rarely opened to get the ideas out and, more likely, if forms have to be filled out, they take too much time and then have to be mailed off. Nine months later, you get a form letter rejecting your idea. Studies have shown that it is very typical for only 10 to 20 percent of employees to submit even one suggestion in their entire careers! Of these, it is also very typical that only 10 to 20 percent are actually implemented.

2. Suggestion programs are usually not linked tightly into the culture of the enterprise or into the job of an employee. Nobody pays attention to the program; once in a while a suggestion is implemented and an employee publicly receives a big check, but the important message is that employees are not expected to submit suggestions as part of their normal work responsibilities.

3. Suggestion programs are not managed as processes with the kind of discipline and focus that important processes require.

4. Employees, managers, and senior executives do not normally recognize how powerful a suggestion process can be in facilitating improvements across the entire organization and in all processes.

As if these four problems were not enough, other difficulties are frequently evident. Too often focus is on cost savings; programs that pay for ideas create a "lottery mentality" that encourages people to submit only those suggestions that might generate a large reward check; and these programs have too many restrictions, such as suggestions cannot be related to your job!!? Management involvement is frequently limited, and evaluators find suggestions annoying to deal with.

On the other hand, if you are going to ask your employees to direct their own affairs, work in self-managed teams, take responsibility for their own actions, and improve processes and increase their effectiveness, then as a leader, you must give them the resources with which to carry out their responsibilities. Many of the tools they require are as simple as methods for getting things done—a concept you understand well in IT. One of these tools is an effective suggestion process, a vehicle for collecting employee ideas for improvement, getting them channeled to whoever can implement them, and then rewarding the generator of the idea for model behavior and an absolute contribution. A suggestion program, as a vehicle for continuous improvement, must be one of the vital processes of the organization. And, ranked with measurements and organizational management, should be implemented sooner rather than later.

How to Make Suggestions Work for You

Companies all over the world are reporting spectacular results when they implement suggestion processes. When suggestions are treated as a process, participation by employees frequently rises to nearly 70 percent per year, while acceptance and implementation rates also rise to over 50 percent per year. Milliken is recognized as the leader in suggestion processes in the United States, but the list of firms that have replaced old programs with new processes reads like a who's who of corporations. There is even a process user's organization devoted to continuous improvement of suggestion processes! Implementation of such a process has been found to be just as effective at the department level (for example, in MIS, sales, manufacturing) as across the entire enterprise.

Companies that have implemented such a process have learned several key lessons about obtaining meaningful suggestions for improvement:

1. Employee participation. All employees are eligible to participate, not just nonmanagement. Teams are eligible and encouraged to play.

2. Recognition. All implemented suggestions are celebrated regardless of size. Just as baseball games are won with single base hits and not just home runs, everyone accepts the idea that thousands of little suggestions are sought, tracked, and celebrated because they have a cumulative positive effect on the efficiency and effectiveness of the organization. They help the enterprise win the game. Blockbusters are wonderful, but you cannot rely on them as an improvement strategy just as a baseball team cannot rely on home runs to win games every day.

3. Management participation. Managers must be involved. Managers of suggesters play the role of advocates and supporters of specific suggestions for improvement until they are implemented. If the employee thought enough to make the suggestion, then his or her manager, in the role of creating and facilitating an environment in which employees can perform their very best, takes the suggestion as one of the most important items he or she can work on. Rather than seeing suggestions as additional work, managers see them as agenda-setting items for their contributions to the organization.

4. Types accepted. Rather than simply emphasizing suggestions that save money, successful organizations seek out suggestions on any topic, from anybody in the organization. If the suggestions save money, great; but they also want ideas on how to improve efficiency and improve the quality of any product, service, or process.

5. Feedback. The most widely heard complaint from employees about suggestion programs is that they never hear what happened to a submitted idea. In a good process, there is continuous communication between the suggester and manager or company until the idea is implemented or discarded. Feedback does more to generate new suggestions than just about any other action because employees see that their ideas are appreciated and, when implemented, that they can make a difference. In MIS, this feedback is crucial because staff members, often focused on narrow activities, need the psychological push to get them thinking and acting on broader departmental issues.

6. Job focus. Quality-driven MIS organizations expect their employees to improve the department as part of their job and, therefore, a suggestion process is a tool, just like a PC or CASE, with which they carry out one of their central responsibilities. It is not uncommon in such organizations to see a line item in an employee's performance plan saying that he or she should submit suggestions (but do not set any target or quota for these, please). When managers or peers do appraisals or bonuses and rewards are extended, they are often in response to the role individuals played with suggestions. Some departments and companies even hold local or annual meetings in which teams and individuals tell each other what improvements were made and at which suggestions are celebrated.

In short, quality-driven organizations treat their suggestion process as one of a half dozen absolutely critical strategies for continuous improvement. The genius of the process is that it can be applied across the entire company or agency, so that ideas that affect other departments can flow back and forth in a format and through a process that is understood, repeatable, and measurable.

Keys to the Design of an Outstanding Suggestion Process

This suggestion process seems to be implemented in hundreds of organizations in a remarkably similar manner. An employee submits a suggestion on-line to his or her manager, who acknowledges receipt within twenty-four or forty-eight hours. Within two or three days, the two talk about the idea and jointly determine how to have it analyzed or implemented. If the suggestion is within the manager's immediate area of responsibility, it can be implemented right away (for example, placing a telephone or a terminal in a conference room on their floor). If it is beyond the manager's responsibility, he or she takes joint (sometimes primary) responsibility for advocating its study and, if appropriate, implementation in a larger organization (for example, across the entire MIS department or company).

Since suggestions are submitted on-line, you can program tracking by individual, unit, suggestion type, quantity, and source. The computer can show whether or not the process is working. For example, it is normal in such a process to have the system trigger a reminder to manager and employee that a suggestion is still "open" (not implemented or rejected by either manager or employee or both) every thirty days so that they can communicate on progress. Trend analysis shows the organization what kinds of suggestions it is getting and which populations provide more or fewer.

Trend analysis gives the enterprise insight on how much commitment employees have for personally suggesting improvements. We do not have significant evidence as to what is normal participation for an MIS community; however, given the participation statistics just cited, one can safely expect high participation and results within technical communities. Manufacturing organizations, which have large technical communities, do participate extensively in such processes.

Once suggestions are implemented, they are communicated back to the suggester and his or her manager and are publicized with appropriate recognition. The latter can come in a number of ways: a better appraisal, a bonus, a small token of appreciation (a plaque, for example), name and picture on a bulletin board, or a promotion. After a while the culture changes, and you actually see posted lists of how many suggestions came from one organization versus another.

You must avoid some known problems, however. The most obvious is not to measure an employee on the number of ideas submitted because that just generates more suggestions, not necessarily better-quality suggestions. This was a common problem early on in Japanese companies that implemented this process, and it took years for some to fix it. Your emphasis should be on quality ideas from the beginning. To improve quality, keep the suggester involved extensively and at least partially responsible for implementing his or her own suggestion.

A second problem now seen in some companies with very high suggestion submission rates, is the encouragement of the trivial suggestion. Moving the proverbial trash can from one end of the room to another might make the measurements look good, but does not really improve things. Emphasize the need for ideas that make a difference by rewarding and complimenting quality, but be careful not to discourage suggestions or to create an atmosphere where only home runs are sought.

What to Measure and How to Expect Improvements

It makes good sense to track a number of items. They are:

- number submitted by department and person, and participation rates
- number implemented by office and person, and percent adopted
- type (for example, process, product, facility, end-user satisfaction, health and safety)
- origin by geography or type of employee (programmer, systems analyst, etc.)
- rejection and acceptance rates and ratios

- cycle times (time from suggestion to implementation by type)
- money saved, revenue generated, customer satisfaction improved, or other benefits derived

Just as important applications are not easy to implement, so it is with suggestion (improvement) processes. The biggest problem, and one that appears in any organization with an existing suggestion program, is simply getting employees to use it. The old paradigm, in which suggestions were not taken seriously, is a real problem. This perception requires extensive management attention for one to three years.

Successful implementation calls for management's focus, recognition of many efforts, use of teams to develop the process, and even local emphasis programs to call attention to the process. Education of employees on the reasons for the process and the expectations that are necessary in terms of roles and results is also a critical task. You must also be patient. It is not uncommon in the first year to see only one suggestion for every four employees. But it will rise to four to five per employee within a couple of years, and then as high as fifteen to twenty per employee per year. Most executives do not understand that constancy of purpose in implementing this process if required—another reason the process fails to take off as quickly as it should in many MIS organizations. But imagine the power you gain if every employee submits ten to fifteen suggestions and over 50 percent are implemented! Imagine if these suggestions overwhelmingly came out of your employees' direct knowledge, out of their jobs! Imagine the effect on the corporation's bottom line if MIS employees, along with others in the organization, make suggestions and implement most of them, all directed at improving the effectiveness of the company or government agency!

Role of Management

Hundreds of books about management's role have been published in the past five years for quality-driven organizations, and now we have over several dozen devoted just to MIS. The book you are reading is yet another on the topic. But I would like to summarize very briefly three fundamental ideas to keep in mind:

1. Managers have to take the initiative in making sure there are links between MIS personnel and those for whom they provide services. You have to ensure that lines of communication and understanding exist within the IT organization and across functional boundaries into end-user departments, suppliers to the company, and finally to customers and the

general public. It is easy for your staff to remain insulated within the MIS community. This role is so important that you must make it a process in itself with adopt-a-department programs; routinely performed reviews of MIS activities with key suppliers, customers, and end-user departments; and through involvement in the community at large, for example, with other MIS organizations in other companies and through professional societies such as local chapters of the Data Processing Management Association (DPMA). These efforts help keep everyone focused on priorities, on adding value through their own work, and on building new skills.

2. Managers own responsibility for sheltering MIS personnel from company politics and bureaucracy so that these employees can spend as much time as possible serving end users. This is not a contradiction of the first idea; management also is responsible for not spreading employees too thin and away from performing their jobs. Management must listen to the needs of its employees and judge how best to satisfy these while being cost effective and profitable. Despite much rhetoric from the quality community about employee responsibility, it is management who is ultimately responsible for creating the environment in which employees can work without fear, with a reasonable level of urgency to get things done, and with utmost efficiency and effectiveness.

3. Managers owe it to their employees to teach and preach continuous improvement, to back up that gospel with good quality process work, ongoing education, and rewards that signal clearly that internal and external customers really do come first. The values of quality must be their values and be the continuously burning issues of the day:

- cycle time reduction
- customer (end-user) focus
- work simplification
- excellence in what is done
- efficiency
- effectiveness

Among the many things the late Dr. W. Edwards Deming pointed out to managers were two simple, obvious, but difficult observations to take advantage of: People really want to do well and enjoy their work, and second, what we do must be a service of value to those who depend upon us. Our job as managers is to make those two concepts reality.

How You Must Change Your Role

These are different responsibilities than most of us had over the past decade. Ten years ago, a good programmer who was personable would have had a real opportunity to become a programming manager; the same was true for systems analysts and operations. The cherished skills of the programmer, along with the ability to control or influence others doing the same kind of work, were the obvious path to management. In the worst of cases, such an individual could always step in and perform the jobs of his or her employees. Today, managers, particularly first-line supervisory personnel, are being asked to relinquish much oversight responsibility while delegating authority to people who know more than they do about specific tasks and technologies and what end users want. Instead of making decisions for employees, or inspecting and authorizing, managers today must become teachers showing employees how to make decisions and how to be accountable for progress in a positive way.

Instead of just fighting technical fires or answering end-user complaints, and criticizing employees for causing problems, managers have to spend more of their time training, coaching, and fostering improvements both within the MIS community and across the enterprise. Suggestions become very important to IT managers playing this new role. So, too, does the effective use of communications processes. In the management literature today, these functions are frequently called leadership skills. Bashing managers continues to be a popular sport; however, true leadership is always in fashion and there never seems to be enough of it. The good news is that we know that leaders are not born to wear the royal purple; they are trained, just as their employees are trained. And how do you train managers to display leadership? Several basic activities make up the practices of good leadership:

- setting strategic visions and "selling" them to employees
- preserving high standards of measurable quality
- modeling the way to customer and end-user focus
- strengthening the heart by supporting teaming, employee initiatives, and individual accomplishments
- fostering a world of continuous improvement

Instead of just criticizing a missed deadline on tested code, managers must also review successes to learn how to increase them. Instead of just appraising employees, they have to teach them to do that among themselves. Instead of being the keyholes through which their organizations are run, they must become doorways for employee initiative.

These activities frequently call for new ways of doing things. Breaking away from old habits requires not the controling we grew up with as managers, but a questioning that leads to a search for new ways and acceptance of those ways. That requires the use of vision-based leadership. Ensuring that continuous improvement in services exists requires that

MIS managers communicate and negotiate well with end users, suppliers, customers, and business partners; that they understand and use statistical measurements; that they initiate the use of process improvement and reengineering techniques; and that they be willing to learn at the same time as they delegate.

Measuring Performance

This chapter has called for a tall order. So how do you know if the process is all working? How do you know what is going well and what is not? Clearly, to answer these questions, the MIS community needs a series of measurements that helps everyone appreciate how well the human resource component of IT is doing. That strategy calls for a broader set of measures than historically have existed and also for an ongoing assessment process. While more will be said about assessments in the final chapter, examples of measurements begin to suggest what is possible for an IT organization.

1. Measure your investment in developing people's skills. That gives you an idea of how these skills are expanding or contracting. You can measure number of hours trained per person and days of training for the department by subject, and then develop a trend chart showing how that amount and type of training has changed over the years. Common subjects that should be tracked (beyond technical skills you normally would monitor, such as programming and data-base knowledge) include quality seminars on the company's business, teamwork, statistical process control, and process improvement.

2. Track what is going on with suggestions, focusing on participation and implementation rates. The most common tracking mechanism is simply to list by month the total number of staff, then in the next column the total number of suggestions, and then in the third column an average. For example, if in October 1993 you had a staff of 84 and they contributed 98 suggestions, you have an average of 1.17. Over time you can see if the average is rising or falling, and that tells you how much the staff is using the process. The actual number of staff and suggestions is not as important as the run rate since that number tells you how much is going on. A similar table/chart can be built by month and trended over time to suggest the number of improvements proposed and the number actually implemented. Since when a suggestion is made and when it is implemented varies, run rates are more important and best calculated on a quarterly basis. You want to see to what extent suggestions are being implemented. If implementation is increasing, that is good; if it is not, ask why.

3. Measure degree of commitment to quality and other strategic initiatives within the department from personnel surveys. Using the technique of asking a core set of questions each year allows you to maintain a trend chart showing the ebb and flow of opinion. Common questions that can be asked and measured statistically are those that can be answered by a number, for example, from one to five with one being "most agree" and five "least agree." For example, "As employees, we are empowered to make decisions and solve problems. To what degree is this true for you? Pick one to five." Track all your questions for years that way.

4. Track the effect of nontechnical training on employees as a way of finding knowledge gaps that need to be filled. For example, one data center for a Fortune 1000 manufacturing company surveyed employees on their knowledge of four topics: customer focused quality; products, customers, and markets; financial performance measurements; and teamwork and employee involvement. The results were presented as percents (in our case, 80 percent, 80 percent, 40 percent, and 55 percent). Training was done in those areas and employees resurveyed; the results were 97 percent, 97 percent, 85 percent, and 73 percent. By using the pre- and post-training surveys, management learned that the biggest knowledge gap was in finance and thus arranged for a series of briefings and training sessions for staff. As a consequence of post-training survey work, one could see that the greatest improvement percent was in the growth in understanding of financial performance issues. This is a good illustration of measuring an activity, learning from the data, taking action to improve something, and then measuring again to see the results. This should be done for all things important to the organization.

5. Track recognition programs: what is rewarded and recognized. For example, if the department has a quality award for individual or team performance, track by month or quarter how many received the award and in what department within MIS. Trended data over time will tell you who is participating (for example, which managers are using the award program) and who needs help in exploiting the tool. If you have an employee recognition program in which individuals can give out recognition (for example, a small gift to a fellow employee for a job well done), track the number of those by quarter and also by department. That information gives you insight into the degree of ownership and empowerment evident in a department. Those using such awards aggressively are well on their way, and those who do not will require you to ask why. Reasons for lack of participation could be that there is less empowerment and team-based activity in the department, that these employees are not well aware of the peer recognition program, or that they do not take it seriously. But whatever it is, until you know why some individuals are participating or not, you will not know what issues to deal with.

6. Collect information about issues that influence morale. Unhappy employees are not going to be effective, empowered associates—a simple reality we must accept. Therefore, we need to treat them with the same razor sharp sensitivity we would apply to understanding customers' opinions about our goods and services. We survey effectively how customers feel about our products, people, and services. Do the same for your employees so that you have an early warning system that leads you to actions that continuously improve morale. Make sure your survey and roundtable approaches are broad enough to capture information that might not be predictable through the routine questions asked in opinion surveys. That is why write-in comments are a useful vehicle.

7. Develop a "top sheet" report card for the entire MIS organization and publicize it. All major processes should have a set of metrics associated with them that describe how well they are working and the results achieved. Over time, you can create a one-sheet report-card-like document to send to all employees listing the processes or measurements along the left side in a column, current data in the next column, last month's or quarter's data in the third column, and so forth. Include in your top sheet personnel-related items such as morale index, commitment to quality management, percent of budget spent on all types of training, number of rewards, and so forth. Try to limit yourself to three to four items as indicators to all employees on how they are performing in such areas as skill development, morale, and recognition (see chapter 11).

References

Byham, William C., and Jeff Cox. *ZAPP: The Lightning of Empowerment: How to Improve Productivity, Quality and Employee Satisfaction.* New York: Fawcett Columbine, 1988.

Larson, Carl E., and Frank M. LaFasto. *TeamWork: What Must Go Right/ What Can Go Wrong.* Newbury Park, CA: Sage Publications, 1989.

Osburn, Jack D., Linda Moran, Ed Musselwhite, and John H. Zenger. *Self-Directed Work Teams: The New American Challenge.* Homewood, IL: Business One/Irwin, 1990.

Ryan, Kathleen D., and Daniel K. Oestreich. *Driving Fear Out of the Workplace: How to Overcome the Invisible Barriers to Quality, Productivity, and Innovation.* San Francisco: Jossey-Bass, 1991.

Shrednick, Harvey R., Richard J. Shutt, and Madeline Weiss. "Empowerment: Key to IS World-Class Quality," *MIS Quarterly* 16, no. 4 (December 1992): pp. 491–505.

Scholtes, Peter R. *Performance Appraisal: New Directions.* Madison, WI: Joiner Associates, 1991.

10
Starting the Implementation of Quality Management

There is nothing more difficult to take in hand, more perilous to conduct, or more uncertain in its success than to take the lead in the introduction of a new order of things.
NICOLO MACHIAVELLI, 1532

In this chapter, I illustrate how to assess where your organization is on the quality journey. I then describe the components of a tactical plan for continuous improvement of operations and the role of ABC accounting. I also review dangers and proven approaches for launching quality management practices.

We have one question to answer in this chapter: How do we move forward in implementing quality business practices and values in an IS organization? As in the previous chapters, I cite examples, but I do not want to be too definitive because no two organizations do things the same way. However, I identify some of the obvious and basic moves you would want to make. For those already on the journey to quality, the issue is more what to do next. That second question will be answered partially in this chapter and more fully in the next.

Determining Where You Are Today

Just as you would not want a doctor to prescribe medicines or surgery until he or she had thoroughly examined you and had convinced you of what was wrong, neither should you accept the advice of any quality expert without first understanding the health of quality in the enterprise. The process begins with assessing the portion of the organization you control, then extends to evaluating the company as a whole. One useful approach I illustrate later in the chapter is to take the Baldrige Award criteria and do an initial "sniff test." As you implement changes, you then can write a formal annual report on progress while identifying areas that require additional focus. Doing this kind of "due diligence" assessment of operations first moves you well down the road to making fact-based decisions about actions to take, while demonstrating the value of this approach to the entire IS staff. In the last chapter, I will demonstrate how this style of management can become a permanent feature of daily activities.

However, before we go through the process of assessing where you are today, it is helpful to understand typical phases of evolution organizations undergo as they implement quality management principles. Your company is somewhere on the bandwidth, and each part of the enterprise is in a different phase. Thus, the engineering community might be well down the road, IS somewhere in the middle, and the enterprise as a whole further behind. Understanding this reality is important because it affects the support and resistance you might receive from various parts of the enterprise as you implement quality practices. In short, if for no other reason than political realities, it is important to appreciate exactly where you sit on a continuum.

Five Stages of Transformation

Figure 10.1 illustrates in general terms five stages evident in enterprises that have transformed themselves into high-quality organizations. I have shown this illustration to many people in a large variety of industries and functions in various stages of evolution and have received very strong confirmation that it is an accurate portrayal of the phases. The evidence keeps coming in, for example, that from start to "superb" takes about a decade. Recent experience by American companies in particular suggests

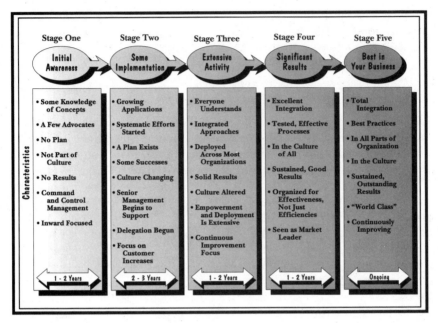

Figure 10.1 Five stages of transformation.

that the targets are moving again, making attainment of a "superb" status even more difficult than in the late 1980s or early 1990s. Encouraging results become evident in the second, or more commonly, the third year, and by the seventh year, results are generally very good.

In Stage 1 there is beginning of awareness, without integration across functions, although some pockets have attempted to apply quality management principles. As yet, there are no results and little evidence that continuous improvement is making a difference. The organization is probably not obsessed with customer or end-user satisfaction, although it may be doing well financially (so far). The management style is very much the old "command and control."

Stage 2 is characterized by growing interest and learning about quality principles. There is some support from senior management and, typically, a real champion has emerged (always an influential executive). Processes are being constructively redesigned and integrated in various parts of the company, and some employee attitudes have changed. Companies claim some success in important areas, although they cannot always say for sure that the quality approach caused them. Employees begin to be empowered with responsibilities and decision making. This is an important stage because during this period, if management lacks constancy of purpose, previous gains can be lost. It is a vulnerable time because the company or government agency has yet to see important enough results to confirm the wisdom of the kinds of profound changes called for in this book. Management has to stay on the quality path for two to three years as it builds up momentum and a track record of results.

A particularly dangerous situation often exists at this juncture if, for example, a senior management change occurs, such as a new CIO or a new senior vice president coming into power. If this occurs, employees collectively pause from the new quality efforts, waiting to see if the new managers supports them. Since many employees at this stage are barely converted to quality processes, lack of immediate and focused reaffirmation of the quality vision by the new manager, along with no tangible evidence of support (for example, personal time invested in quality initiatives), results in a return to old habits. It can happen in less than a month! If this happens, it can take years to reverse the situation and get back on the quality path. To recover, the company might even have to bring in a new functional executive, such as a different vice president of IT. By Stage 3, the risk declines because a particular manager, regardless of placement in the organization, is outnumbered by quality proponents already deeply immersed in renovations. Young employees also will have little or no memory of what the "old ways" were and, thus, can be counted on to be part of the emerging quality culture.

In Stage 3, the head of steam is clearly evident all over the enterprise, not just in IS or even a part of the department. There are effective, well-documented plans for improvement, evidence of systematic approaches to business, and all important areas are being worked on. The culture and its values have undergone important changes, and few parts of the enterprise remain unaffected. Employees are making many decisions, and the attitude of continuous improvement is healthy and very evident. By now, solid results can be demonstrated with positive trends that people are beginning to prove are a consequence of new ways of doing things. In other words, employees are living the Baldrige approach.

Stage 4 is the beginning of a golden age in a company's history. By now, all the major business journals are featuring articles about the firm because results are excellent and sustained. You are achieving significant competitive advantages, increasing market share and profits, and evidence is mounting that your approach to and deployment of quality principles brought in the good news. Processes are well-integrated, tested, and innovative across the majority of the enterprise, including IS. You are organized more for effectiveness and customer/end-user service than for simply improving efficiency or ROI. Employee surveys show very high buy-in for the company approach (above 80 percent approval), while customers, end users, and suppliers are applauding with approval ratings usually above 90 percent. You got to Stage 4 because your company sustained its faith and patiently paid its dues in Stage 3.

In Stage 5, books are written about your company, senior executives are routinely presenting the quality story at business conferences, and you win the Baldrige or some other comparable quality award. How you do business (processes) is considered unique and innovative. At this time, how you do business is often called "world-class" or "best of breed." In other words, it is as good as anybody does in any industry or the best in your industry. Your approach is systematic and continuously measured and refined. Efforts are deployed across the entire enterprise in all departments and divisions, and you now have a culture that espouses continuous improvement and customer/end-user service. Management expects, and regularly gets, outstanding results. You are one of the best in your industry and continuously outperform competition. Results are clearly due to approach and deployment. Beginning no later than Stage 2, IS has played a critical leadership role in facilitating the entire corporation's business transformation.

Is it possible to move backward through these stages? Sadly, yes, and it happens frequently. The greatest movement back and forth occurs most frequently in Stage 2; backsliding decreases as one moves forward. However, since a test of how well a company is doing involves the degree to which it gains and sustains market share, revenues, and profits, if you lose any of these then you have important proof that the company is sliding backward. IS is as guilty as any other part of the enterprise in letting that happen. So far, we have evidence of at least one Baldrige winner, possibly two, and one Deming Prize recipient, that have slipped significantly backward. Because there are no guarantees of continued success, all of the quality experts argue the case for continuous improvement forever as the way to keep a company in the game. This approach is made even more urgent by the fact that as customers, suppliers, and end users come to expect higher levels of quality in goods and services, the bar continues to rise.

How to Assess Where You Are

Where are you on the spectrum? Using the Baldrige criteria is a convenient way to arrive at a believable answer. Figure 10.2 is a modified list of the Baldrige criteria in a worksheet and Figure 10.3 has guidelines. Get your staff around a table, give them a copy of each, and have them fill out Figure 10.2. Using Figure 10.3 (which gives them guidelines for judging how well their organization is doing at each stage), they can judge what percent to assign each item and calculate the points earned. You want to do this because some of your activities will be more advanced than others, and you want to know more than simply what stage you are at as a whole.

It is possible that for a particular category your approach would be

Self Assessment Worksheet			
	Max. Pts. Possible	% Achieved	Points Earned
1.0 Leadership			
1.1 Senior Executive Leadership	45	_____	_____
1.2 Leadership System and Organization	25	_____	_____
1.3 Public Responsibility and Corporate Citizenship	20	_____	_____
2.0 Information and Analysis			
2.1 Management of Information and Data	20	_____	_____
2.2 Competitive Comparisons and Benchmarks	15	_____	_____
2.3 Analysis and Use of Company-Level Data	40	_____	_____
3.0 Strategic Planning			
3.1 Strategy Development	35	_____	_____
3.2 Strategy Deployment	20	_____	_____
4.0 Human Resource Development and Management			
4.1 Human Resource Planning and Evaluation	20	_____	_____
4.2 High Performance Work Systems	45	_____	_____
4.3 Employee Education, Training, and Development	50	_____	_____
4.4 Employee Well-Being and Satisfaction	25	_____	_____
5.0 Process Management			
5.1 Design and Introduction of Products and Services	40	_____	_____
5.2 Process Management: Product and Service Production and Delivery	40	_____	_____
5.3 Process Management: Support Services	30	_____	_____
5.4 Management of Supplier Performance	30	_____	_____
6.0 Business Results			
6.1 Product and Service Quality Results	75	_____	_____
6.2 Company Operational and Financial Results	130	_____	_____
6.3 Supplier Performance Results	45	_____	_____
7.0 Customer Focus and Satisfaction			
7.1 Customer and Market Knowledge	30	_____	_____
7.2 Customer Relationship Management	30	_____	_____
7.3 Customer Satisfaction Determination	30	_____	_____
7.4 Customer Satisfaction Results	100	_____	_____
7.5 Customer Satisfaction Comparison	60	_____	_____
Total Assessed Values		_____	_____

Figure 10.2

Quality Self-Assessment Guidelines

	Approach	Deployment	Results	
Stage 5	• World class approach; sound, systematic, effective; continuously evaluated, refined, and improved • Total integration across all parts of organization • Proven innovation	• Fully in all of organization • Ingrained in culture	• Exceptional, world class, superior to all competition • Sustained, clearly caused by approach	100% 90%
Stage 4	• Well developed and tested • Excellent integration • Innovative	• In almost all of organization and functions • Evident in culture of all groups	• Excellent, sustained in all areas with improving competitive advantage • Much evidence that they are caused by approach	80% 70%
Stage 3	• Well planned, documented, sound, systematic; all aspects addressed • Good integration	• In most of organization • Evident in culture of most parts of organization	• Solid, with positive trends in most areas • Some evidence that they are caused by approach	60% 50%
Stage 2	• Beginning of sound, systematic efforts, not all aspects addressed • Some integration	• Begun in many parts of organization • Evident in culture of some parts of organization	• Some successes in major areas • Not much evidence they are caused by approach	40% 30%
Stage 1	• Beginning of awareness • No integration across functions	• Beginning in some parts of organization • Not part of culture	• Few or no results • Little or no evidence that any results are caused by approach	20% 10%

Figure 10.3

valued more than your deployment or results. In determining what percentage to assign to a category, balance approach, deployment, and results equally. Thus, if you thought approach was worth 30 percent, but deployment only 20 percent, and results only 10 percent, then judge the category to be worth 20 percent. Using category 1.1 on senior leadership, if our CIO had a good plan (30 percent), but had just started to implement it (20 percent), and had no evidence that he or she had yet made a difference (10 percent), I would conclude that under his or her leadership so far, we were exhibiting Stage 1 behavior.

To help with the mechanics of filling out the worksheet, let us use, for example, the same category 1.1 in the self-assessment, which is leadership of the senior executive. Based on what I have said throughout this book, you would go to Figure 10.3 and find the words that best describe leadership on quality today. Suppose, for example, that you determine that there is some beginning of awareness on the part of senior management, but no quality results of that leadership. That would mean you can assign only 20 percent of the 45 points on the worksheet to that question. Fill in 20 percent in the Percent Achieved column and 9 points in the Points Earned column of Figure 10.2. Go through the same exercise for all the items and tabulate the point totals at the bottom. Collect the worksheets from everyone and come up with an average for each of the seven categories and as a whole. Figure 10.4 gives a rough indication of how many points you should have for each of the five stages.

Look at where your points fit to see in which stage you are. For example, if you have 198 points, you are still in Stage 1, and if you have 600 points, you are in Stage 4. Warning: The worse you are, the more inaccurate is your self-assessment. Those who know more about quality management

Baldrige Assessments Compared to Stages		
Points	**Stage**	**Comments**
0–200	Stage 1	Slight attention to quality
201–400	Stage 2	Some evidence, limited efforts
401–600	Stage 3	Fair; good prevention-based processes
601–800	Stage 4	Good to excellent; more improvements needed
801–1,000	Stage 5	Superb in all categories

Figure 10.4 Baldrige stages correlated to points received.

principles tend to grade themselves harder than those who do not. Appendix A will help refresh memories about what to value in this exercise. Some managers go the extra step and give each participant an actual copy of the Baldrige Award criteria published by the American Society for Quality Control (ASQC), which is short and easy reading. To get a copy call the ASQC in Milwaukee, Wisconsin, at 414-272-8575, fax 414-272-1734.

Evaluating categories takes up most of the time in this exercise. You should look for the extent to which plans exist to improve operations continuously, and then the extent to which a system exists for accurately measuring those improvements. Look for benchmarking to compare your performance with that of other enterprises to insure that you have close links with your suppliers (for example, your manufacturing plants), and to assess to what degree the organization uses such methods as surveys and other fact-gathering efforts to understand customers. To what extent are relations with customers transitory (for example, one transaction at a time or infrequent) as opposed to ongoing? Finally, to what extent are you committed to preventing mistakes rather than just correcting them? Is your approach a focus or a wish? A commitment to quality must run from the top of the house to the bottom.

Organizations that do self-assessments have found it useful to draw up sets of questions to ask themselves as part of the process of evaluating each function (in Baldrige these are grouped into seven chapters). Every handbook on Baldrige contains useful questions. Each enterprise that develops an internal Baldrige-like assessment package also develops questions in language familiar to employees.

An example from the Baldrige assessment illustrates the process. Using leadership (Chapter 1), section 1.1 calls for the assessor to describe the senior executive's leadership, personal involvement, and visibility in maintaining a customer focus and quality in all that gets done. A perfect score is 45 points. Questions that might be asked to determine whether or not certain activities were present are:

- What evidence is there that the CIO is involved in the quality effort?

- How many hours did the CIO spend last year on quality-related activities?

- What is the breadth of quality-related activities in which executives are involved?

- How much training did the CIO receive in quality last year?

- How much time did this executive spend with customers, suppliers, and end users discussing quality issues?

- What percent of the budget or other resources was devoted to quality improvement efforts this year and over the past three years?

Over time, these kinds of questions become clearer and more relevant to the enterprise. For instance, in Baldrige Chapter 5, Process Quality, section 5.1 focuses on design and introduction of products and services. Typically IS personnel look at this section and say it affects manufacturing, not them. In reality it affects both. However, in 1990, IBM's internal version of the document asked personnel to focus on their "leadership of goods and services based primarily upon process design and control, including control of procured materials, parts, and services." Two years later, the topic included language concerning "service-related requirements" and "use." IBM wanted to know about processes associated with the introduction of products to customers and services to end users— making the language more relevant to service-focused organizations.

The previous questions from section 1.1 on executive leadership were paraphrased from IBM's self-assessment in 1993. In 1990, the assessment had no questions, just statements of what needed to be addressed. For example, "Areas to address: (b.) senior executives' approach to building market-driven quality values into their leadership process and the organization's culture." Feedback from employees led to development of the laundry list of questions, beginning in 1992.

Assess Your Approach to Improvement

When thinking about results, it is not unusual for managers to conclude that their organizations are not as well run as they might be. Guiding subsequent discussions around the three aspects of approach, deployment, and results is very consistent with how many managers perform their jobs. The issues are very basic:

- Are a management system and a defined, repeatable process focused on end users and customers? If the answer is yes, are these approaches prevention-based rather than designed to detect problems and then react to them? Think, for example, of how software is developed and help desks managed.

- Is the approach grounded on quantitative data that is reliable and objective? If not, the approach is faulty.

- Does the approach to quality include such elements as evaluation and feedback, and encourage continuous improvement? Related to that is the whole issue of what tools are available and to what extent they are used effectively to support the evaluation process.

Deploying Your Quality Efforts

Issues of deployment usually focus on the extent to which actions are taken to support customers and end users. They involve the degree to which quality initiatives are embedded in business transactions and interactions with customers, suppliers, end users, and the community at large. When you look at processes, are quality features evident in all internal activities and operations, products and services? To a large extent, the debate is over the extent of quality deployment in these areas.

Finally, there is the issue of results. In the world of quality, results that happen by accident do not count. Results that occur because you applied an approach that was effectively deployed and could be measured do count. Put another way, what you planned to do, then did, caused specific, measurable results. Questions often asked about results and quality include:

- Was there a defined baseline?
- Was there relative improvement?
- To what extent were achievements sustained as gains?
- How much benchmarking takes place against the best?
- How are results linked back to approach?

These are tough, no-nonsense questions, and answers to them form the basis for the desire to build or improve quality strategies in any organization. Armed with the insight gained from your exercise (although it was not as rigorous as a formal Baldrige-like assessment, which Stage 3 through Stage 5 organizations perform routinely at least annually), you can begin to plan what to do next.

What the Assessment Teaches You

While Figure 10.3 tells you roughly at what stage you are, you can next appreciate in more detail where you are on your journey to a transformed IS operation. Using the Baldrige point system helps.

- If you have 125 points or less, you should conclude that there is no evidence of effort in any of the seven categories and that hardly any attention is given to quality, even as a management concept. Sad to say, many organizations fit this profile.
- If you are between 126 and 250 points, you would be given some credit for slight evidence in some categories. Quality is probably still a very low priority as a disciplined approach to running the business.

- At a range of 251 to 400 points, some evidence exists of efforts under way in a few categories, but none of the efforts is outstanding. In this range, you would expect to see limited integration of efforts. People are still reacting to problems, not preventing them in the first place.

- Between 401 and 600 points, the first important corner on quality has been turned. You see evidence of effective efforts in a number of the Baldrige categories. By now prevention-based process redesign is under way, although many new procedures are still young and being stabilized. One normally would recommend at this stage that additional deployment of quality principles be required, and you should be looking for continuity in the application of new processes.

- Between 601 and 750 points, you can feel good about where the organization is on quality because there is considerable evidence of effectiveness in each of the seven categories and, typically, outstanding performance in a number of them. There is good deployment and lots of results. Pockets of improvement become very obvious, while some processes remain too immature to show significant results.

- A 751-to-875 point assessment indicates an outstanding commitment to quality, excellence in approach and deployment, and significant results tied back to approaches. In short, wonderful things are happening in all seven categories with industry leadership in some.

- Above 876 points, your firm would be breathing pure oxygen! Since probably no firm in the United States has gone much above 875, one could imagine that a company with such a high score as 900 or more would be characterized as having operations with effective integration, sustained results in all facets of the business, and recognition as either a national or world leader in its industry. If your IS organization scored here, software maintenance would be virtually nonexistent, end-user satisfaction would have been near 100 percent for years, and you would be designing the applications written about in all the leading journals!

Figure 10.4 showed a slightly different model of improvement, based on assessments of customer service organizations—not too dissimilar to IS enterprises.

Elements of a Tactical Approach

The following discussion is aimed primarily toward those in early stages of implementing quality because the majority of IS organizations have only barely started to deal with the issue. Those further along would instinctively want to know how others would recommend approaching quality and, thus, would find these ideas useful because they are based on experiences from industry.

Quality always begins with leadership. The individual who introduces quality management practices into an organization has to follow the same steps as other leaders have done elsewhere.

1. The senior IS manager establishes a vision of what quality is in the organization by explaining that it is a company-wide and department-wide initiative, that it is supported by the top of the house, and that it will implement well-known business practices. The vision should be tied to corporate values that cherish customer service, employee involvement, and dignity in a world of continuous improvement.

2. Leaders work within their IS organization to document and establish challenging objectives for the transformation that lead to better understanding and fulfillment of customer and end-user requirements. This is typically a good stage at which to demand documentation of existing processes and then start using benchmarking methods to find better ideas.

3. A master plan is developed. Like any other IS initiative, quality implementation will only come from a well-ordered plan of action that is implemented as a well-managed application project.

4. Tools with which to practice quality are provided to employees. The primary tools continue to be education on quality practices, training in the use of its tools, and practice in deploying such skills as teaming and statistical process control. Associated with the deployment of training is the early establishment of teams to gain experience working on processes.

5. Leaders find they need to create an environment conducive to improvements. The four critical elements here are quality plans, progress reviews of those plans, recognition for achievement of quality improvements, and then appropriate rewards. Many of the sample processes described throughout this book were chosen to give you examples of these important activities.

6. Leaders must "walk the talk," leading by example. Beyond making presentations, IS leaders must also go to classes on quality, sit in on quality reviews at staff meetings, be team leaders on important processes, and approach problems as opportunities to learn and to improve. Leaders who spend 15 to 25 percent of their time on quality-related activities are probably in Stages 2 to 4.

How IS Management Should Perform Personally

The management structure surrounding quality initiatives can either support the early education and process reengineering efforts or hurt them. Successful approaches typically involve the senior IS manager (for example, CIO, vice president of IS) treating his or her immediate direct reports as the quality board of directors of the enterprise. In such a scenario, each staff member would own a critical process (end-user feedback, application development, etc.), would be expected to report progress at staff meetings, and would be held accountable for improvements. Ideally, a process owner would also be given authority to spend resources of the organization to deploy his or her own process plan. Staff meetings in such an environment begin with quality reviews, which take between 20 and 100 percent of staff meeting time.

In the beginning, work should be done to identify critical processes, lay plans in place, and deploy. By Stage 3, process owners and their senior executive would be spending time reviewing results, tuning plans, and ensuring that focus remained on customer service and continuous improvement. Much of the discussion would involve skills and activities of employees focused on processes.

The key point is that line managers, reporting to senior managers or executives, own quality, too; they are process owners and dedicate considerable portions of their time to continuous improvement as a process of planning, executing, inspecting, replanning, and redoing.

A common strategy is to implement at each level of the organization a similar structure in which every manager who has employees is responsible for processes. Each staff member focuses time continuously on quality improvement. At each level of the enterprise, a quality plan is documented and inspected.

How to Use Quality Councils

In addition to the personal role of managers is the useful concept of deploying quality councils populated with individuals from multiple organizations and backgrounds, but all bound together by better-than-average understanding of quality management practices. Members of councils serve as "technical" advisers to line management on quality and may have several levels of employees. They act as the quality conscience of the organization, often do quality audits (for example, conduct Baldrige-like assessments), may be given responsibility for training employees on quality management, and serve as advisers to process teams. There is no ideal approach on how best to deploy such councils. Stage 2 firms typically create them.

Another approach is to establish quality-focused councils that concern themselves less with the mechanics of how critical processes function and more with the relationships between IS and critical communities. For example, councils made up of IS personnel and end users who work with a particular application (for example, order entry) or function (for example, sales, accounting) are frequently used. Yet another twist is to host a council that focuses on how IS can support a particular corporate strategy or initiative (marketing, customer service, downsizing, etc.). Finally, a council made up of peer executives meeting with their IS counterparts to discuss the application of technology in more general terms is perhaps the most frequent and oldest approach. Each approach brings differences in emphasis, but when disciplined through the rigors of quality management practices, each gives IS feedback on needs and results.

Stage 3 organizations usually have a combination of councils, some of which meet monthly (for example, the more tactical), others quarterly, and perhaps the senior executive councils meet twice yearly. Such organizations also have cross-functional teams looking at processes in very broad terms. For example, a common type of cross-functional team, made up of customers, IS, accounting, and sales, might look at the company's billing practices. EDI activities inevitably generate the need for such teams since more than just technical issues crop up. The most difficult issues are often cultural and process oriented.

Members of quality councils should have more training on quality methods of management than the average employee and should be given the opportunity to advise senior line management on what processes are most broken or in need of reengineering. They should help those managers determine the most critical processes. General quality councils are frequently assigned responsibility for training employees, provided you give team members time to devote to the project. Since training in Stage 2 and 3 companies is extensive, you may have to put in place full-time instructors.

Organizations with fewer than 1,000 employees probably can use part-time instructors, providing there are close to a dozen who can devote up to 25 percent of their time to the task over a two- to three-year period. A good rule of thumb is one part-time instructor for about every 100 employees or up to a half dozen active process teams. For bigger organizations, a small full-time instructor/coaching staff works better. Full-time instructors can act as coaches to process teams to help figure out measurements, apply statistical analysis, do benchmarking, and conduct assessments.

Quality councils are teams and, thus, should be populated carefully. Besides the obvious requirement of personal compatibility, communicating well and persuading others of the value of quality techniques are essential, along with a real fire in the belly over quality. Good solid skills in process improvement are also a must. Ideally, such councils should represent major stakeholders and enjoy the absolute support of the senior IS executive. In some enterprises, the senior executive is the chairperson of the council and attends all meetings.

Watch out for mistakes. Some members play politics, others do not devote sufficient time to the project, and yet others have insufficient experience to bring value to the table. Common mistakes also include the senior executive not defining in detail what he or she expects from the council or coaches or why individuals were selected to serve. And, as with any team, council members have to learn to work together as a team.

Role of Effective Quality Managers

In previous chapters, I have discussed the quality audit function, suggesting that inspecting could be reduced in the development of new software if quality were designed into the programs. However, quality managers in IS organizations are being appointed whose responsibilities extend far beyond inspecting software. Typically reporting to the senior IS executive, often having many years of experience (particularly in programming or operations), these individuals are responsible for coordinating quality activities of the senior staff, including the quality council and organization-wide assessments (such as Baldrige). In addition, they advise all levels of management on process improvements. They also play the part of a "booster" in helping senior IS management sell quality and articulate the vision of the department.

The more effective quality managers also ensure that quality implementation plans do not take on a life of their own, that they do not work on the mundane or trivial activities, and that quality activities are kept tied intimately to the business plan. They spend considerable time talking to other enterprises, end users, and customers about their quality efforts, articulating to them their own organization's efforts in the field of quality.

How to Focus on What Needs to Be Done

Three experts on organizational behavior and human resource management (Michael Beer, Russell A. Eisenstat, and Bert Spector) have identified six critical activities that emphasize focusing on the work at hand rather than on more abstract concepts such as employee participation or culture change. Their work is relevant to IS operations and is confirmed by my own experiences.

They studied six organizations for four years and concluded that in these enterprises, as well as in others, senior management incorrectly assumed that company-wide programs caused transformation and that employees changed their behavior when management simply modified formal structures or systems. In reality, education and attitudes alone will not do the job. Rather, people will do different things because of the organizational roles they are asked to play. Put another way, to make people change, put them into new organizational contexts, as I demonstrated in Chapter 3. To do that requires coordination, commitment, and competencies all managed in an interrelated manner. Focus on the work at hand, not on some concept that is ill-defined such as "quality," "empowerment," or "market-driven." Ignore my suggestion if those terms are very well defined and communicated in your organization!

These researchers observed that organizations that are effective in changing their corporate culture—which is what Stage 1 and 2 companies have to worry about the most—tend to take the same half dozen actions.

1. They found specific business problems and engaged those affected by them to diagnose issues, thereby gaining their commitment to change. They changed a specific process or set of processes because of a specific business problem.

2. They shared a vision of how one should organize and manage for competitive advantage. A leader can get employees to reorganize "toward a task-aligned vision," which then leads to new roles and responsibilities. They can define new organizational structures, jobs, and measurements of success.

3. Management needed to foster consensus for the new vision, which emerged as a result of attacking specific business problems. Typical examples included loss of market share, declining customer satisfaction, etc. I envision a situation in IS in which a 20 percent cut in budget or the need to get a multimillion-dollar system up quickly could result in the same behavior. Consensus must also extend beyond vision to define the competencies needed to implement it, and finally to develop the cohesion required to "move it along." This requires general management to provide support, tools, education, reorganization, and protection as people assume new roles. An IS executive must also maintain constancy of purpose in this phase as people buy in to the new vision at various speeds. You may have to replace some managers as you go through this conversion because a few will not be able to make the change.

4. They focused next on extending changes horizontally and vertically across the enterprise, but avoided a top-down approach. Cross-functional teams and quality councils, among other steps, help. IS managers at this

point are tempted simply to force the issue, but to make it stick they must let employees convince each other that the vision makes sense.

5. As the revitalization process emerged, management institutionalized changes through such traditional methods as policies, organization, systems, and standardized procedures. For example, if a team is in place and has a process for accomplishing its goals, then recognize it as such on the organization chart. Over time, the organization and its practices mirror a structure and tasks that are focused on what the business considers important.

6. Taking a page from the quality gurus, management measured, monitored, inspected, and then adjusted the game plan in response to problems that surfaced as the organization moved from one stage to another. The authors argued that "the purpose of change is to create an asset that did not exist before—a learning organization capable of adapting to a changing competitive environment."

Their survey of general managers turned up other lessons relevant to the IS world. One was that effective executives create a need for change by setting very high levels of expectations and accountability. That tactic forces individuals to find better ways to get their jobs done without senior management having to articulate what methods to use. They also discovered that successful business unit organizations proliferate around the enterprise. The most effective general managers early on identify with organizations with the greatest likelihood of success in transforming or achieving new results; then they offer support and resources to speed them along. Finally, new career paths are created that foster and reward leadership in transformation, not simply for managing efficiencies. "Corporate renewal depends as much on developing effective change leaders as it does on developing effective organizations." They conclude that:

- A process focus was crucial.
- Organizations change best on a unit-by-unit basis.
- Programs do not cause significant change.
- Persistence over time (instead of the quick fix) leads to positive results.

Their observations represent a very different mindset than the average IS manager has grown up with in the western world.

Figure 10.5 illustrates an actual improvement process plan that applies the steps they identified. I have found that it helps answer the question: Who does what? Each function and individual has a set of responsibilities. Publish a chart like this for your organization and you, too, reduce confusion about who is responsible for what.

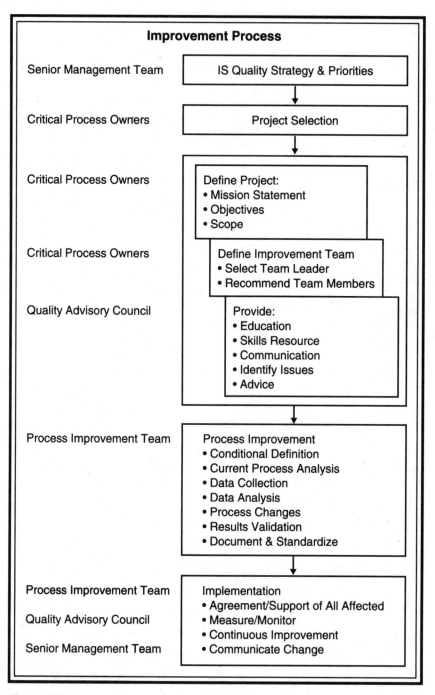

Figure 10.5

Role of ABC Accounting

Floating around the edge of quality management practices is a relatively new body of accounting practices called activity-based cost accounting, or ABC. It is identified with quality practices because these accounting activities are used to measure the cost of steps within processes. A more formal definition of ABC is the body of accounting practices, sometimes also called a method, by which one measures cost and performance of activities, processes, and cost objects. With such an approach, you can assign costs to activities or processes based on their use of such resources as people and supplies. A recognized byproduct of ABC is the acknowledgment that there is a causal relationship between cost drivers and activities.

For example, salary costs are allocated within ABC by percent of time expended and by person to an activity, not by the cost of making a product (the more traditional approach). If you are paid $10 per hour and you spend one hour per week filling out time sheets and expense reports, then those activities are assigned a cost of $10 times the number of weeks you do that activity during the course of a year, times the number of employees in the company, and so forth. Armed with that kind of accounting information, one might be able to cost justify a faster, less complicated expense reporting system or reengineered process.

With ABC, activity costs are assigned to cost objects (the reason for an expense) based on an accurate accounting of how much an activity is consumed. ABC provides information about activities such as the number of tasks performed and measures of quality (for example, errors, defects, successful completions) of a nonfinancial nature. In short, it is the ability to establish the cost of steps within a process that makes ABC methods attractive to proponents of quality management.

In addition to its attractiveness as a way of measuring process activity, there is the very real issue for IS that, as organizations implement quality practices, they will frequently want computerized ABC accounting systems. ABC is a new facet in quality management and, because it is spreading so quickly, you will be hearing more about it over the next several years. IS organizations are beginning to install applications in support of ABC for their end users, but also in some cases, for their own purposes. In addition to costing out processes, it is also being applied to costing out the expense and results of strategic initiatives, probably the one source of motivation that will drive increasing numbers of end users to turn to IS for ABC.

Unless your company is already attempting to implement ABC, any IS organization should begin to understand what ABC is about—it has a growing body of terms and concepts that cannot be ignored. Second, a dialogue should begin between IS and accounting to see if there is an opportunity to work with ABC as a way of increasing the organization's appreciation for this type of accounting. While ABC proponents would argue that you cannot implement half-way measures, the reality is that no company is going to change fundamentally its accounting practices without some sense of what the benefits are. Picking a process that is being improved or reengineered is the easiest way to get started.

Conclusions

Anytime an organization determines to change in a substantial manner how it manages activities, it is important to determine where to begin. It is difficult enough to lay out a strategy for business transformation, let alone to implement it, so understanding what that journey will probably look like is an early step. IS organizations functioning within enterprises that have undergone enormous change know that management philosophies, personnel practices, technical methods, and business strategies all change. Quality management practices provide a useful set of techniques and experiences to facilitate that transition. Talk to any IS executive at Xerox, IBM, GE, or even at much smaller companies, and you hear the same story. Quality management practices helped because they forced them to understand how they were performing today, to identify the gap between where they were and where they had to be, and then to define a strategy for changing how they performed their tasks. The body of management practices under the umbrella of quality is also expanding—witness the arrival and growing popularity of ABC accounting. There will be other enhancements to quality practices in the years to come.

One final suggestion on getting started with the implementation of quality management practices: benchmark. There are two ways to go about this. First, talk to other IS shops that have started down this path to get insights and suggestions; much of what you will hear is similar to what is in this book, except it will be more personal and specific. There probably are IS organizations in your community that have been on the path for a number of years who are willing to help. Second, once well down the path, recruit a half dozen IS organizations at your stage of evolution and meet with them on a regular basis (for example, twice a year) to compare progress among yourselves, share war stories, and craft strategies for further continuous improvement. These should be formal meetings with presentations of well-prepared material. Emphasize measuring performance. Add more informal discussions about such ambiguous issues as personnel attitudes, political frustrations, and corporate cultural barriers, all of which are important positive and negative influences on anybody's ability to implement quality practices.

References

Beer, Michael, Russell A. Eisenstat, and Bert Spector, "Why Change Programs Don't Produce Change," *Harvard Business Review* (November-December 1990): pp 158–166 (Reprint No. 90601).

Cartin, Thomas J. *Principles and Practices of TQM*. Milwaukee: ASQC Quality Press, 1993.

Collins, Brendan, and Ernest Huge. *Management by Policy: How Companies Focus Their Total Quality Efforts to Achieve Competitive Advantage*. Milwaukee: ASQC Quality Press, 1993.

Cortada, James W. "Quality Movement Is Here to Stay," *The Total Quality Review* (March/April 1994): pp. 7–9.

Fried, Louis, and Richard Johnson. "Gaining the Technology Advantage: Planning for the Competitive Use of IT," *Information Systems Management* (Fall 1991): pp. 7–13.

Lederer, Albert L., and Veronica Gardiner. "Strategic Information Systems Planning: The Method/1 Approach," *Information Systems Management* (Summer 1992): pp. 13–20.

Turney, Peter B.B. *Common Cents: The ABC Performance Breakthrough*. Portland, OR: Cost Technology, 1991.

11
Making Quality Your Management Process

We have to undo a 100-year-old concept and
convince our managers that their role is not
to control people and stay on top of things,
but rather to guide, energize, and excite.

JACK WELCH

This chapter is for those who are at Stage 2 in their quality journey and want to move forward. Much of what is described here is Stage 3 and 4 activity, where process improvement, quality criteria, and measurement systems are applied. How to weave the Baldrige criteria into the management process is a major focus, along with some of the obvious problems to overcome in quality management.

After the first year of the quality discovery is about over, after the Deming videotapes have been misplaced, and after the realization that changing your culture can really be an uncomfortable job, especially for the management team, come years of hard work. The work is hard mainly because it is different: more analysis, more decision making based on facts not just experience, and convincing each other and employees that there are better ways to run IS. It is no surprise, therefore, that Deming's message so strongly emphasizes the gospel of "constancy of purpose," meaning "stick to it" because so many organizations start and never carry through their business transformation. That is why you will read from time to time that Baldrige is flawed, that the quality movement is a fad, that there are too many people doing quality for the sake of quality and not to improve the business. However, those who stick to the game plan have told an opposite story: one of lower expenses, better quality products and services, and improved sales.

The biggest problem for most IS shops is that they are just starting the effort and very few IS organizations have positive histories at this time. Even in companies like IBM and Xerox that have been at it a while, their IS shops were late getting into the game and thus the reports, while beginning to appear, are still too few. So the image is yet to form. Another problem is a common error by management that allows people to work on processes for the sake of processes without demanding results. You have to set some expectations, otherwise, why bother? Another problem in almost every organization in the beginning is that quality has been assigned to a quality staff, not to the people who really do the work.

Too many managers, including almost all IS managers and supervisors, still have short-term views of the world, when in fact quality is a process that takes years, which is difficult for American and European executives to accept. I liken the disciplines of quality to those needed for weight reduction: You have to change your diet, eat less, exercise properly and consistently, and avoid temptations. That is simply hard to do. And in very large organizations, like major manufacturing companies and state and federal government agencies, there is also the problem of bureaucracy, which may be focused on improvements important to the enterprise, but are of little or no relevance to the customer or taxpayer. One quick example using state governments: IS comes in and suggests that people can pay for their license plates by telephone using a credit card. Sounds great: The agency gets money quicker and with less risk of a bad check, and it appears convenient to the taxpayer—except the agency makes the mistake of also charging the taxpayer an extra several dollars for the convenience of renewing license plates this way! Why charge the taxpayer when in fact the new approach saves the state the cost of handling the renewal?

The fundamental fix to implementing real quality-focused practices is to keep the faith until these new approaches have led you to a better-run organization. Pay attention to interim and long-term results of any process reengineering work and do not do anything that ultimately is of little or no value to your stakeholders (customers, end users, management, fellow employees, or stockholders).

Managing Process Improvement and Reengineering

Much has been said about processes in this book, and there are thousands of articles and books on the topic. Therefore, I will only address in very general terms a strategy for implementing processes appropriate to IS. My underlying approach is to conduct process improvements quickly and look for results early. While that may seem like an obvious strategy, the reality often is that, depending on which stage you are in, quick implementation may not be possible. A fundamental objective of Stage 1 organizations is to introduce concepts of quality and to defend the need for change.

Beginning in Stage 1 and continuing through Stage 2, organizations must expose employees to the concept of process management, teach them how to improve or reengineer processes, and persuade them to adopt permanently a new set of values and working principles. Invariably, management concludes that it is better to expose employees to the concepts and let them try them out than it is to also demand results. Often a shotgun approach is taken so that employees can get their proverbial feet wet. At first the strategy works great, but sometime in Stage 2, employees want to see results also or they lose faith in the transformation.

Management, now worried, but also concerned about how much time teams are spending in education, in process documentation, and other related activities, and also impatient for results, correctly concludes that it is time to change tactics. Now it sets priorities on processes in need of improvement, focusing resources only on these, and expecting results. Its ability to set priorities on what needs to be reengineered is a result of experiences gained in Stage 1 shotgun approaches and of paying attention to what end users are saying. IS managers are then in the market for all the techniques that consultants and authors recommend to improve processes.

Emphasize improvement overwhelmingly and save reengineering for processes that are really unsalvageable.

At this stage, you can see approaches becoming more realistic, deployment more effective, and results more apparent. At this stage, the disciplines discussed by quality experts concerning how tasks and processes should be managed come into play as relevant and necessary.

To a large extent, understanding what to fix or improve is the hardest step to take. One IS organization surveyed its end users to determine from outside of IS how application development was viewed. Figure 11.1 illustrates the output from the survey. IS management now had confirmation that its application development process needed improvement.

They broke the development process into eight steps in the cycle (it could just as easily have been six or ten) and narrowed down the steps

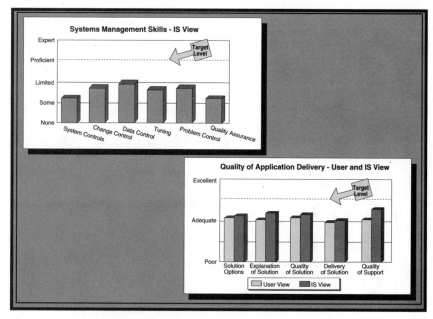

Figure 11.1 End-user view of application development.

that were in real trouble (see Figure 11.2). Going into this exercise, the process team assigned responsibility for improving the effort consulted with experts on application development and learned that there were seven key software quality components they needed to work with. Figure 11.3 lists the components, their definition, and defines their significance.

Now the process team could look at each aspect of application development and begin to improve incrementally pieces of the process, set goals for that improvement, measure results, and study what effect they had on end users.

Not all processes have to be selected based only on what end users think.

You know that some processes require work in order to do other things for end users. Two obvious examples that typically are in desperate need of improvement in most IS shops are the skills development and the strategic planning processes. Once a process is selected, studied, and understood, then you need to set specific targets for improvement. For example, you could set a target that calls for the design phase of application development to shrink by x percent of total project time; even easier to implement is reduced calendar time to write code (using software tools).

Teams can be assigned target dates for completion of certain steps in their process work (end-user surveys, benchmarking completed, pro-

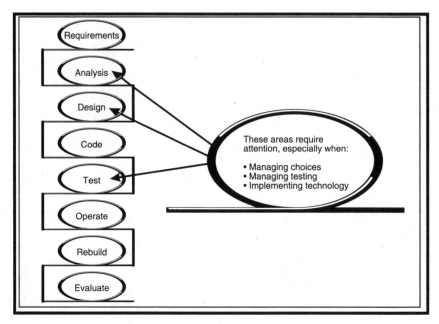

Figure 11.2 Application life cycle.

Component	Definition	Importance
Flexibility	Continuous Evolution and Changing Needs	Response to Users
Maintainability	Quick Repair and Replacement	Improves Customer Service
Reusability	Optimal Productivity and Quality of Software	Lowers Development Cost
Integration	Coupling One Product to Another	Easier to Use Applications and Get Access to Data
Consistency	Ease of Learning and Use	Reduces Training Needs
Usability	Optimal User Productivity	Exploits Power of Applications and Reduces User Technical Training Interface
Reliability	Optimal System Productivity	Supports End-User Processes

Figure 11.3 Seven key software quality components.

posed changes, pilots under way, etc.). Breaking down the effort into steps empowers employees, incrementally drives up confidence since many little reinforcing successes are achieved, and generates results that make sense to the organization.

Think of this approach as a just-in-time quality improvement strategy.

Whatever needs to be improved the most is worked on first, with tools and resources applied in exchange for specific results. As a little victory occurs, treat it as an empirical exercise by learning what worked or did not and then apply the lessons to the next process improvement task. This approach leads to continuous learning by all individuals and the organization as a whole, and always with some rewards and results earlier rather than later.

Focus on Specifics

By making sure that the quality movement in your organization is tied to a business plan, it becomes easier to select the processes to work on first and to know what to expect of them. One company, for instance, found that it took over an hour for end users to get to a warm body at a software help desk. It studied the types of phone calls that came in, when, and from whom. It discovered that a large number of calls could be reduced in length by just announcing on the sign-on screen in E-mail what the system's performance status and problems were that day and also allowing end users on the help telephone line to dial 1 for a recorded message concerning system availability. That cut the wait time for a caller down to less than two minutes.

Teams learn to expect short-term results. Many short-term accomplishments do add up to long-term results. You can boil the ocean; just get everyone to do it one teacup at a time.

Effective process improvement or reengineering methodologies—and every organization seems to have its own five-step, seven-step, or ten-step approach—does include establishing early exactly what is to be accomplished and what results to expect. That step forces fluff out of the process quickly:

- Education is focused on matters important to a specific team.
- Processes are broken down into manageable pieces.
- Incremental benefits are earned.

This approach works well in all parts of the IS organization; however, management can improve upon the effort if it instills the same sense of urgency to accomplish that exists in sales organizations and among senior executives. Little successes in the beginning help to build momentum, particularly for Stages 1 and 2; later, experience will have reinforced the notion that continuous improvement approaches are worth the time they take and are accented with a long stream of incremental results.

I particularly like the sense of urgency that is fostered in quality projects; it is an atmosphere that frequently infects members of a team with an enthusiasm otherwise not evident in the organization—these are people with a purpose.

Weaving the Baldrige Management Criteria into Yours

Ultimately, your transformation into a quality-focused IS organization will depend on having a way to weave the kinds of values and concerns raised in this book into the daily lives of all concerned, from IS professionals to end users, to their customers and suppliers. What you measure and how you reward, after all is said and done, will do more to drive the entire organization in one direction than anything else. Using a model of ideal behavior for the organization, then applying measures and inspections against that model is a practical way of moving forward. While there is no perfect model, and many variations are touted as ideal for IS, it is more important to have *a* model than *the* model because then you have a perspective against which to compare results.

Since I have used the Baldrige model throughout this book, the process of developing a management model can be illustrated with it. Many organizations take the Baldrige criteria and craft their own variation of a management model; do it if it makes sense to you. Often management will do precisely that to give employees a sense of ownership for a model that they built. However, there are four rules of thumb to keep in mind.

First, have clear objectives of why and how you want to use your management model. These normally should include:

- weaving quality practices and values into the fabric of the business
- developing a management process based on the model's criteria
- causing continuous evaluation of progress in fulfilling your vision, strategies, and quality objectives

This approach moves you away from reaction to a focus that prevents problems through planning and forces closer coordination of the various parts of the business.

Second, assign management owners to each Baldrige chapter or function. Take the most senior managers or team leaders of your enterprise and assign each to at least one year's monitoring of a chapter. Their role for that year or longer would be to look at the organization constantly through the lens of their topic and then to report problems, improvements, and suggestions. Specifically, their responsibilities would be to:

- inspect performance and advise on how to improve

- advise and support peer organizations within the firm (for example, other IS organizations or departments of comparable size and scope)

- perform an annual assessment of the entire IS organization

- report results of that assessment to the entire IS organization through both presentations and a written report

- become experts on their subjects by dint of working on them in their organization, by attending seminars and reading, and by benchmarking.

Each of these chapter or topic owners should form a miniteam to help them track and respond all year long, and each should be able to train and support a replacement should he or she move on.

By making the senior leaders of the IS organization the chapter owners, we have in one group those who have sufficient power and resources to modify measurement systems to conform to the requirements of their chapter and who have the capability to reward or punish. That is why ownership cannot be delegated to lower staff; only the data-gathering activities and the actual improvement actions should be delegated.

Third, define a simple process for the flow of activities that occur during the course of a year. A simple flowchart would do the trick. More important is deciding what gets done. Figure 11.4 illustrates an example of a strategic planning process used by one IS organization—again, it is not the specifics of a model that counts, rather having one that makes sense for you.

Let's apply an example using Baldrige. One sales organization that I am familiar with used an approach that in varied form is beginning to appear in IS departments. It determined that each fall it would write a formal self-assessment along the Baldrige lines. Therefore, it appointed next year's chapter owners in the summer, conducted its first written assessment in the fall, and reported conclusions to senior management and to the entire sales organization in December. Then once a month over the next seven months, a chapter owner would present a detailed analysis of his or her topic at the monthly senior staff meeting. These discussions included analysis of problems, anticipation of future changes, processes that needed improvements, and ultimately what such changes would mean to future assessments. Each chapter owner was required to develop

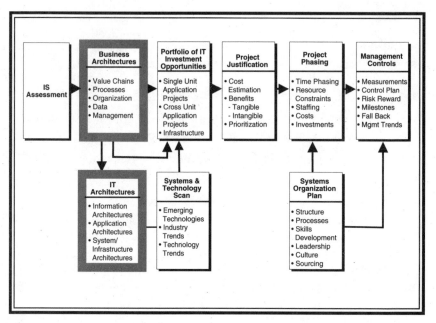

Figure 11.4 Sample strategic planning process.

a Baldrige forecast that said, "If we do such and such, our Baldrige assessment next year would go up by so many points." By spring, the organization was able to forecast next year's Baldrige assessment in points much as sales management forecasts business based on the probability of certain changes or recommendations taking place. Those approved for action were then tracked, just like sales leads, until they were completed.

If a sales organization can be so disciplined, then an IS department can be, too, since what has just been described is closer in style to how an IS organization operates than sales. Moreover, it is an excellent example of how an IS organization can acquire management tips and techniques by comparing its way of performing to those of another function. In this case, the approach was transferrable across functions.

Fourth, have your chapter owners network with other chapter owners in your enterprise or in other companies. If you are part of a large corporation, this process may be forced on you by necessity. For instance, if a number of departments each followed a similar process to the one just described, and the senior vice president to whom these departments reported was also preparing an annual self-assessment, all of the customer feedback owners (Chapter 7 of Baldrige) would be comparing notes and then feeding observations up to whoever was watching this chapter for the vice president. Thus, they would be learning from each other and getting ideas about how to improve the enterprise at the department and national levels. The same can be done by finding similar counterparts in other companies. What a wonderful way to get closer to some of your better-run customer IS organizations!

Once you have this initial chapter owner process up and running, the IS department can then move to a second phase in which a set of "top sheet" measurements can be implemented along the lines described throughout this book. Monthly or quarterly, each chapter can report to all the one or few measurements most relevant to its topic, just as financial data are presented.

Baldrige Certification Process

Once an organization starts functioning in Stages 3, 4, and 5, a new phase becomes evident, making it possible to certify an organization. Such a certification process allows a company to measure and compare one department to another in Baldrige terms. This approach is more important in large organizations that have multiple IS departments.

The typical objectives for a certification process include:

- establishing minimum actions and activities that an organization must take (defined in Baldrige terms)

- tying together local and national goals and activities

- providing a vehicle for recognizing and rewarding approved behavior

- conforming to certification standards of a major customer (for example, U.S. Department of Defense)

Minimum chapter expectations can be set nationally and, when met, can result in more budget dollars invested in certified organizations for education and expanded services, for example. Let us illustrate an example using end-user satisfaction. You do national surveys and conclude that next year you want each data center to have end users, on average, happy with the services of a data center 91 percent of the time. IS shops that meet or exceed that percent would obtain x number of points toward the following year's certification; if they missed, they would receive fewer or no points in this category. You can do this for all the chapters, add them up, and if an organization is not at a minimum, it receives no certification.

Each year the bar can be raised. So, for example, if in the first year certification requires 400 Baldrige points, the next year it could be 450, the following year 500, and so forth. Your highest point earners serve as benchmarks of "best of breed," telling senior management how fast one can increase the points next year.

The highest point getters have their budgets expanded faster than their peers, more promotions and bonuses are earned, and greater opportunities to attack company-wide problems through IT are assigned to high performing organizations. Poor performing organizations are given extra attention by management and, if necessary, key managers are replaced.

Certification strategies are relatively new; however, three "best practices" are beginning to appear, mainly outside of the IS world so far.

Certification should begin with the senior manager of the organization. Just as the first chapter of Baldrige calls for transformation to a quality-driven organization to begin with the personal leadership of the local executive, so too should the certification process. Only when that individual is personally performing well in Baldrige terms can the rest of the enterprise be expected to follow suit. Using the issues listed in Baldrige Chapter 1 (Leadership) in Appendix A, you can quickly draw up the criteria of expected behavior of all executives and managers.

The IS executive or manager should conduct an annual self-assessment followed by an outside audit of the assessment. Using the same process that accountants in companies employ, the executive or manager subject to certification should prepare a self-assessment (for example, using the Baldrige approach) and submit it to whoever does the certification (probably the vice president if IS, the CIO, or even the president of the company). That senior executive then must have the assessment audited to validate its contents and to make observations about how to improve processes and general operations. That assessment can be done by peer managers from other parts of the organization or by Baldrige-trained examiners. Where this kind of audit is done, management reports that the experience is very positive, a learning event, and nothing as negative or disturbing as a traditional accounting audit. Unlike an accounting audit, where the hunt is normally on to identify deviations from practice (a negative experience for most), a quality audit searches out suggestions on how to improve operations (a positive experience).

Broaden what you measure to determine success. As you move toward a process of certification, traditional measurements of success (such as end-user satisfaction or lines of tested code produced) become only parts of a larger mosaic of measurements, rather than just the most critical ones. Ultimately, one can end up with a Baldrige-like score that is a statement of how the entire IS organization functioned as a team and serviced customers, end users, suppliers, and other stakeholders, all within the context of the seven major Baldrige categories. Many types of success are required in order to meet minimum goals ranging from skills development to improved programming and telephone handling, to better management of expenses and appreciation of end-user issues.

Role of Other Quality Certification Approaches

Throughout this book, I have used the Baldrige criteria to frame discussions, particularly concerning how management functions and organizations assess performance. Baldrige is particularly useful for this purpose because it is applicable to service organizations, and IS is service-based. Second, the Baldrige criteria is rapidly being adopted in one fashion or another across American industry, particularly in service parts of an organization. Even the Baldrige Award is currently evolving into a Baldrige certification process. But Baldrige is not the only quality model available.

In the programming community, there is the work done by the Software Engineering Institute (SEI), which has established detailed guidelines for how software can be produced. SEI's model is important because it has been endorsed by a very large user of software—the U.S. Department of Defense—and a growing number of companies. SEI argues that somewhere between 75 and 85 percent of all software development projects run into significant problems, hence the need for standard "best practices." SEI has developed procedures and assessment practices covering three important aspects of programming and software design:

1. organization and resource management
2. software engineering processes
3. tools and technology

The first concentrates on functional activities, personnel, and assets to ensure that roles are clearly defined and effectively deployed. It calls for a precise understanding of who the work is done for (such as, customers and end users). The second focuses on how the actual software development process functions, is measured, and is managed. The last addresses application of tools. Using a scoring mechanism, one can rank an organization along a "maturity scale" at five different levels. SEI has reported that only about 20 percent of the software development operations it has assessed have reached the second of five levels; few have gone beyond.

While the SEI approach is very useful for software development, its focus limits its attractiveness to the entire IS organization. For assessments and guidelines covering more than software development, you still have to use some other model, hence the value of Baldrige.

What about ISO-9000? Originally created to help manufacturing companies in ninety-one countries standardize quality assessment practices, it has become a badge of quality for companies around the world. It consists of guidelines for documenting activities, not for standardizing quality systems implemented by companies. They are:

- ISO-9000 quality management and quality assurance standards guidelines for selection and use

- ISO-9001 quality systems model for quality assurance in design/development, production, installation, and servicing

- ISO-9002 quality systems model for quality assurance in production and installation

- ISO-9003 quality inspection and test

- ISO-9004 quality management and quality systems elements guidelines

- ISO-8402 quality terminology and definitions

The ISO-9000 process was designed and is used to ensure that a supplier conforms to specified customer requirements, which means ensuring a predetermined level of quality. For a manufacturing company, that always required IS participation in documenting its role in helping end users conform to standards (for example, through the supply of IS applications). Sounds very similar to Baldrige, so where are the differences?

1. ISO and Baldrige are not mutually exclusive. Many companies use both. IBM, for example, won a Baldrige award at its Rochester, Minnesota, plant. The same facility is also ISO-9000 certified. The same is true for many other Baldrige winners and users of the Baldrige criteria.

2. Baldrige focuses on your being competitive in operations, while ISO concentrates on conformity to practices you specified in your own quality model.

3. Baldrige emphasizes organizational learning to improve operations; ISO-9000 emphasizes conformance to buyer's requirements.

4. Baldrige defines quality as customer-driven; ISO defines it as conformity to documented requirements.

5. Baldrige emphasizes results of quality activities in its assessment; ISO places less emphasis on results and more toward conformance to standards.

6. Baldrige covers all operations and processes; ISO tends to emphasize more design/development, production, installation, and servicing.

The pros and cons of both Baldrige and ISO-9000 have been debated since the start of the 1990s. One is not necessarily better than the other, although managers tend to take sides in favor of one over the other. If pressed, I choose Baldrige for IS because it is broader in scope. However, ISO provides a strong discipline for documenting what you do. Each has much to offer an IS organization. Since IS is part of a much larger enterprise, it makes practical sense for the technical community to adopt a quality audit model that is consistent with the rest of the company. If the rest of the firm, for example, is working with Baldrige, IS had better also because in time the impulse of senior management is to have a common approach across the entire enterprise. In fact, both quality approaches, and even the one surrounding the Deming Prize in Japan, encourage a commonality of approach.

How to Use Measurements Effectively

Today, nothing seems to be so mismanaged as measurements and, yet, probably not a single executive or responsible manager would argue against the importance of good measurements. Measurements in most organizations simply appeared in some helter skelter fashion over time, growing on the enterprise like barnacles on the hull of a ship. Often measurements of performance were developed in response to specific situations in earlier times. Rarely is an organization equipped with a set of measures that reflect today's values and objectives of the enterprise. A manager or employee comes into a job and begins using whatever measures are already there; rarely does a manager do more than simply add additional measures.

All of that is beginning to change. In the first place, as organizations move toward process management approaches, with emphasis increasing on fact-based decision making, old measures are giving way to new sets. These include measurements of results (the more traditional approach), but also others defining how a process works. Second, new business strategies call for different measures. The largest body of new measures concern cycle time, the amount of time that it takes to do a task, a process, or accomplish a strategy. Third, new business practices are generating whole new bodies of measurements, such as ABC accounting, which provides data on the costs of tasks.

But perhaps most evolutionary is that management teams are beginning to treat performance measurements as a process. Once down that path, managers in general want a coordinated set of measurements that reflect 1990s issues and values; that document performance of processes, quality practices, and more traditional outcomes (for example, revenue and budgets); and that do it in new ways, such as through on-line systems and extensive graphical representation.

Hard issues are measured (such as, number of lines of clean code), but also many soft ones (such as, extent of employee participation in quality-focused activities). While IS organizations have a large number of measures, they are overwhelmingly a collection of related and unrelated measures that have evolved over time. The IS manager, in short, faces the same problem every other functional leader does: how to create a new meas-

urements process that is effective. I have yet to see an IS organization that
has completely figured this one out. However, a growing set of experiences across American, European, and Asian industry concerning measurements are transferrable to IS.

Measurement Goals and Criteria

As in any good process, some clear thinking up front is helpful. Effective
goals for any measurement process typically are:

- must identify benefits of a process
- should document rate and quality of changes in plans
- controls projects and activities
- facilitates acquisition of skills and resources
- facilitates an organization's capacity to change

Put another way, answering the question "why measure?" influences
what measures you get. Typically, the answers to the question are:

- You cannot know if there are any improvements in quality or perform-
  ance without measuring results. Feelings and impressions are too im-
  precise.
- Measurements can keep you focused on what really has to be improved.
  They lead to more relevant actions tied to specific goals.
- Measurements avoid randomness in improvements in cultural changes.
  For example, they help you avoid restructuring organizations without
  first having a baseline and targets for improvements while linking
  changes in your culture to specific, desired outcomes.
- Measurements give everyone an occasion to celebrate results.

We are learning in IS and in other organizations that measurements are
excellent tools for facilitating change. They encourage people to become
involved in changes because they get feedback on their work and insight
on what to do next, and they like to see results rather than vague goals
and objectives that are not actionable. By linking improvements and measurements, various types of activities do not get mixed or confused, thereby
avoiding contradictions, while increasing the odds of ensuring effective
linkages of rewards, compensation, promotions, and improvements.

A second set of experiences with measurements concerns level of detail.
When you begin to treat measurements as a process, one of the first questions is how much information do we need and at what level. Different
levels of function and of the organization require varying degrees of in-

formation. Figure 11.5 illustrates a hierarchy of measures going from the subprocess all the way up to a department report card. Figure 11.6 is a summary of the kinds of measures you can find at each level. For each of your major IS processes, you can develop subprocess and process measures, then a package of measurements for the entire department and, finally, the one to three measures per critical process included on a monthly one-page report card that goes to everyone.

While this is not the place to conduct a tutorial on how to develop measures—that would require its own book—some suggestions that other organizations have implemented successfully are applicable in IS. From the point of view of criteria or trends in types of measures, the most widely accepted are:

- data trended over time
- information belonging to key processes
- movement toward measuring variances from targets
- increased use of root cause analysis of defects
- more emphasis on measuring defects and less on simply achieving targets
- cycle time reduction as a major design point

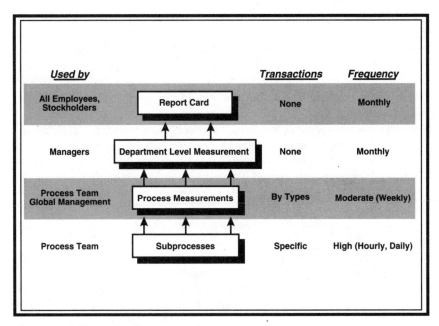

Figure 11.5 Hierarchy of measurements.

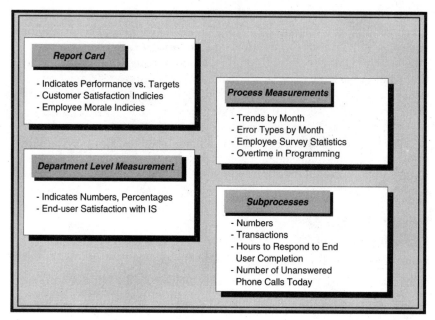

Figure 11.6 Type of measures by level.

Understanding Your Management Process Helps Measurements

Most managers do not realize that what they do as managers is, in fact, a process; it just is not documented or articulated in some conscious way. But it does exist. Understanding that process and then articulating how it should function puts measurements in context. For example, Figure 11.7 shows a management process as it exists in one organization that, until its managers saw this chart, did not know it had a management process. External pressures were recognized, but poorly understood, which led to problems and opportunities for management to work on, then to decisions, and finally to activities that the organization was asked to perform. Whatever measurements existed played some influence on these activities.

By building a measurement-centric management process, you take a dramatic step forward in continuously improving how management of the organization occurs. Figure 11.8 suggests what that looks like. External pressures and strategy cause information to be gathered, problems and opportunities to be identified and decided upon, and processes engaged to execute management intents. Organizations then simply become institutional supply cabinets that contain people, money, computers, and so forth, to get the work done. But at each phase of the management model,

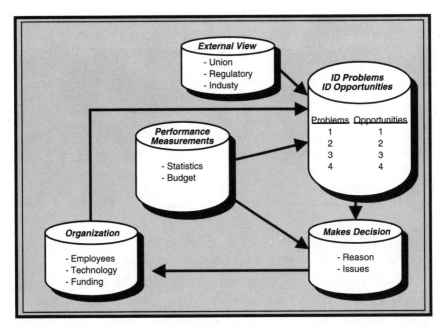

Figure 11.7 Actual management process.

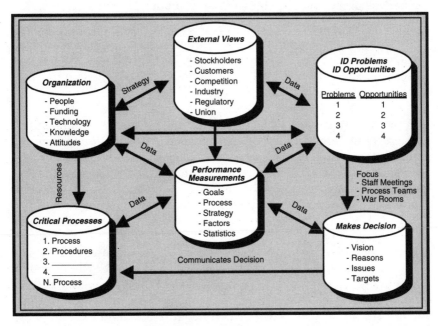

Figure 11.8 Measurement-centric management process.

measurements of performance play a significant role in making decisions and actions fact-based. Measurements viewed this way can help IS operations. A number of actions become possible; these include:

- Identification of problems and opportunities are driven from an analysis of external business environments, internal processes, and current performance.

- As problems and opportunities are recognized, changes to the performance measurements process can be made to capture information to assist in making decisions.

- Business levers (such as computers, people, funding) are affected by the external business environment as new management techniques, technologies, and competitive strategies are introduced.

- Decision making is driven from an understanding of problems and opportunities and is reflected in a change to processes and measurements.

- Changes to measurements are made to track the effectiveness of decisions and impact of decisions on the IS organization.

- By measuring continuously the capabilities of each process, these processes can be tuned. Decisions that impact processes then drive reevaluations of the organization's ability to support changed processes.

- Organizational structures are determined by the performance requirements of the processes in response to external factors and needs of end users and customers. This approach makes organizations more responsive to change with minimal disruption to work done within the processes.

In practice, when you look at management activities this way, measurements are developed by process teams for process improvements. Second, report cards or "top sheet" measures emerge out of what management needs to coordinate across the entire organization. Third, measurements are carefully designed to be clearly understood by all who need to use or know about them. They make sense, they are relevant to the business, they are supported, and they encourage improvements, not enhance fear of failure.

But how do you respond to the basic purpose of measurements, which is to answer the question: What constitutes a win? In other words, where are we making money and losing it, and why? Where are we succeeding or failing, and why? The answer lies along the nine attributes axis and key processes axis, first introduced with Figure 6.2; Figure 11.9 reminds us of what they are. Build measures along the nine attributes exis and for

	Growth	Stakeholder and Customer Satisfaction	Productivity	Cycle Time	Waste	Reliability	Quality	Flexibility	Financial
System Requirements Analysis/Design	# Preventative Processes, Files Needed	% of End-User Involvement (FTEs) in Design	% of Total Project Spent on Design		# End-User Design Changes	Complaints	Actual vs. Planned ROI		Planned vs. Actual Cost
Software Requirements Analysis	# New Changes to Design	Enhancements by Module	# Interfaces with Existing Software	Time to Acquire Requirements	# of Changes Required	# Omissions Noted in Review of Objectives		Speed of Changes	Cost of Phase as % of Total
Preliminary Design		End-User Satisfaction	# Data Items Passed between Modules		# of Changes to Specifications Due to Design Requirement	# Changes to Project Plan, Test Plan after Review	# Changes to Design after Review Due to Error	# Screens/ # Required User Interfaces	Cost of Phase as % of Total
Coding and Testing	Modules or Lines of Code in Excess of Original Design	% Grade by User	% of Time Spent on Coding	Time to Code a Module & by Type	% of Code Changed Due to Reliability Errors	Errors/Module	Defect Rates (Improvement vs. Plan)	# Lines of Code Reused	Estimated Hours vs. Actual
Integration and Testing		# User/Tester Mis-understandings	# PTF Steps Reduced	Time to Train User, Tester of Documentation	# of Recoded Modules	Problem Rate	Errors in Coding Problems/ Month	Rate of Speed to Change	Defect Fix Time
End-User Acceptance Testing	# of Modifications by Type, Module	Time Spent on Walkthroughs	% Features Tested at Alpha Sites	Time to Performance vs. Planned	# Defects Total	Complaints	% Grade from Usability Lab Testing	% Resolution of Defects	# of Delivered Errors
Overall	Growth in Customer Acceptance of End Product	Complaints, Customer Satisfaction	Ratio of Work Days per System/Lines of Code/Module	Timeline of Finished Code	Defects by Program	% of Missed Deadlines	% Improvement in Inspection Effectiveness	% Changes Mode/Work Day of Effort	Cost of Executable Instructions

Figure 11.9 Examples of software development measures by type.

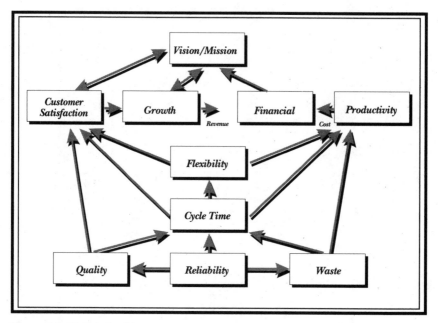

Figure 11.10 Relationship among measurements.

each of your major processes (for example, top six to ten) and you will probably get the answer to the question, "Is it a win?"

With these measures in place, you can get to the heart of how to use measurements. Very quickly, you will discover that the true genius of measurements is understanding how they interact with each other. Research that other colleagues and I have conducted within the IBM Consulting Group suggests a pattern of influence of one type of measures over another regardless of type of organization. You can be a bank, an IS shop, a sales organization, or a customer service department, and these relationships seem to hold true. The table in Figure 11.10 illustrates how different types of measures affect each other and, more specifically, which ones influence which measures. We have found this table to be very useful because it is important to understand what effect a measure can have. You will, over time, change measurements as your measurements process reflects more of what the organization wants to accomplish and as you learn how measures affect behavior in the organization. The table gives you a head start in understanding their implications.

Sustaining Your Measurements Process

The first step is simply to begin treating measurements as a key process, not as an eclectic collection of data. They are the heart of your management process and, therefore, they should be balanced and comprehensive. I would take into account five factors in applying them to an IS organization:

1. Timing: When are they needed and by whom?
2. Detail: How much data and for whom?
3. Change: When should they be changed and by whom?
4. Accuracy: To what extent do people believe the numbers?
5. Improvement: How can measures provide more insight?

Managing these five factors as part of the measurements process sustains your measures as a viable management tool. Figure 11.11 illustrates how the process functions when properly managed.

Benchmarking your performance against that of other IS shops then becomes a viable management exercise. Increasingly, reports are also appearing about the results of various IT benchmarking projects. For example, researchers have begin to report in articles and books what "average" IT organizations look like from consolidating measures. That kind of information can be useful. While measures are often of more numeric types (costs, devices per location, etc.), surveys of this kind are becoming

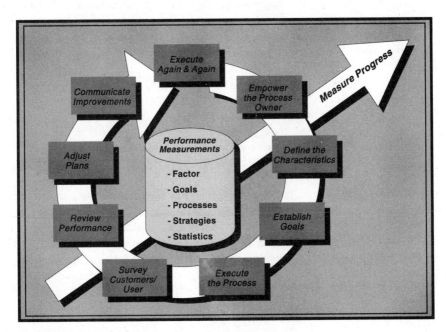

Figure 11.11 Performance measurements process.

more available. Various benchmarking consortiums are also measuring the following kinds of performance and issues:

- critical success factors in IS
- best practices in IS
- most influential cultural factors
- performance by critical processes
- effect on customers and end users by process
- measurements being employed
- how budgets are spent

Conclusions

This chapter has been devoted to the implementation of quality management practices as an overall management process. I have assumed that a philosophy of transformation exists, functioning in an organization that recognizes it must perform better work more quickly, and whose priorities will continue to change rapidly. That is a tall order, but the promise of quality management practices is that it can be delivered. There are too many cases where that has already occurred to be any longer an issue of debate. The heart of the change is looking at the enterprise as a collection of processes making up a system, and then managing these processes through use of rigorous disciplines and tools. Such change is nothing less than profound for the IS community. Most communities have various barriers to be overcome.

The first barrier is conceptual because these are new ideas. It is overcome through training of senior management and its developing a vision of what the IS organization should be doing.

The second is frequently financial because the transformation costs money (training alone will drive expenses up initially). "Quality is free" is a nice slogan, but it is made believable by cost justification and benchmarking.

A third problem is cultural, although IS has historically used many of the quality improvement tools and techniques in programming, but not in the overall management of the organization. Education, communication, new incentives, and rewards all help to overcome this barrier.

Fourth, there is the elusive problem of inertia or lack of urgency. It takes a while for an organization to recognize that it needs to get on with the transformation, and even then, it takes times to build momentum. Benchmarking, education, and some severe business shocks all help to get around this problem.

A fifth issue involves technical capabilities. Legacy systems that block the way, lack of data, and the time it takes to develop new applications are real impediments. Your requirement is to respond quickly to new systems and data. The most successful response to the problem has been to develop and implement a phased evolution in architectures, data bases, and programming and query tools.

Sixth, support around the rest of the enterprise, and specifically by end users, is always a chronic problem. They accept your need to transform in various degrees. The response to this problem has varied, but the most effective strategies have been to co-develop new processes and applications, jointly develop IS plans, and communicate success as a way of demonstrating benefits of the new approach.

Seventh, people are slow to change. The human resources community argues with evidence that you can do several things: train and communicate the need and the "how" of the changes called for, change how you measure performance, reorganize people into different types of teams and groups, reward model behavior, punish the opposite, and recognize that some people will not make the transition and so find a graceful way to exit them out of your organization.

Eighth, regulatory problems exist in some industries. For example, in the U.S. utility industry, each of the fifty states has a regulatory body that influences how companies can operate. The most effective techniques here are the same ones used by companies with recalcitrant unions (as was the case years ago in the automotive industry): Get them involved in helping to define what the transformation needs to look like and engage their involvement in implementing it.

A ninth problem is institutional. Organizations are like silos made worse by the fact that they have lives of their own. These have to be broken up early in the process or they will prevent the transformation. In order to change, programming has to work with end users, operations with programming, and so forth. To fix the organizational problems, companies have gone to such extremes as outsourcing (a popular strategy to use on IS). Other strategies include flattening the organization and moving to team-managed processes.

To a large extent, everything talked about in this book represents common sense and longstanding good business practice. For instance, focusing first on customers made your company successful. Focusing on fact-based management—by collecting data and improving incrementally—can be seen in how management practices have improved over the last half century, and how they have helped Japanese industry in the past two decades. Focusing on services and support has made it possible for information processing to become a trillion-dollar industry with its tool—the computer—serving as the symbol of our age.

References

Beer, Michael, Russell A. Eisenstat, and Bert Spector. "Why Change Programs Don't Produce Change," *Harvard Business Review* (November-December 1990): pp. 158–166 (Reprint No. 90601).

Champy, James A. "Mission: Critical," *CIO* 6, no. 15 (January 1992): p. 18.

Cortada, James W., and John A. Woods. *The Quality Yearbook*, Annual 1994 and subsequent years. New York: McGraw-Hill, 1994 and subsequent years.

Grady, Robert B., and Deborah L. Caswell. *Software Metrics: Establishing A Company-Wide Program.* Englewood Cliffs, NJ: Prentice-Hall, 1987.

Schaffer, Robert H., and Harvey A. Thomson. "Successful Change Programs Begin with Results," *Harvard Business Review* (January-February 1992): pp. 80–89 (Reprint No. 92108).

Tapscott, Don, and Art Carson. "IT: The Sequel," *Journal of Business Strategy* 14, no. 4 (July/August 1993): pp. 40–45.

Appendix A

Malcolm Baldrige National Quality Award

The award promotes "awareness of quality as an increasingly important element in competitiveness, understanding of the requirements for quality excellence, and sharing of information on successful quality strategies and the benefits derived from implementation of these strategies." Awards are given in three categories: manufacturing companies, service companies, and small businesses. Nominations are by the companies themselves submitting an application. Finalists are also judged on site visits to confirm the contents of the nominations. Award criteria purposes are "to help elevate quality standards and expectations; to facilitate communication and sharing among and within organizations of all types based upon common understanding of key quality requirements; and to serve as a working tool for planning, training, assessment, and other uses."

The award's core values and concepts are:

- customer-driven quality
- leadership
- continuous improvement
- full participation
- fast response
- design quality and prevention
- long-range outlook
- management by fact
- partnership development
- public responsibility

The seven categories (think of them as chapters) share common themes. The criteria are designed to produce results ranging from customer satisfaction to cycle time reduction to increased market share, and to contributions to national and community well-being. Trends, current levels, and benchmarks and evaluations are important. The criteria avoid prescriptions in the belief that each organization has to travel a different path to quality improvements. Processes must be linked to results; successes by accident do not carry weight in this assessment. The criteria call in any organization is for a diagnostic system that focuses first on requirements (such as those of a customer) and on those factors that should be employed to assess strengths and areas for improvement across an enterprise. The criteria are intended to be comprehensive, covering all departments, divisions, organizations, processes, and work units.

Feedback and learning based on experience defined by facts provide a closed loop of continuous improvement. "These cycles of learning, adaptation, and improvement are explicit and implicit in every part of the Criteria." The cycles have stages: planning, design of processes, selection and deployment of indicators, their execution, assessment of results and progress, and plan revisions to take into account progress, learning, and new information gained in the cycle. Finally, the criteria emphasize cycles of improvement to occur at all levels and across all parts of the organization. Overall aims and purposes have to be consistent so that nobody is working at cross-purposes.

The Baldrige approach places emphasis on "incremental and breakthrough improvements" with more concentration on what needs to be enhanced. Financial performance is crucial via results that lead to superior market performance, lower operating costs due to process improvements and better use of assets, and "support for business strategy development" and decisions. Invention, innovation, and creativity are recognized as "important aspects of delivering ever-improving value to customers and maximizing productivity." The seven sets of criteria, which are organized as chapters, are:

1. Leadership. This category focuses on the role senior executives play personally "in creating and sustaining a customer focus and clear visible quality values."

2. Information and Analysis. This category focuses on the "scope, validity, analysis, management, and use" of information to improve quality and competitiveness.

3. Strategic Quality Planning. This category focuses on a company's planning process and "how all key quality requirements are integrated into overall business planning."

4. Human Resources. This category focuses on how the firm realizes the full potential of its employees in the pursuit of the organization's quality and performance objects.

5. Management of Process Quality. This category focuses on the "systematic processes" used to seek ever-higher quality and performance.

6. Quality and Operational Results. This category focuses on quality levels and improvement trends in quality, operations, and suppliers.

7. Customer Focus and Satisfaction. This category focuses on a company's relationship with customers, knowledge of their requirements, and factors determining marketplace competitiveness. Emphasis is on results.

In each chapter, assessments are done on approach taken, deployment, and results achieved. Many companies do internal self-assessments each year using these criteria without necessarily submitting a nomination for the award because the process is a useful way of taking a snapshot of internal operations. At IBM, for example, there is a Market-Driven Quality (MDQ) self-assessment process in which all major business units complete an annual assessment that looks much like a Baldrige nomination. The company recognizes outstanding results by presenting three classes of awards to business units when they achieve certain levels of performance as measured by the Baldrige point system.

The criteria and point values by category continue to evolve each year, so you will want to work with the latest edition. Each year, for example, the Baldrige becomes more demanding as it continues its shift toward results and less on deployment or intent. In other words, if you were assessed this year at 450 points and next year performed exactly the same as this year, your score would be lower. The second biggest change to watch out for is the growing emphasis on the customer (Chapter 7). This chapter has undergone considerable change in the past five years. For an IS organization, the customer should include customers, clients, end users, suppliers, and other significant stakeholders in your success (Fig. A.1).

Because the Baldrige criteria and award nomination are applicable across many industries and organizations within companies, they have become a de facto certification process for many enterprises. In fact, there has been a discussion among quality experts and the administrators of the Baldrige Award about evolving the criteria into a formal certification process. That would allow many more companies to be publicly recognized for their quality efforts once they had achieved a certain level of quality performance, instead of competing for only six slots on the award roster.

The award is administered by the American Society for Quality Control (ASQC). You can obtain copies of the Baldrige criteria, descriptions of the nomination process, and additional information on the award by writing to them at:

American Society for Quality Control
611 East Wisconsin Avenue
P.O. Box 3005
Milwaukee, WI 53201-3005 USA
Telephone: 414-272-8575 or 800-248-1946
Fax: 414-272-1734

Baldrige Award Criteria

1995 Examination Categories/Items		Point Values
1.0	Leadership	90
	1.1 Senior Executive Leadership	45
	1.2 Leadership System and Organization	25
	1.3 Public Responsibility and Corporate Citizenship	20
2.0	Information and Analysis	75
	2.1 Management of Information and Data	20
	2.2 Competitive Comparisons and Benchmarking	15
	2.3 Analysis and Use of Company-Level Data	40
3.0	Strategic Planning	55
	3.1 Strategic Development	35
	3.2 Strategy Deployment	20
4.0	Human Resource Development and Management	140
	4.1 Human Resource Planning and Evaluation	20
	4.2 High Performance Work Systems	45
	4.3 Employee Education, Training, and Development	50
	4.4 Employee Well Being and Satisfaction	25
5.0	Process Management	140
	5.1 Design and Introduction of Products and Services	40
	5.2 Process Management: Product and Service Production and Delivery	40
	5.3 Process Management Support Services	30
	5.4 Management of Supplier Performance	30
6.0	Business Results	250
	6.1 Product and Service Quality Results	75
	6.2 Company Operational and Financial Results	130
	6.3 Supplier Performance Results	45
7.0	Customer Focus and Satisfaciton	250
	7.1 Customer and Market Knowledge	30
	7.2 Customer Relationship Management	30
	7.3 Customer Satisfaction Determination	30
	7.4 Customer Satisfaction Results	100
	7.5 Customer Satisfaction Comparison	60
TOTAL POINTS		1000

Figure A.1

Appendix B

How to Do Benchmarking

Benchmarking is a method for finding how to improve processes quickly by learning from others dealing with similar issues. It is a critical tactic used by organizations interested in continuous improvement. It involves sharing of ideas and descriptions of processes. Benchmarking is done between organizations, within an enterprise, and also between firms. The latter approach frequently is the most productive since no two firms seem to approach processes quite the same way. David T. Kearns, former CEO at Xerox, called benchmarking "the continuous process of measuring products, services, and practices against the toughest competitors or those companies recognized as industry leaders." His is a good definition, coming from an individual who has spent his whole life in highly competitive industries and who has a profound knowledge about the world of IS and IT. In fact, his company is recognized as the leading user of benchmarking because of its own success with it and as a result of some employees writing important books and articles on the topic. IBM's formal definition is "the continuous process of analyzing the best practices in the world for the purpose of establishing and validating process goals and objectives leading to world-class levels of achievement." IBMers have also published on the subject, primarily on the more tactical aspects of benchmarking based on experiences in IT manufacturing.

Either definition, however, leads to some clear objectives. Benchmarking allows one to set process improvement goals that exceed those of the best as measured quantitatively. Such an approach increases your confidence that the best approach is continuously being developed and shared across the enterprise. Another appropriate goal is to ensure that benchmarking becomes part and parcel of all management systems. These are goals widely shared. Today, nearly half the Fortune 500 companies do benchmarking. Companies and industries are also forming benchmarking consortiums to examine specific issues such as the relative cost of IT.

In addition to using the approach to see how your processes are doing as compared to those of acknowledged leaders, benchmarking has other uses. It lends itself to objective assessments of the strengths and weaknesses of existing processes. It stimulates thinking and acceptance of new ideas and approaches. Benchmarking frequently helps the process of justifying changes either in quantitative or qualitative ways, even pushing aside internal resistance to change by legitimizing new ideas.

In its simplest form, benchmarking is not a difficult process. First you define the process to be benchmarked. You measure how you are doing it today, documenting the process. Then you select benchmark partners who also have documented a similar process and you compare notes, either one time or on a regular basis over time. Discussions center around how to improve each other's processes, share what you are learning, and then experimenting with improvements. Assessments are fact-based relying on measurable results. Findings become the basis for changes in your process as you continuously improve their effectiveness. This is time consuming so most firms pick the most critical processes to benchmark.

Benchmarking. can be as simple as reading an article about a process and comparing it to your own. Another approach is to hire a consultant to conduct the benchmarking activity. Often, the process owners of two or more organizations will personally lead the benchmarking activities, complete with joint meetings, site visits, and sharing of process documentation. Benchmarking can be of peer organizations within your company (such as, how one IS organization does against another). Comparing common processes across multiple firms in different industries is useful (such as, how end-user feedback is done). A third approach is to compare your performance against competitors. In IT common benchmarking themes are expenditures, help desk performance, operations, and programming effectiveness and efficiency.

Experience suggests some basic rules for effective benchmarking:

1. Train people in the process of benchmarking to ensure effectiveness.

2. Make sure company secrets that could damage your firm are not at risk.

3. Coordinate benchmarking with other parts of your enterprise so you avoid two or more groups benchmarking on the same process (a real problem in large organizations enthusiastic about the application of TQM principles).

4. Share benchmarking results widely within your enterprise for the same reasons as in number 3.

5. Document all benchmarking results in detail so that processes can be improved and lessons learned along the way are not lost.

From a tactical point of view, workable approaches include setting up an internal clearinghouse or benchmarking competency team and designating benchmarking coordinators in each organization (such as in each IS department or one individual for the whole IS organization), focal points for dealing with outside companies, and some process for documenting and communicating benchmarking activities. At IBM, for example, there is now an electronic bulletin board with a data base of such projects. Benchmarking education becomes a real necessity once an organization has gone down the quality management path for a year or more and is deeply involved in process improvement or reengineering, so offer it to employees as needed. Best practices also involves looking at benchmarking as a process in itself, subject to continuous improvement. Figure B.1 is a model of the process that incorporates the approaches taken by such companies as IBM, Xerox, and AT&T.

Since the primary purpose for benchmarking is to accelerate the process of improving business practices, it can be employed early in the development of a new process to get ideas on which way to go before investing a lot of time reinventing the wheel or, worst case, just improving existing practices slightly. Looking at other processes early on definitely gets your teams thinking in bolder, more effective terms because there is always somebody who has developed a process far better than yours. The fastest way to get these ideas is from the American Productivity and Quality Center, which has been building a data base for benchmarking for many years. If you are a member of this organization, it will do research on how other people do a process and get you articles, names, and telephone numbers. Its work is fast and effective. Process teams find it very useful early on. The address is:

American Productivity and Quality Center
123 N. Post Oak Lane, Suite 300
Houston, TX 77024-7797 USA
Telephone: 800-324-4673
Fax: 713-681-5321

APQC is one of the best things to come along to help those wanting to do process reengineering. Members of its staff will tell you that over half of the Fortune 500 companies do benchmarking, including many of your competitors. They also can show you that companies doing ongoing benchmarking have more profitable performance—on average a third better than those who do not.

Good benchmarking practices follow classical process improvement strategems of plan, do check, and act by planning studies, collecting data, analyzing them, and then adopting improvements on a continuous basis.

Benchmarking, while effective with all processes, tends to do best when applied to key business processes, areas causing customer dissatisfaction,

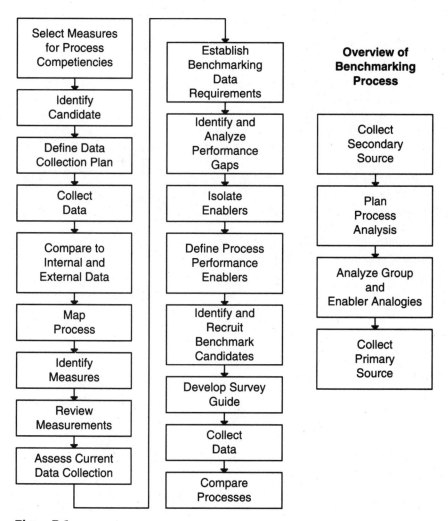

Figure B.1

applications subject to rapid changes in technology, areas causing employee dissatisfaction, and, of course, for the sake of efficiency, with processes that cost more than the benefits they generate.

The common benefits currently being achieved by benchmarking, based on surveys on those who have applied this approach, include:

- leads to stretch objectives
- makes goals realistic and actionable
- encourages pursuit of excellence and breakthrough thinking

- forces study of competition and other firms
- focuses attention on customer needs
- represents one of the most effective ways to energize process teams
- illustrates need for change and how to achieve it in manageable and precise terms

Benchmarking is in itself a process to be learned, not a single event or a tool. Good process management builds continuous benchmarking into it.

For additional details on benchmarking, see Robert C. Camp, *Benchmarking: The Search for Industry Best Practices That Lead to Superior Performance* (Milwaukee: ASQC Quality Press, 1989); Gregory H. Watson, *Strategic Benchmarking* (New York: John Wiley & Sons, 1993).

Since the Appendix A concerns the Baldrige criteria, it should be noted that benchmarking is specifically mentioned in that criteria in 2.0 (Information and Analysis), 3.0 (Strategic Quality Planning), 5.0 (Quality Assurance of Products and Services), and in 6.0 (Quality Results).

How to Learn More about Quality

This appendix provides tips on how to learn more about topics discussed in this book. The field of "quality" is growing. The number of books, seminars, and knowledge about processes are in themselves a growth industry. Have you checked your junk mail lately? Everyone is offering seminars, tapes, and yes, even books!

For Those New to Quality

For those honest enough to admit they have everything yet to learn, I would begin by reading one or two general books on the topic, then follow up by attending a conference. There is nothing like attending a conference in which people who make more money and are more successful than you are preaching the gospel of quality to get you fired up!

Quality Or Else, by Lloyd Dobyns and Clare Crawford-Mason (Boston: Houghton Mifflin, 1991) is an excellent introduction that addresses the changing nature of the world economy, the quality movement, and its basic tenets. It has lots of war stories and is easy to read. Follow that book, with three other books: Thomas H. Davenport, *Process Innovation* (Boston: Harvard Business Press, 1993), which does an excellent job of showing the relationship of processes to IT; Lowell Jay Arthur, *Improving Software Quality* (New York: John Wiley & Sons, 1993), a detailed "how to" book for software development applying TQM principles; and G. Gordon Schulmeyer and James I. McManus (eds.) *Total Quality Management for Software* (New York: Van Nostrand Reinhold, 1992), which is a large collection of articles on principles and war stories. For an ongoing collection of best articles, chapters from books, and very current general reference materials (bibliography, organizations, etc.), see the annual publication

The Quality Yearbook (New York: McGraw-Hill, 1994 and published annually), edited by James W. Cortada and John A. Woods. We have also published an encyclopedic book on hundreds of quality concepts that works as a dictionary but has entries the size you would find in a reference book, complete with bibliography: James W. Cortada and John A. Woods, *McGraw-Hill Encyclopedia of Quality Terms and Concepts* (New York; McGraw-Hill, 1995).

I would invest in membership in the American Society for Quality Control (ASQC). This used to be just for engineering and manufacturing people wanting to apply statistical measures, and so forth, but over the past fifteen years has evolved into the leading organization providing literature and education on all aspects of quality, including for the service functions. They produce a monthly magazine, *Quality Progress,* that contains short case studies in easy-to-read formats, keeps you up-to-date on seminars and shows, and advertises and reviews books on quality. See Appendix A for the address of the ASQC.

When you join ASQC, you will wind up on everyone's mailing list so expect a lot of junk mail on quality from all quarters of the economy. At least you will learn about what is available. Both the ASQC and every other major management society in the United States, Europe, Asia, and Australia/New Zealand have been developing local chapters specializing in topics relevant to its membership. In the United States, for example, in every state, there are local quality councils in which you can meet others interested in quality, where local managers make presentations on their work, and hold conferences and workshops. These tend to be worthwhile. See *The Quality Yearbook* for details.

The American Productivity and Quality Center (APCQ) is another source of quality information. Like ASQC, it sells all the major books on quality and presents seminars. APCQ is also the major source of benchmarking information. APCQ is an association of companies and so is very focused on "how to" education and strategies and is a wealth of information on applying quality in services and sales. You can find APCQ's address in Appendix B.

In addition to the seminars and publications offered by these two organizations—and today almost every other professional management association—there are other useful sources. Among my favorites are the seminars taught by community colleges aimed at businesses. Check them out, along with those offered today by just about every business school at your local university. The most outstanding example of local education that I have seen are the courses taught by the Quality Academy at Fox Valley Technical College in Appleton, Wisconsin. It has been offering the usual short seminars on the basics of quality and how to apply its principles, and providing consulting for nearly a decade and, therefore, has a well-matured program. But it is not alone in such offerings; you will find equally good offerings in your area.

A recent development has been the creation of consulting services by major corporations in which they offer to transfer their best quality practices to clients. Almost every Baldrige winner, for example, provides these kinds of services for topics in which they specialize. These are valuable because of their experience in actually implementing the quality practices. For example, if you need help in developing a new customer satisfaction feedback process, you might go to IBM, or if you want a reservation system, you would go to one of the major hotel chains or airlines. These pockets of real competencies are developing rapidly, and you see them emerging through the various quality conferences and articles in *Quality Progress* and as tracked by the APCQ.

For Those Already Familiar with Quality

Your needs are probably very specific. Membership in ASQC is important, along with involvement in industry specific organizations. I also recommend several books that go beyond the basics. First read Christian Gronroos, *Service Management and Marketing: Managing the Moments of Truth in Service Competition* (Lexington, Mass: Lexington Books, 1990). It is a serious academic study that brings you up-to-date on what the business school community has learned about services during the late 1980s and, as such, is a practical reference book. Next, read Kenneth and Edward Primozic's *Strategic Choices* (New York: McGraw-Hill, 1991). This is a hands-on, no-nonsense guide to strategic planning in this world of changing technologies and global competition. Its value is the linkage it offers between basic planning principles and the realities of a more quality-focused global economy. You will find it short, to the point, and streetwise. The third book is Mary Walton's *The Deming Management Method* (New York: Putnam, 1986), which summarizes Deming's ideas in a short book. This book is more theoretical, but if you are in a Stage 3 company, you are ready for this one. Deming's own book on the subject, *Out of the Crisis* (Cambridge, Mass.: MIT Press, 1986) I find impossible—it is some 600-plus pages long. Walton can get you where you need to be very quickly. If you are at Stages 1 or 2, you may think of Deming and some of the other quality gurus as unrealistic for an IS environment; by Stage 3 you understand from experience how to translate many of their useful insights into IS realities.

You would also benefit in establishing linkages in your community and across the nation with like-minded IS managers and executives to compare notes on quality activities. In many cities, professional associations have started to form roundtables, and so forth, to facilitate dialogue. I find most of these not very effective. Therefore, I suggest you find a dozen peers in various local companies, all in IS, and form a roundtable. Meet once a quarter for a half day to review either quality programs at each others' firms or to discuss in depth a specific issue (end-user surveys, employee training, compensation, and so forth). Take turns putting the agenda together and hosting the event. These councils invariably get wonderful reviews and are easy to launch. One other suggestion: Populate the council with IS representatives from many industries so you avoid the problem of sharing information with a competitor; you can get data on rivals in other ways.

The last suggestion is that you "pitch" at local and national meetings on quality and even write on the subject. Those exercises will force you to clarify your thinking and effectively reflect back on your successes and failures. Such activities rapidly spur forward your education on quality.

Index